The Complete Idiot's Reference Card

Frequently Found Violations on Application Forms

- ➤ Age or date of birth
- ➤ Marital status
- ➤ Number or ages of children
- ➤ Year of graduation or dates of attendance at schools
- ➤ Arrest records
- ➤ Maiden name
- ➤ Person to notify in case of emergency, or next of kin
- ➤ Ownership of automobile
- ➤ Health-related questions

Internet Job Listings

Every listing should include the answers to these questions:

1. What is the nature of the job?
2. On what aspects of the job will the employee spend the most time?
3. What skills will the employee use on the job?
4. What are the key requirements to be considered for this job?
5. What training will the company give the new employee?
6. What is the range of compensation?
7. What are the advantages of working for this company?
8. Who can I speak with for more information?

Top 10 Internet Referral Services

1. Monster.com
2. Careerpath.com
3. CareerMosaic.com
4. HeadHunter.net
5. JobSearch.org
6. HotJobs.com
7. Dice.com
8. CareerBuilder.com
9. NationJob.com
10. Jobs.com

alpha
books

Questions to Ask Applicants

➤ Describe your present responsibilities and duties.

➤ How do you spend an average day?

➤ How have you changed the content of your job from when you assumed it until now?

➤ Discuss some of the challenges you encounter on the job. How do you deal with them?

➤ What do you consider to be your chief accomplishments at your present or previous jobs?

➤ How do you view the job for which you are applying?

➤ What in your background particularly qualifies you to do this job?

➤ If you were to be hired for this job, in what areas could you contribute immediately?

➤ In what areas would you need additional training?

➤ In what ways have your education and training prepared you to do this job?

➤ What disappointments did you experience in your previous jobs?

➤ In what areas did you need help or guidance from your boss?

➤ For what actions or qualities have your supervisors complimented you? Criticized you?

➤ What do you like most about your current (or most recent) job? What do you like least?

➤ What do you seek in a job?

➤ What is your long-term career objective?

➤ How do you plan to reach this goal?

➤ What type of position do you see yourself in five years from now?

➤ What are you seeking in your next job that you are not getting now?

Seven Questions to Ask a Reference

1. What is your opinion of the applicant's work in relation to other people assigned to similar work?

2. What do you consider to be his or her strengths?

3. In what areas does he or she need to improve?

4. Why did he or she leave your company?

5. If the applicant were to reapply for a position with your company or another company where you had the power to hire or reject, would you hire him or her? If not, why?

6. Is there anything else of significance we should know about (applicant's name) that will help us make him or her more effective if we should hire him or her?

7. Do you have any further comments you'd like to make about (applicant's name)?

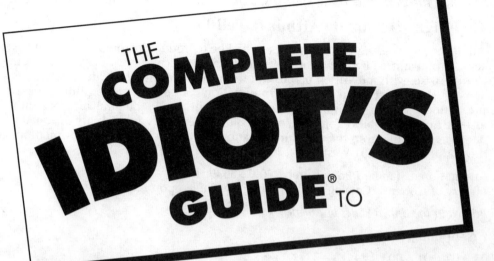

THE

COMPLETE IDIOT'S GUIDE® TO

Recruiting the Right Stuff

by Arthur R. Pell Ph.D.

alpha books

Macmillan USA, Inc.
201 West 103rd Street
Indianapolis, IN 46290

A Pearson Education Company

To my children and their spouses: Hilary and Mark, Douglas and Geri.

Publisher
Marie Butler-Knight

Product Manager
Phil Kitchel

Managing Editor
Cari Luna

Acquisitions Editor
Amy Zavatto

Development Editor
Nancy D. Warner

Production Editor
JoAnna Kremer

Copy Editor
Amy Lepore

Illustrator
Jody P. Schaeffer

Cover Designers
Mike Freeland
Kevin Spear

Book Designers
Scott Cook and Amy Adams of DesignLab

Indexer
Lisa Wilson

Layout/Proofreading
Angela Calvert
Svetlana Dominguez
Gloria Schurick
Betsy Smith

Contents at a Glance

Contents

9 Headhunters

Part 4: Weeding Out the Unqualified   167

13 Resumés—The Applicant's Sales Tool   169

14 The Application Form   179

17 Face to Face with the Applicant   221

18 Barriers to Good Interviewing   237

Foreword

Recruitment is estimated to be a $180-billion industry, and it's no wonder why. With the booming economy and competitive business environment, corporate America is experiencing a severe talent drought—and talent is the competitive edge needed for success. Companies nationwide are thirsting for talented workers, and the right recruiting practices can mean the difference between success and failure.

A generational labor shortage is changing the landscape of recruiting—here's why:

➤ There's a reduction in employee *tenure,* and jobs are becoming vacant more often—my grandfather worked for one employer for 37 years, but my kids will work for 10 or more over the course of their careers.

➤ The *baby boomer* population is exiting from the workforce faster than entry-level workers are coming.

➤ There's a *university deficiency*, especially relevant to the IT industry, in which major universities across the country are not producing enough technically skilled workers to fill demand in the marketplace.

➤ The *dot.com revolution* has introduced a paradigm shift— companies are facing new business models and more competition than businesses have had in the past 50 years. This means the existing workforce needs to acquire new skills to effectively compete.

➤ Employee confidence is at an all-time high! We're moving to a *free agent world*. About one in six workers is working in a nontraditional—non-9-to-5—job, and this area is growing.

These are the concepts that are changing and shaping the human capital marketplace. And they're changing the way we staff our companies and retain talented workers. At Monster.com, we're always innovating with new products to meet evolving staffing needs. Last year, for example, we launched Monster Talent Market (talentmarket. monster.com), the online auction that brings companies together with freelancers, contractors, and independent professionals.

The economy is about change, and we're all facing the same challenges. Whether you're at a start-up looking to hire your first employee or you're at an established Fortune 500 company and are looking to get more out of your recruiting practices, this book can help.

The Complete Idiot's Guide to Recruiting the Right Stuff offers insightful advice to keep you ahead of the hiring curve. This book looks at the process of recruiting start to finish—developing a strategic recruiting plan, getting what you need out of the interviewing process, writing job postings—both on- and off-line—that attract quality candidates, making it easier to make good hiring decisions. Special consideration is also given to avoiding hiring pitfalls, recruiting and attracting college candidates, and recruiting via the Internet.

In this book, you'll find practical ideas you can start implementing immediately to improve your recruiting processes. So read on—and start recruiting and retaining the best talent.

Jeffrey C. Taylor
Founder and CEO of Monster.com
www.monster.com

Introduction

Adding a new person to your team or department can be one of the most important decisions you make on your job. Hiring the wrong person will not only cost you money in wasted time and lost productivity, it can be an emotional drain on you and others in the company.

This is especially true now. In an expanding economy when qualified applicants are in short supply, it has become more and more difficult to locate, screen, and hire men and women who have the right stuff.

You can't depend on personal referrals, running a want ad, or calling an employment agency alone. You have to use your creativity and think "outside the box" to even attract good applicants. That's just the beginning. Once you have identified viable candidates, picking the best is not easy. Good screening, superior interviewing, and careful selection must follow.

As you read this book, you'll learn tricks and techniques that will get you better results in this complex procedure.

Here's a challenge for you. Before you begin reading this book, turn to Appendix C, "Interviewer Quiz." Take the "How Good an Employment Interviewer Are You?" quiz. Don't check the answers yet. After you finish reading the book, take it again. Compare your responses and check them against the answers listed.

How to Use This Book

Reading a book like this one can be interesting, enlightening, and amusing. I hope this book will be all of these things to you. More importantly, it should provide you with ideas you can use on the job. You'll find lots of these ideas in the following pages.

It will all be a waste of your money, time, and energy, however, if you don't take what you read and put it into effect in the way you recruit and select staff members.

Following these five steps should ensure that this book isn't just a reading exercise but also a plan of action for you:

1. After you read each chapter, create an action plan to implement what you've learned. Indicate what action you will take and when you will do it.

2. Share your plan of action with your associates. Get them involved.

3. Set a follow-up date to check whether you did what you planned to do.

4. If you didn't follow through on your plans, reread the chapter, rethink what you did or didn't do, and make a new plan of action.

5. Review what you have done periodically. Renew your commitment.

What You'll Find in This Book

This book will provide you with the tools and techniques of recruiting and selecting new employees. Here is a quick overview of what you will learn:

Part 1, "Setting the Stage—Starting the Process"

After a review of the most common mistakes made in hiring people, you'll study how to determine exactly what is needed to fill the open position. You'll learn how to conduct a job analysis that will bring out what qualities—both tangible and intangible—an applicant must have to perform the job successfully.

Part 2, "Complying with the Laws—And There Are a Lot of Them"

Before starting the hiring process, it's essential that you know what you can and cannot do under equal employment and related laws. In addition to learning what the laws entail, you'll be given guidelines that will help keep you out of trouble.

Part 3, "Sources for Candidates"

Sometimes the best place to look is within the company. You'll see how job banks and job postings can identify qualified people already on your payroll. You'll learn how to write effective want ads, use employment agencies and headhunters, recruit at
colleges and schools, and use the Internet as a source for filling jobs.

Part 4, "Weeding Out the Unqualified"

Good prescreening enables you to eliminate unqualified people before wasting time interviewing them. In this section, you'll pick up prescreening techniques including how to evaluate resumés, use company application forms effectively, and conduct telephone interviews.

Part 5, "Making the Interview More Meaningful"

Interviewing is by far the major technique in choosing the person you will hire. Interviewing is both an art and a science. You'll learn how to structure an interview to get the most and best information about the candidate, how to get the applicant to talk freely, and how to avoid common blunders in this process.

Part 6, "Making the Hiring Decision"

The interview is just part of the process. In this section, you'll learn when and how tests can be used to determine an applicant's qualifications and how to get real information when checking a reference. You'll learn how to make an objective comparison of candidates. Once the decision to hire is made, you'll be shown how to make a job offer that's likely to be accepted. Once the new employee starts, the book will conclude with some tips on how to keep him or her from quitting.

Extras

To add to the material in the main text, a series of shaded boxes throughout the book will highlight specific items that can help you understand and implement the material in each chapter:

Words to Work By

You may have an idea of what most of these expressions mean, but you don't have to guess about their meanings and implications. These definitions will put you in the know so that, when your boss throws these terms at you, you won't have to bluff your way through.

Hiring Hints

These are tips and techniques to help you implement some of the ideas you pick up in this book. Some come from the writings of management gurus; others come from the experience of managers like you, who are happy to share them.

Employment Enigmas

These are common mistakes made by supervisors and team leaders that could cost you time, money, energy, and embarrassment.

Recruiting Residuals

This miscellaneous information and tidbits may add to your knowledge or just amuse you.

Acknowledgments

Special thanks to B.K. Nelson, my agent, for introducing me to the editors of *The Complete Idiot's Guide* series.

To Dr. Franklin C. Ashby for his counsel and guidance.

To Richard Beck for his patience in helping me overcome the computer hurdles in preparing the manuscript.

To my editors, Amy Zavatto and Nancy Warner, for sharing their expertise; and Amy Lepore, copy editor.

And to my wife, Erica, for many years of peace, support, and love.

Trademarks

All terms mentioned in this book that are known to be or are suspected of being trademarks or service marks have been appropriately capitalized. Alpha Books and Macmillan USA, Inc. cannot attest to the accuracy of this information. Use of a term in this book should not be regarded as affecting the validity of any trademark or service mark.

Part 1

Setting the Stage—
Starting the Process

In order for any enterprise to thrive—perhaps even survive—it depends to a great degree on the people who work there. As a manager or team leader, you have the awesome responsibility of bringing to your team or department the best qualified people for the jobs for which you are responsible.

Hiring cannot be a haphazard procedure. There are lots of jobs out there seeking to be filled and good people are hard to find. To assure that you not only can locate qualified applicants, but select the ones that are best for your job openings takes planning. You have to develop and then follow a systematic process.

In this first part of the book, we'll look at the more common errors companies make in their hiring activities. Then we'll get into the first step of the hiring process—examining the jobs we want to fill and determining just what kind of person we need to fill them.

Chapter 1

20 Mistakes Companies Make in Hiring People

In This Chapter

➤ Making mistakes when getting started

➤ Failing to use all available sources

➤ Wasting time with unqualified applicants

➤ Getting inadequate information in interviews

➤ Making the wrong hiring decisions

➤ Losing the candidate you really want

"I hate having to hire people. Not only do I worry about whether the person I hire will make the grade, it also takes a tremendous amount of time away from my regular job."

During the many years I've counseled companies on their personnel policies, I have heard this complaint over and over again from team leaders, department managers, and company executives. They complain about the extra hours spent reading resumés and the time it takes to interview innumerable applicants. They always keep in mind, however, that these decisions are important; they have a direct impact on the future of their team, department, or company.

In most large companies and many smaller firms, recruiting and selecting new employees starts with the human resources or personnel department, but line managers, team leaders, and department heads must be involved in every aspect of the process. They are the people who will have to work with the person hired. They will be responsible for the new member's success or failure.

Recruiting and selecting staff is both an art and a science. As good as managers and team leaders may be in performing their jobs, they often don't have the special skills needed to hire people. I have had the opportunity to observe the hiring process in hundreds of organizations, and I have witnessed countless mistakes.

This chapter will point out 20 of the most frequently made hiring errors. In the balance of this book, you will learn how to avoid these errors and how to replace them with sound, solid, proven techniques that will enable you to make better hiring decisions.

Recruiting Residuals

Human resources experts estimate that hiring an employee costs a company 1.5 times his or her salary—the combination of recruiting costs, training time, and lost productivity as co-workers and supervisors pitch in during the time the job is left unfilled.

Poor Planning

Some companies don't have any plans in place. They don't even think about open positions—until someone quits, is fired, or additional staff is needed. Other organizations may have established procedures for hiring that are inadequate or, worse, totally wrong. Let's look at three planning boo-boos.

1—Waiting for Vacancies

Sometimes you know when a team member plans to leave. He may be reaching retirement age; she is expecting a child and has chosen to remain at home. This gives you weeks or months to find a replacement. Often, however, it's a complete surprise. Sarah finds a better job and gives you two weeks notice. Tom is badly injured in a car accident and will be out for months.

Some jobs are more difficult to fill than others. Unless there's a plan for hiring new people, the job may remain unfilled for a long time.

Such problems can be minimized by having an ongoing hiring program. Developing and using such a program will be discussed in Chapter 6, "Your Best Bet May Be Close By."

2—Looking For the "Dream" Candidate

Ideal candidates rarely exist. To find their "dream" candidate, companies often establish unrealistic specifications (job specs) that are not really needed to do the job. By including them, you may eliminate the best candidates for the wrong reason.

For example, when the Property Development Corp. expanded its Minneapolis division, one of the jobs created was Divisional Controller. The job included managing the company's accounting department, dealing with banks and other financial institutions, and coordinating financial matters with the home office. When determining the *job specifications*, in addition to comprehensive experience in performing similar work, the company required that candidates have a degree in accounting, have an MBA, and be certified as a CPA.

Are these educational requirements truly meaningful for success in the job?

Because the job calls for extensive knowledge of accounting, the degree in accounting is most likely an essential factor. But why an MBA? Graduate degrees in business may provide a good deal of knowledge and analytical skills that may not be acquired by experience. However, depending on the program undertaken by the student, the specific skills needed for being a successful controller may not have been learned. In many cases, the skills needed may have been acquired by work experience. If an MBA is a requirement, men and women who have the necessary skills but not the degree will be eliminated. To avoid this, the MBA may be considered as *one* of the means of acquiring the skills needed to do the job, but the lack of the degree should not eliminate an otherwise viable candidate.

Let's look at the requirement for certification (CPA). Certification is required for accountants working as *public* accountants, whose work involves dealing with clients' accounts. Having this certification is needed for a career in public accounting but not for accounting positions in companies or organizations. Having a background in auditing and other public-accounting activities

Hiring Hints

Make friends with the human resources staff. When you need that extra push to fill your job vacancies, you'll be one step ahead of other team leaders.

Words to Work By

Job specifications are the qualifications a person should have to perform a job.

may be a valuable asset for controllers, and it certainly is not a negative factor, but to make it a job requirement may again eliminate the best-qualified applicants.

Analyzing the job and developing meaningful specs will be discussed in Chapter 2, "Do You Know What You're Looking For?"

3—Cloning the Incumbents

In seeking to replace an effective employee who has moved on, use as your model that person's mirror image. Or if he or she was not effective, search for the exact opposite.

Hiring Hints

If you don't require having an MBA/CPA and you are down to a few similar applicants, perhaps the MBA may be the better choice because he/she has that one extra "thing." But, if you make it a requirement, you may eliminate a the person who is better qualified due to his/her experience.

You loved Diane. You wished you had 10 like her. When she left because her husband was transferred to another city, you were devastated. Your goal: to hire another Diane. So you used her background as the specs for her replacement. Diane graduated from an Ivy League college. Therefore, her replacement must come from an Ivy League school. Diane always dressed in bright colors—she really made the place more cheerful; thus, applicants wearing bright clothes will be preferred. Before she worked here, Diane worked in a bank. Bank experience is important, and so on, and so on.

You fired Alfred. Alfred was from New York. His successor should come from a smaller community. Alfred was an avid sports fan—he always talked about sports. People like that don't really concentrate on their work. No sports fans. Alfred had a background in Macintosh computers. Although he did learn our PCs, he always complained that Macs were better. No Mac users, and so on, and so on.

Such trivial factors often enter into the unofficial job specs. Using the incumbent or a predecessor's personal characteristics as significant factors in determining the qualifications for a job not only can keep you from hiring the best-qualified person, it may overly influence you to hire an unqualified person just because he or she is like (or unlike) the previous holder of that job.

Limiting Sources

To get the best possible candidates for your job openings, it's smart to use as many sources as possible. Just because you found a terrific guy or gal from your alma mater (or when you had a tough job to fill, a friend recommended a great candidate), that's no reason to hope that this time around you can depend on the same resources to come through again. Open your mind, open your rolodex, use your imagination, and broaden the market.

4—Only Promoting from Within

Promoting or transferring a current employee to a new position is commendable and should be encouraged. Internal candidates are known factors. The company has seen them in action. It knows their strengths and weaknesses, their personality quirks, their work habits, their attendance and punctuality patterns, and all the little things that months or years of observation uncover. It also is good for employee morale and motivation. This will be covered in detail in Chapter 6.

The problem, however, is *limiting* the candidates for a position to current employees only. In this highly competitive world, a company should attempt to find the very best candidate for open positions—and that person may not be currently on your payroll.

There was a time when companies boasted that, when the Chairman retired, they hired a junior clerk. Everybody moved up a notch. It is likely that, in a large organization, there are many highly competent people available for filling the new openings, and of course, they should be given serious consideration. However, a search for outside candidates may bring to the company new skills and expertise that is currently lacking and new ideas that often elude people in-bred within the organization.

Employment Enigmas

When companies use current employees as their primary source for new teams, it tends to perpetuate the racial, ethnic, and gender makeup of the staff. Companies whose employees are predominantly white and male and that rarely seek outside personnel have been charged with discrimination against African Americans, other minorities, and women.

5—Relying on Personal Contacts

Personal contacts are excellent sources for referrals. People you know from your business and social worlds often may be ideal candidates themselves or may recommend highly qualified people from their networks. Indeed, networking can be a prime source of potential applicants. In Chapter 11, "Using the Internet as a Recruiting Source," you will learn how to develop your own networks.

But using personal contacts has its downside. First, the people you contact may not know anybody at this time who is qualified. Or worse, they may palm off a friend or relative who needs a job but has limited abilities for your opening. Turning down a friend of a friend may jeopardize your relationship with that person.

Another problem is that you may be overly impressed with the personality or sociability of a person you know and not consider his or her true capability for the open position.

A good example of this is Harry L., the sales manager of Amalgamated Products. Harry was always looking for good salespeople. He knew Jim D. for years. They belonged to the same golf club and occasionally played together or socialized in the restaurant or bar. When Harry learned that Jim was looking for a job, he offered him a position on his sales force. It didn't take long for Harry to realize that Jim needed considerable training and supervision if he were to succeed. It was only after months of wasted effort and frustration that Harry finally let him go. Had Harry used even minimal screening, he would have learned that Jim had a pattern of failures in his previous jobs.

Employment Enigmas

Even people who come highly recommended should not be hired unless you learn at least as much about them as you would a person who answered your help-wanted ad.

Many companies encourage their current employees to recommend friends and acquaintances for open jobs. This can be a valuable resource and should be used. It should be made clear, however, that the referral by another employee is not a guarantee of a job, and the applicant will be treated the same as any other applicant. More on this in Chapter 6.

6—Writing Ads that Don't Pull

Help-wanted advertising is expensive. Whether you are running a classified ad in the local paper to fill a clerical or blue-collar position or a display ad in a national publication for a technical expert or an executive, the results can range from just a few replies or a deluge of resumés.

No matter how many responses you receive, the key is whether the respondents actually fit the job. Too many companies place ads that either do not pull at all or bring in a plethora of responses from unqualified people.

Too many managers write help-wanted ads without giving them adequate thought. They scribble the ad on a scratch pad while waiting for a phone call to go through or on a paper napkin while eating lunch. Writing and placing effective ads will be covered in Chapter 7, "Writing Employment Advertising."

Poor Screening

Whether candidates respond to an ad or are referred by the other sources you use, it takes time—lots of time—to screen out the unqualified and to select the ones you think are worthy of being interviewed. Once an applicant is invited for an interview, depending on the type of position involved, an initial interview can take anywhere from 10 minutes to over an hour.

How much time do you have to devote to interviewing? Even if you are a full-time interviewer in the human resources department, there are only so many hours each day you can schedule. If you are a team leader, a department head, or a senior executive, your day is probably already full, and interviewing means putting in extra hours.

You must be able to prescreen candidates so that the ones you do interview are viable prospects for the open position.

Recruiting Residuals

Studies show that, when screening responses received from an ad, employment specialists spend an average of 30 seconds reading each resumé and deciding whether the applicant should be given further consideration.

7—Paper Tigers: Resumés That Sound Ideal

Most employers ask prospective employees to provide a resumé either before they meet with them or at the interview. Because resumés are written to impress prospective employers, you must learn how to separate the facts from the fluff.

Beware of the functional-style resumé. In this format, the writer describes the functions performed in previous jobs. This is very helpful in learning about the applicant's background, but often it is used to play up functions in which the applicant has only superficial knowledge—and it may not indicate the duration of the experience or the name or type of company in which it was attained.

For example, Gertrude S. used a functional format. She listed four functions: administration, data processing, personnel, and secretarial. Although 80 percent of her job was secretarial, her resumé gave the impression that she was equally involved in all four functions.

This doesn't mean you should not consider Gertrude for the job, but it does mean you must be prepared to ask very pointed questions about the specific details on her experience in each of the functions listed.

When seeking an information technology position, Ted L. used the more traditional chronological resumé. Instead of listing the dates of his employment, however, he just noted the number of years of in each position followed by a description of the duties performed.

> Systems Specialist, ABC Co. (5 years)—(description of duties)

> Programmer, XYZ Co. (3 years)—(description of duties)

> Sales Representative, Apex Insurance Co. (8 years)—(description of duties)

This gives the impression that he spent the past eight years in computer work, but in reality, the most recent job was the last one listed—selling insurance. He has been away from computer work for some time, and the field has changed significantly during those years.

In Chapter 13, "Resumés—The Applicant's Sales Tool," you'll be given guidelines for how to decipher resumés and prescreen candidates so you can use your limited interviewing time effectively.

8—Wasting Time on Unqualified Applicants

Sometimes, when companies are in a rush to fill a job, they may ask applicants to telephone for appointments or to come right to the office.

Despite all the problems that come with reading and evaluating resumés, they serve the purpose of helping to eliminate unqualified people and saving interviewing time. When no resumé is used, it is more difficult to weed out time-wasting candidates.

Dealing with these potential time wasters will be covered in Chapter 13.

Poor Interviewing

The interview is still the most frequently used selection tool. Although there are courses, seminars, books, and workshops on how to interview applicants, a great percentage of interviews are badly constructed, are poorly conducted, and fail to accomplish their objectives.

9—The Unstructured Interview

The interview is more than a polite conversation. Yet many interviewers sit down with the applicant and expect that, by asking a few questions and conversing about the applicant's background and the job requirements, they will get enough information to make a decision to hire or reject the candidate.

To ensure that you obtain significant information about a candidate, ask very specific questions that will bring out whether the person can perform the job and what he or she offers in comparison with other applicants for the same position. This may or may not develop in a pleasant conversation. A definite structure must be designed to elicit the key points, to give the candidate the opportunity to expound on his or her credentials and accomplishments, and to enable the interviewer to size up the applicant's personal characteristics.

Designing structured interviews for the types of jobs you seek to fill will be discussed in Chapter 16, "Planning the Interview."

10—The Overly Structured Interview

Some interviewers, in their efforts to cover all the bases, overly structure their interview plan. They make a list of questions and read them to each candidate. In this way, they will get responses that enable them to determine basic qualifications, and because the questions asked are the same for each applicant, answers can be easily compared and the differences among the candidates clearly defined.

Sound good? Maybe. The problem is that, quite often, answers require follow-up questions. If you stick to the structure—with no flexibility—you may miss an important point.

For example:

> **Interviewer:** What was your greatest accomplishment on that job?
>
> **Applicant:** I saved the company a lot of money.
>
> **Interviewer:** What was your greatest disappointment on that job?

Note that the interviewer asked the next question on the list instead of following through and finding out what the applicant did to save the company money. The answer might have opened the door to even more questions that would have given considerable insight into the prospect's qualifications before moving on to the next question on the list.

Hiring Hints

Make every question count. If the answer is vague or unclear, ask an appropriate follow-up question. Refer to Chapter 17, "Face to Face with the Applicant," for more information about these types of questions.

11—Asking Unlawful Questions

It's been 35 years since the federal Equal Employment Opportunity law went into effect. You'd think that, by now, companies no longer would be asking applicants questions that are considered unlawful. Yet every day some interviewer in some company—maybe yours—will ask a question that shouldn't be asked.

Why? Sometimes it's ignorance of the laws. Most employment professionals know the laws and abide by them. However, as previously noted, team leaders, managers, and even team members often participate in the interviewing process. Many of these people have only vague concepts of the laws. And, as in many matters with legal implications, it's not always clear just what the law allows and prohibits.

You may feel that, to determine whether the candidate will be available for overtime work, you need to ask if she has any young children. Uh-uh! Illegal! The applicant has an unusual name. You're curious so you ask, "What kind of name is that?" When the applicant is rejected for whatever reason, he files a complaint against you claiming discrimination because of national origin. This may not have had anything to do with his rejection, but because you asked, the burden is on you to prove otherwise.

In Chapters 3, 4, and 5, you'll learn what the laws require and how to get much of the information you need to make a hiring decision without violating any laws.

12—Telling Too Much About the Job

One of the major errors interviewers make is telling the applicant all about the job early in the interview. They may even give the applicant a copy of the job description before the interview begins.

Why is this bad? It enables the smart applicant to tailor his or her background to fit the job description. For example, the open job calls for somebody who has extensive experience in administering employee benefits. In her last job, Shirley had some exposure to benefits. Knowing that this is an important aspect of the open position, Shirley might play up—perhaps even exaggerate—her background in this field.

Of course, the applicant should have some concept of the job for which he or she is being interviewed. Accomplishing this without prepping the applicant to feed you responses designed to fit the job requirements will be covered in Chapter 17.

Poor Selection

The bottom line in the hiring procedure is selecting the best candidate for the open position. Sometimes there are very few qualified people, and you may be tempted to hire "a warm body" just to fill the vacancy. This almost always is a mistake. It's better to keep looking. But often there are several good candidates. You want to pick the best, so watch out for the following mistakes in making this important decision.

13—Inadequate Reference Checks

The applicant has presented you with a slick resumé and has come across well in the interview. Before you make the decision, you should verify that what the applicant claims is true.

The purpose of the reference check is to verify the applicant's statements and perhaps to catch the "artful liar."

Unfortunately, this essential part of the employment process is often disregarded or treated much too casually.

Often, the background check is assigned to a junior employee who may send reference letters to previous employers or may telephone them—with little training or know-how in asking probing questions and interpreting the responses.

In recent years, many companies have been advised by their attorneys not to give any reference information for fear of defamation suits. They limit responses to reference inquiries such as the dates of employment and some generalized information about job duties.

Because of this, some organizations don't bother to check out potential employees and take them at face value. This can be a costly mistake. There are ways to obtain meaningful information. They will be discussed in Chapter 21, "Checking References."

Employment Enigmas

Don't accept vague answers to reference questions. Probe for meaningful information. Refer to Chapter 21 for ways to find the answers you seek.

14—Overly Impressed by Superficial Factors

There's an old saying that the decision to hire or not to hire is often made in the first 30 seconds of the interview. There is some truth to this. One of the major factors in hiring is the first impression made by the applicant—and that is primarily physical appearance.

Studies have verified that good-looking people are far more likely to be hired than equally qualified but less attractive people. In an informal exercise that I conducted at a series of seminars a few years ago, I distributed a job description and several resumés of more or less equally qualified prospective candidates. Half the class received resumés with photos of the applicant attached; the other half had no photos. In virtually every instance, the participants who received photos selected the more attractive candidate, while the choices of the nonphoto group were about equally divided among all the candidates.

Common sense tells us that a person being is attractive is no assurance of competence, yet both men and women may decide in favor of the better-looking applicant. Perhaps we just like to have nice-looking people around us.

Some first impressions create a *halo effect*. Because you are so impressed by some superficial facet, it is assumed that all other aspects of his or her background are outstanding. He's so charming; he must be a good salesman. She speaks so well; she'll make a great supervisor. Halo effects are not limited to first impressions. Sometimes, because an applicant is highly competent in one aspect of a job, it is assumed that he or she is equally competent in others. Charles could type on the word processor at 90 words per minute. With that speed, the supervisor figured he had hired a winner. It wasn't until after Charles started work that the supervisor realized speed was his only asset. He was a poor organizer, he was temperamental and didn't work well with others, and he had other unsatisfactory work habits.

Poor first impressions may cause you to reject an otherwise well-qualified candidate, creating the *pitchfork effect*. An applicant may be downgraded in your mind because he or she does not speak well—this is important if the job calls for oral communication, but it should not be a factor for jobs in which oral communication is not required. One of my clients wouldn't even consider an applicant who had a straggly beard and long, unkempt hair. Only after the person who referred the applicant persuaded my client that the man was a computer whiz did he hire him. This man has since solved countless problems for the company and has saved it tens of thousands of dollars.

Smart employers don't make hiring decisions based on one or two factors. No matter how impressed you may be by an applicant, learn as much as you can about him or her. Conduct a thorough interview and use the other hiring suggestions made in Part 6, "Making the Hiring Decision," before choosing the new employee.

Words to Work By

The **halo effect** is the assumption that, because of one outstanding characteristic, all of an applicant's characteristics are outstanding. (That person "wears a halo.") The opposite is the **pitchfork effect** (the symbol of the devil). You assume that, because one characteristic is poor, the person is not satisfactory in every aspect of his background.

15—Subconscious Biases: Pro or Con

We all have biases. Biases are not limited to prejudice against people because of their race, religion, or sex. They may be based on long-held beliefs or stereotypes—whether they're true or false. They may be caused by our personal tastes or idiosyncrasies.

At one of my seminars, I asked participants to share with the group some of their hiring mistakes. Most people told about people they hired who didn't make the grade, but one of the participants told about a salesman he had rejected. He said, "At a luncheon meeting of our trade association, the sales manager of one of our competitors was bragging about his top sales rep. He said that in his first year, he broke all records for bringing in new accounts. When me mentioned his name, it rang a bell. I recalled interviewing him some time ago. When I returned to my office, I checked my files. Sure enough, I had interviewed and rejected him. Why? My notes on his application just said "not suitable." Then I remembered. I turned him down because he was wearing a bow tie. My stupid bias against bow ties had kept me from hiring a potential winner."

Many people have biases in favor of people like themselves. I knew a manager who preferred to hire people who graduated from the University of Michigan and would never—no matter now qualified he or she may be—hire a Michigan State grad.

To get the best people, you have to identify your own biases and compensate for them in making the decision. You'll learn more about this in Chapter 22, "Making the Decision."

16—Mismatching Candidates with Job Specs

Earlier in this chapter, we commented on the importance of having realistic job specs. The whole purpose of developing a list of specifications is to ensure that the person hired can do all (or most of) the facets of the job.

Often it is difficult, if not impossible, to find somebody with all the requirements. In such cases, choose the specs that are absolutely essential and decide in which areas a new employee can be trained after employment.

The big mistake organizations make is hiring a candidate who qualifies in several of the specs but is weak in the essential areas. There are certain aspects of most jobs in which experience or technical know-how is essential and cannot be taught on the job. This will be discussed in Chapter 22.

Hiring Hints

When you set up specs for a job, ask yourself, "What must the applicant be able to do that other members cannot do." Keep in mind that your team will be stronger if it includes people with different but complementary skills.

17—Overlooking the Intangibles

When making a hiring decision, it's just as important to evaluate the intangibles as to determine the candidate's capability to perform the job.

Too often, the employer limits the selection procedure to determining whether the applicant is technically qualified and overlooks such factors as whether the person can work in a team, communicate ideas, work under pressure, be flexible, and the countless other personality factors that make up the human being.

Employment Enigmas

Choose new members carefully. The men and women you select for your team must not only have the technical skills to do the job, they must be able to work in a team environment and must relate well to the other team members.

The intangibles that make for success on a job are just as important as education, skills, and experience. In making your job analysis, be as diligent in determining the intangible factors as you do the tangible factors.

Determining these intangibles in the interview is not easy. Some suggestions for how to identify intangibles will be found in Chapter 17. This can be augmented in several other ways. There are some psychological evaluations or tests that may help (see Chapters 19, "Special Types of Interviews," and 20, "Using Tests"). In addition, much can be learned by using assessment centers (see Chapter 19).

Losing Good Candidates

You have screened hundreds of resumés, interviewed dozens of applicants, tested or sent many of them for evaluation, and checked references. You finally make up your mind—make an offer—only to have it rejected by the applicant. This is the most frustrating experience one can have in the hiring process. Why should this be?

18—Making Job Offers That Won't Be Accepted

The terms of employment should be well-thought-out long before an offer is made. Too many companies, however, have a preconceived idea of the offer before they even interview applicants. This makes for sound business, but unless the offer is shaped to fit the needs of the applicant, there's a good chance it will not be accepted.

One major part of the job offer is the salary. We'll talk about this in the following section.

Other factors that should be clearly understood prior to making a job offer are such key aspects as the amount of travel required, the hours of work including the likelihood of extensive overtime, whether the job will call for relocation now or in the future, and any other special aspects of the position. Don't surprise the applicant at the time of the offer with "By the way, you will have to go to our plant in California for three months of training."

Making a job offer that will most likely be accepted will be covered in Chapter 23, "Making the Job Offer."

19—Negotiating the Financial Package

With lower-level employees, salary is nonnegotiable. It's take it or leave it. But when the position is hard to fill, you must be more flexible, or you'll lose the best applicants.

It's not necessary or even advisable to commit to a salary too early in the interviewing process. There may be many factors that should be considered in determining the final financial package. It makes sense, however, to have an approximation of the salary range clearly established early on. If you and the applicant are far apart on salary, there's no point in considering the applicant seriously.

Another aspect of compensation is your benefits package. If your package is significantly poorer than other firms in the community or industry, you might have to compensate in other areas. Despite the increasing cost of health insurance, unless your medical plan is in line with those of other firms, many applicants will turn you down.

Most benefits plans are standardized. However, more and more organizations are constructing individual benefit programs for each employee. The amount paid into the package may vary with the position and pay scale. The specifics of what is covered within the package can be tailored to fit the desires of the employee. You'll learn more about this in Chapter 23.

Recruiting Residuals

The benefits package for each employee of most large organizations costs between 30 and 50 percent of that person's salary.

20—Current-Employer Counteroffers

Talking about frustration? This is the worst example. After all the time, energy, thought, and emotional turmoil you have experienced in the hiring process, you offer the job to Tom, and he accepts it. You think your troubles are over and you can get back to work. A week later, Tom calls and tells you he gave notice to his boss and was made a counteroffer, so he decided to stay. You have to start all over.

You must expect that counteroffers will be made to good workers. You probably have done the same when one of your best people gave notice. To beat this, you have to be proactive. You must prepare the person to whom you make a job offer to expect and reject a counteroffer.

How do you do it? You'll learn how in Chapter 23.

Hiring Hints

Good people are hard to find. Once you've chosen the person you want, make every effort to sell him or her to accept your job offer.

The Least You Need to Know

➤ Plan the hiring process before you even look for applicants and stick to the plan.

➤ Develop job specifications that are realistic and that have direct bearing on job success.

➤ Prescreen candidates so that those you do interview are viable prospects for the open position.

➤ Interviews must have a definite structure designed to elicit the key points, to give the candidate the opportunity to expound on his or her credentials and accomplishments, and to enable the interviewer to size up the applicant's personal characteristics.

➤ Learn what types of interviewing questions are considered unlawful and steer clear of asking them.

➤ Don't tell the applicant too much about the job too early in the interviewing process.

➤ Verify the applicant's background using a well-planned check of education and experience.

➤ Smart employers don't make hiring decisions based on one or two factors. No matter how impressed you may be by an applicant, learn as much as you can about him or her.

➤ In addition to salary and benefits, factors that should be made clear before making a formal job offer include the amount of travel required, the hours of work including the likelihood of extensive overtime, whether the job will call for relocation now or in the future, and any other special aspects of the position.

➤ You must expect that counteroffers will be made to good workers. Be pro-active. Prepare the person to whom you make a job offer to expect and reject a counteroffer.

Do You Know What You're Looking For?

A job is open. Why? It may be that the incumbent quit, retired, was transferred, or was fired. It may be a brand new spot created in a reorganization, an expansion, or a diversification of the organization. No matter how the job opening developed, the first step in filling it is to study the job, learn exactly what the position entails, and then determine what characteristics the person(s) you seek must bring to the job to perform it successfully.

In this chapter, you will learn several ways to analyze jobs and to write job descriptions that truly depict what the person would be doing day to day, week to week, year to year. You will also learn how to determine what education, experience, and personal traits candidates should bring to the job to perform the duties effectively.

A Job Is Open

Jobs develop for a variety of reasons. What is needed to fill a particular job depends to a great degree on why the vacancy exists. The process differs significantly depending on whether you are replacing a worker who has left or expanding the team or department.

When Refilling a Position

Lisa, a customer service representative, notifies you that she's decided to go back to school and will leave the job in two weeks. What do you, as her team leader, do? If you work for a medium- or large-size organization, you will probably notify the human resources department and request a replacement. In a smaller company, you notify your boss and start the process rolling to find a new employee.

Words to Work By

The **job description** is a list of duties, responsibilities, and expected results that a job entails. Other terms used for the job description are **position results description** or **job results description.**

It's not always necessary to refill a job immediately. In some cases, it may be a slow period in your business, and you may want to wait until things pick up. However, if the job is to be refilled, you have to start at once. It takes time to find good candidates and even more to time to make a new person productive.

It may seem that the "logical" way to start is to pull out the current job description and specifications and start the search for somebody who qualifies. But is this "logical?"

Jobs change over time. The *job description* may have been written several years ago. What is being done today may be somewhat different from what was done then. It's a good idea to review carefully and critically every job description before starting the search to refill it.

You will recall that one of the hiring mistakes noted in Chapter 1, "20 Mistakes Companies Make in Hiring Pepole," was cloning the incumbents. You were cautioned not to base the criteria used to choose a replacement on the background of the individual who left. Here is your chance to reevaluate the job and to determine if what the former employee performed was really what should have been performed—and you should adjust the requirements accordingly.

For example, when Lisa was hired, customer service reps wrote out customer complaints on a form, checked them out, and then telephoned or wrote to the customer with the results and suggested solutions. During her tenure, all this was computerized so that many of the problems could be checked and adjusted during the first telephone call. Although Lisa was very good in her dealings with customers, her computer skills were poor, and she was much slower than other reps. The job description and job specs should be rewritten with more emphasis placed on computer, skills.

When It's a Brand New Position

Your team is overworked. You need a larger staff. You succeed in persuading your manager to add one or more positions to your team. What kind of jobs will you add?

On some teams, all members do the same kind of work. On a data entry team, they all enter much of the same kind of data; on a quality-control team, all members may perform the same function. In these cases, you can just review the job descriptions to ensure that they are current.

On other teams, one or a few members may perform a specialized type of work. On a multifunctional team, part of the team may study market trends, and another part may study production capabilities. Now you have been given the added responsibility of studying financial implications. An entirely new job description is needed for the new assignment.

> **Hiring Hints**
>
> If you use the same systematic approach to analyzing a replacement job as you would a new job, you'll get a more accurate job description.

What Does This Job Entail?

The technique by which you obtain information about what a job entails is called *job analysis*. In some companies, specialists perform these analyses. They may be industrial engineers, systems analysts, or members of your human resources staff. If your company employs these people, use them as a resource. The best people to make an analysis, however, are those closest to a job—you and your team members.

There are several ways to develop information for the job description.

> **Words to Work By**
>
> A **job analysis** should include a description of the responsibilities that fall within a job (job description) and a list of the skills and background required to perform the job effectively (job specification).

Observing the Action

For jobs that are primarily physical in nature, watching a person perform the job will give you most of the material you need to write the description. If several people are engaged in the same type of work, observe more than one performer.

Even a good observer, however, may not understand what he or she is observing. Sometimes it involves much more than meets the eye. Additional steps must be taken to get the full picture. For jobs that are not primarily manual, there is little you can learn from observation alone. Just watching someone sitting at a computer terminal, for example, isn't enough to learn what's being done.

Interviewing the Worker

Ask the people who perform a job to describe the activities they undertake. This technique fleshes out what you're observing. You must know enough about the work, of course, to understand what's being said and to ask appropriate questions. It's a good idea to prepare a series of questions in advance. Below are a few questions that will elicit good information. Only ask those questions that are pertinent to the job. In addition, you should prepare questions that are specific to the job being analyzed.

The following are some of the questions you should ask:

➤ Tell me about how you spend a typical day.

➤ Tell me about some of the other work you occasionally do. How often and when do you do this work?

➤ What positions do you supervise (if any) and how much of your time is spent supervising others?

➤ What responsibilities do you have for financial matters such as budgeting, purchasing, authorizing expenditures, and similar decisions?

➤ What equipment do you operate?

➤ What performance standards are you expected to meet in this job?

➤ What education and experience did you have prior to taking this job that prepared you for it?

➤ What training did you get on this job to help you do it effectively?

Employment Enigmas

When several people perform the same type of job, don't select the most or least experienced or skilled workers to observe. Studying a few mid-level performers will give you a more realistic concept of what is actually done on that job.

Hiring Hints

If you are a team leader evaluating a job performed by a member of your team, review in your mind how you view the position, what you believe the performer should be doing, and the standards that are acceptable.

The people who work day by day on a job can give you more insight into the job than you can pick up just observing it. The information gleaned from these interviews will be invaluable in writing the job description

Interviewing the Supervisor or Team Leader

If you're analyzing a job other than the ones you supervise, speak to the team leader to obtain that person's perspective of the position. Ask the supervisor or team leader questions about his or her perception of the job; these questions should be similar to those you asked the worker. Note variations in their answers. Probe to determine which is the more accurate description.

If you are evaluating a job that you personally supervise, try to take an objective view of the position and review it as if you were a stranger. It's not easy to do, but you'll be amazed at the results. You'll see things you never noticed before, and you'll interpret some of the aspects of what is being performed and how it is done in a different light.

Make It a Team Project

When work is performed by a team, job descriptions cover the work of the entire team. The best way to develop a complete job description is to get every team member into the act.

Have each member write a job description of the job as he or she views it. It's amazing how various people who do what ostensibly is the same job describe the work. Sure, basic aspects will be the same, but the differences between what each person considers to be important to the job should be examined.

Bring the team together and discuss the differences. From this discussion will evolve a true picture of the entire job—duties, responsibilities, special activities, and performance standards. Combine this with your own observations and obtain a consensus from which the final job description will be drawn.

Indicate Performance Expectations

Some companies prefer to call the job description a *position results description* or a *job results description*. They feel that the true objective of this document is to determine what is expected of the people performing the job. Each description should include the major goal (why the job exists), the key results areas (KRAs)—aspects of the job on which the performer should focus attention—and the standards on which performance will be measured.

Hiring Hints

A good job description is not a rigid depiction of functions. It should allow for reasonable deviations, additions, and variations.

Employment Enigmas

Don't base your job specifications on your version of an ideal team member. That person probably exists only in your mind. Be realistic. Your specs should reflect any factors the new member should bring to the job that will contribute to the team's successful performance.

Recruiting Residuals

Companies have found that when performance standards are developed collaboratively by managers and the people who perform the work, they are more realistic and are more likely to be accepted and achieved.

By indicating the results expected and the performance standards by which they are measured, both managers and performers are given not only a standard against which they can continually measure their performance but a motivational instrument impelling action that will lead to desired results.

The following job description worksheet is a helpful tool. Tailor the form you use to the type of job you're analyzing.

Job Description Worksheet

Job title: _____

Reports to: _____

Duties performed: _____

_____

Equipment used: _____

_____

Skills used: _____

_____

Leadership responsibility: _____

_____

Responsibility for equipment: _____

_____

Responsibility for money: _____

_____

Other aspects of the job: _____

_____

Special working conditions: _____
_____

Performance standards: _____
_____

Analysis made by: _____

Date: _____

What You Seek in a Candidate

After you know just what a job entails, you can determine which qualities you seek for the person who will be assigned to do the job.

The job specifications in some situations must be rigidly followed; other situations may allow for some flexibility. In civil-service jobs or in cases in which job specs are part of a union contract, for example, even a slight variation from job specs can have legal implications. In some technical jobs, a specific degree or certification may be mandated by company standards or to meet professional requirements. For example, an accountant making formal audits must be a certified public account (CPA); an engineer who approves structural plans must be licensed as a professional engineer (PE). On the other hand, if there's no compelling reason for the candidate to have a specific qualification, you can deviate from the specs and accept an equivalent type of background or experience.

Components of a Job Specification

Most job specifications include the elements in this list:

➤ **Education:** Does a job call for college? Advanced education? Schooling in a special skill?

➤ **Skills:** Must the candidate be skilled in computers? Machinery? Drafting? Statistics? Technical work? Are any of the skills necessary to perform part of the job?

➤ **Work experience** What type and duration of previous experience is necessary in related job functions?

➤ **Physical strength or stamina:** Does the job require heavy lifting or hard physical labor? If so, is it a significant part of the job or does it only occur occasionally?

Employment Enigmas

There are all kinds of tests available that purport to measure an applicant's ability to do a job. Do they really work? You'll learn more about this in Chapter 20.

➤ **Intelligence:** Some jobs call for a high level of intelligence. Decisions must be made that require deep thinking, solving complex problems, or being able to think on one's feet. Intelligence can be measured by standard tests. For such jobs, the specs might indicate a high score on these tests. In addition, some jobs call for specific types of intelligence such as working with intricate mathematical calculations, dealing with spatial relationships, or using sophisticated vocabulary. All these skills are measurable.

➤ **Communication skills:** The job specs should specify exactly which communication skills you need such as one-to-one communication, the ability to speak to large groups, innovative telephone sales methods, or creative writing skills.

➤ **Accuracy of work:** If a job calls for "attention to detail," specify what type of detail work. In some jobs, there is no room for error. Work must be done right the first time or serious problems may result. Examples include working on a nuclear reactor or piloting a jet plane.

➤ **Dealing with stress:** If a job calls for "the ability to work under pressure," indicate what type of pressure (for example, daily deadlines, occasional deadlines, round-the-clock sessions, difficult working conditions, or a demanding boss).

Hiring Hints

To ensure that the person you hire can do a job, the job specs should emphasize what you expect the applicant to have accomplished in previous jobs—not just the length of his or her experience.

➤ **Extroversion or introversion:** A sales representative or an office receptionist should have an outgoing personality. Shy, introverted people will be ill at ease in such jobs. On the other hand, if the job is one in which the individual works alone in a confined space with little contact with others, the extroverted person is sure to be unhappy and most likely will fail.

➤ **Special factors:** Among the many other factors that may be included in the job specification are such requirements as fluency in a foreign language, willingness to travel, willingness to work on weekends, willingness to work overtime on short notice, and anything else an applicant must comply with to perform the job satisfactorily.

Eliminating Good Prospects for the Wrong Reason

One of the most common problems in determining the specifications for a job is requiring a higher level of qualification than is really necessary, thus knocking out potentially good candidates for the wrong reason. This problem frequently occurs in the following areas.

Education

Suppose certain job specs call for a college degree. Is that degree necessary? It often is, but just as often, having the degree has no bearing on a person's ability to succeed in a job. Requiring a higher level of education (or for that matter, any qualification) has more disadvantages than advantages. You may attract smart and creative people, but the job may not challenge them, resulting in low productivity and high turnover. Even more important, you may turn away the best possible candidates for a position by putting the emphasis on a less important aspect of the job.

Duration of Experience

Your job specs may call for 10 years of experience in accounting. Why specify 10 years? No direct correlation exists between the number of years a person has worked in a field and that person's competence. Lots of people have 10 years on a job but only one year of experience. (After they've mastered the basics of the job, they plod along, never growing or learning from their experience.) Other people acquire a great deal of skill in a much shorter period of time.

It's not that years of experience don't count for anything. Often, the only way a person can gain the skills necessary to do a good job, make sound decisions, and make mature judgments is by having extensive experience. Just counting the years, however, isn't the way to determine that ability.

Rather than specify a number of years, set up a list of the factors a new employee should bring to a job and how qualified the person should be in each area. By asking an applicant specific questions about each of these factors, you can determine what he or she knows and has accomplished in each area.

Type of Experience

Job specs often mandate that an applicant should have experience in "our industry." Sure, there are some jobs in which the skills and required job knowledge can only be acquired in companies that do similar work. In many jobs, however, a background in other industries is just as valuable and may even be better because the new associate isn't tradition-bound and will bring original and innovative concepts to a job.

Preferential Factors

Some job specs are essential to perform a job, but often there are other factors that are not essential but would add to a candidate's value to your company. In listing preferential factors, use them as extra assets and don't eliminate good people simply because they don't have those qualifications.

Employment Enigmas

Don't clone your current team. When you set up specs for a job, ask yourself, "What must the applicant be able to do that I either cannot or do not want to train him or her to do?" Your team will be stronger if it includes people with different but complementary skills.

For example, it may be an extra benefit if a candidate already knows how to use a certain type of computer software, but because that knowledge can be picked up on the job, eliminating a person who is otherwise well qualified might be a mistake.

Be Flexible

Job specs can be so rigid that you're unable to find anyone who meets all your requirements. Sometimes you have to make compromises. Reexamine the job specs and set priorities. Which of the specs are nonnegotiable? These requirements are the ones a new team member absolutely must bring to a job or else there is no way the job can be done. For example, a candidate must have a jet pilot's license to fly the company plane, or the candidate must be able to do machine work to precise tolerances or the work will not pass inspection.

Hiring Hints

The intangibles that make for success on a job are just as important as education, skills, and experience. In making your job analysis, be as diligent in determining the intangible factors as you are in determining the tangible factors.

Suppose your specs call for sales experience. One of the applicants has no job experience in selling but, as a volunteer, was a top fund-raiser for the local community theater. That person may be able to do the job. In seeking to fill a job, the employer should make every effort to abide by the job specs but should also have the authority to use his or her judgment to determine when deviation from the job specs is acceptable.

What Do I Have to Pay to Get the Person I Need?

Another part of job analysis involves determining the pay scale for a job. Most organizations have a formal job-classification system in which various factors are weighed to determine the value of a job. These factors include the level of responsibility, the contribution of a job to the company's bottom line, the type of education necessary, and the required training and experience to perform the job. Notice that the classification applies to a job, not to the person performing a job.

Determining the Pay Package

The pricing of a job in smaller organizations is often done haphazardly: You pay what you have to pay to hire the person you want. You must have some guidelines about what a job is worth, however, so you don't pay more than necessary or offer too little and not attract good applicants. You have to determine the *going rate* for a job you want to fill.

You have to research the market to find out what the going rate is. This list shows some of the sources for obtaining information about the salary scales in your community or industry:

➤ **Trade and professional associations.** Many of these groups conduct and publish periodic salary surveys. Members of the associations can discern how their pay scales compare with other companies in their field and in their geographic area. These surveys are best used when you seek salary information for specialists in your industry or profession.

➤ **Chambers of commerce.** Some chambers of commerce publish salary surveys for their locations. Because these surveys include several industries, you can obtain salary information about jobs that exist in a variety of companies such as computer operators and clerical personnel.

➤ **Employment agencies.** These agencies can inform you about the going rate for any type of position in which they place employees.

➤ **Networking.** Ask people you know who are managers in other companies in your community or industry. They often are willing to share information about going rates.

➤ **The Internet.** Several Web sites provide salary information. Often trade associations, local governments, or chambers of commerce sponsor them.

Words to Work By

To attract and keep good employees, your pay scale must be at least as high as the **going rate,** which is the salary paid for similar work in your industry or community. Another definition: What you have to pay an employee to keep him from going to another company.

Setting the Salary Range

Once you have a clear understanding of what the job is worth, you are in a position to negotiate the specific starting salary with the candidate. In some cases, there is no negotiation. You make an offer, and the candidate takes it or leaves it. However, when the salary is flexible, there may be some give and take.

Usually the salary is set within a range. Jobs are classified according to a set procedure with a range based on the salary survey. For example, a company may have six salary grades, the lowest being basic clerical workers, the next being more-skilled office jobs, then technical specialists, first-line supervisors—all the way up to senior managers.

Salaries within the range are dependent on the people performing the job. Employees start at the bottom of the range and move up within the range. When promoted, they move into a higher classification. Usually, new employees start at a salary at the low end of the range, but managers may have flexibility to offer a higher amount within the range for better-qualified people.

When hired for a new job, most people are offered a moderate increase over their current or most recent salary. Occasionally, a higher increment is warranted for improved credentials, an advanced degree, or a professional license the candidate has received since starting the previous job.

In the current market, for example, information technology (IT) personnel are in very short supply. To attract a candidate, you may have to offer him or her a significant increase over what is currently earned. Sometimes companies are so desperate to fill some jobs that they have to create new job classifications with a higher salary range to reach out to qualified people.

In some jobs, the compensation package is negotiated at the time of the job offer. Dealing with this type of negotiation will be discussed in Chapter 23, "Making the Job Offer."

The Least You Need to Know

➤ Base your job requirements on job factors, not on the background of people currently doing the job.

➤ When you analyze a job, observe the people performing the job and discuss with them and their managers what they do.

➤ Job descriptions, the details of what the job involves, are more than just guidelines. You should take them very seriously. To avoid stagnation, provisions for flexibility should be built into the description.

➤ Job specifications, the qualifications a person should have in order to perform the job successfully, should be based on the job description. This technique enables you to choose people for a position who are capable of doing the job.

➤ By over qualifying a job, you eliminate otherwise qualified people for the wrong reasons.

➤ Know the going rates for your jobs so you don't over- or underpay your associates.

Part 2

Complying with the Laws—And There Are Lots of Them

You're scared! Of course, you believe in fair treatment of everybody regardless of their color, gender, ethnic background, or age. But you are concerned that somewhere along the line you might inadvertently make a comment, ask a question, or do something in good faith, but still be accused of violating the law.

Like all laws, the laws governing equal employment opportunity are subject to interpretation. What appears clear and simple, therefore, easily becomes vague and complex.

This part of the book looks at these laws and provides you with some suggestions and guidelines to help you cope with some common problems. You'll learn what questions you can and cannot ask an applicant, how to get the information you need to make a good hiring decision without violating the law, and many other of the ramifications of the laws relating to hiring people.

Chapter 3

What the Laws on Employment Cover

In This Chapter

➤ Discrimination because of race, religion, and national origin

➤ Discrimination because of sex, marriage, and pregnancy

➤ Discrimination because of age

➤ Discrimination because of disability

➤ Equal pay for equal work

➤ Hiring undocumented aliens

➤ Discrimination because of union membership

As a manager, laws governing employment affect most of the decisions you make about the way you hire, supervise, compensate, evaluate, and discipline personnel.

This chapter looks at these laws and discusses some of the problems you may have in applying them in your job. It explores some of the problems that have plagued other employers and what you can do to avoid similar troubles.

The laws governing equal employment affect every aspect of your job as a manager. It begins even before your first contact with an applicant, and it governs all your relations with employees: how you screen candidates, what you pay employees, how you treat employees on the job, how you handle employees' separation from the company, and sometimes even after that.

Although these laws cover *all* aspects of employee relations, in this book, we will only discuss the parts of the laws that apply to the hiring process. For a discussion of how the laws deal with supervision, discipline, evaluating employees, and terminating them, I suggest reading my book *The Complete Idiot's Guide to Managing People*.

The Civil Rights Act of 1964

The Civil Rights Act of 1964, as amended, prohibits discrimination in employment on the basis of race, color, sex, religion, or national origin. The section of the law that covers employment (Title VII) is usually referred to as the Equal Employment Opportunity (EEO) law and is administered by the Equal Employment Opportunity Commission (EEOC). The EEOC also administers the Age Discrimination in Employment Act (ADEA) and the Americans with Disabilities Act (ADA).

Discrimination—Race, Color, National Origin

Among the areas covered by Title VII of the federal Civil Rights Act of 1964, as amended, is the prohibition of discriminating on the basis of race, color, or national origin. All companies or organizations with 15 or more employees are included in these requirements.

Although many states already had passed fair-employment laws—some as far back as the 1940s—this was the first all-inclusive federal law in this area. How the law is enforced will be discussed in Chapter 5, "More on Employment Laws."

Most companies recognize the importance of these laws and have made strong efforts to train and work with their staffs to comply with them. Many larger organizations have added equal employment officers to their human resources departments to be responsible for compliance with the laws. Smaller firms have assigned this activity to a member of the management team.

The law made companies rethink and change many of the myths that kept them from hiring minorities. Such myths included …

> "White people will never work for a black supervisor."

> "To have a harmonious department, employees should all come from the same ethnic group."

> "You invite trouble if you put Poles and Germans, Irish and Italians, or Xs and Ys in the same unit."

> "Blacks can only do menial work."

The law changed more than just stereotypes. Many of the practices and procedures had to be rethought.

➤ Questions on application forms and in interviews that directly or indirectly queried national origin had to be deleted (more on this in Chapter 4, "Watch Your Language").

➤ Employment tests often discriminated against minorities. These tests had to be dropped or rewritten to overcome this problem (more on this in Chapter 20, "Using Tests").

➤ Provisions for training all employees who interview or process applicants should be provided. More on this in Chapter 19, "Special Types of Interviews."

Religion

Prior to the passage of this law, it was not uncommon for companies to refuse to hire people whose *religious practices* and beliefs differed from their own. Help-wanted ads often specified such requirements as "Protestants only." Application forms included questions on religion. The law now prohibits such requirements.

In addition to prohibiting religious discrimination in hiring, the law requires companies to make reasonable accommodation for a person's religious practices unless doing so results in undue hardship on the company.

What do we mean by "religious practices" and "reasonable accommodation?" Religious practices include Sabbath worship, obligations to pray during the work day, wearing special clothing, and similar rites. For example, observant Jews and Seventh Day Adventists cannot work on Saturday, their Sabbath. Some religious Christians will not work on Sundays. Orthodox Jews must always have their heads covered—usually with a small skull cap called a kippah or yarmulke. Some Moslem women are required to wear special types of garments and have their hair covered. Many Moslems pray several times a day, including times when they are a their work places.

> ### Words to Work By
>
> According to the Equal Employment Opportunity Commission Guidelines, **religious practices** include traditional religious beliefs, moral and ethical beliefs, and beliefs that individuals hold "with the strength of traditional religious views."

Sometimes accommodation for these practices is easy. Suppose your company is open seven days a week and members of your team take turns working on Saturdays and Sundays. One of your employees, David, who is Jewish, can never work on Saturdays. The accommodation: Just schedule him for Sunday work. If you're not open on Sundays but you have other employees who can work Saturdays, you're still required to excuse David from Saturday assignments even though it may require other employees to work on Saturdays. They may resent this, but the unhappiness of other employees doesn't qualify as "undue hardship."

On the other hand, if your business is small and there aren't enough people who can do the work to cover the Saturday shift, it may be considered an undue hardship, and you would not have to hire David.

Here are three other religious considerations in the workplace:

➤ **Religious holidays:** Employees must be given time off to observe their religious holidays, although you're not required to pay them for these days. These holidays are usually considered excused absences and may be charged against personal or vacation days.

➤ **Prayer facilities:** Companies that have a significant number of Moslem employees often provide a place for them to conduct their prayer service—usually a conference room or break room. If you have too few Moslems to warrant a special facility, you must allow them time for their prayers and grant access to a private place.

➤ **Proselytizing on company premises:** Margaret, a devout member of her denomination, believed that it was her mission to convert people to her religion. She continually pressed her religious beliefs on her co-workers and distributed tracts and other religious literature. At the request of team members, her team leader asked her to refrain from this behavior. She refused, claiming that the religious accommodation law and the First Amendment gave her the right to proselytize. Margaret was wrong. Just as a company can prohibit political campaigning on company premises and during working hours, it can restrict religious behavior that disturbs other people in the workplace.

When interviewing a prospective employee, it is not lawful to ask about his or her religion or religious requirements. Once you have decided to hire the person, you may ask if he or she can work Saturdays or Sundays.

Employment Enigmas

If you ask about the need for time off for religious practices *prior* to making the hiring decision and then reject the applicant, even if it is not a factor in your decision, it can be perceived as one and a complaint can be filed. It becomes your burden to show it was not discrimination.

Sex and Pregnancy

In addition to the prohibition of discrimination on the basis of race, religion, and national origin, the Civil Rights Act of 1964 also prohibits discrimination on the basis of gender.

Traditionally, many jobs were generally associated with gender. For the most part, skilled artisans such as carpenters, machinists, and plumbers were considered to be men, as were engineers, accountants, outside sales, and virtually all management positions. Women's jobs were usually lower-paid positions such as nurses, typists, retail sales clerks, and low-skilled factory jobs. Although there have always been exceptions, until this law was passed, few men were hired as secretaries and receptionists, and few women were hired or promoted to supervisory or management jobs.

This law changed the gender structure of most companies radically. You will now find women in most job types and more men performing jobs that were formerly considered women's work.

Recruiting Residuals

When the Civil Rights Act of 1964 was introduced in Congress, it covered only race, color, religion, and national origin. An opponent of the act added sex discrimination to it because he believed that such a radical provision would make the law unpassable. As they say, the rest is history.

The sex provision of the law, however, has an additional element not found in the other categories. There are some positions for which a company is permitted to specify only a man or only a woman for the job. Clear-cut reasons must exist, however, for why a person of only that gender can perform the job. In the law, these reasons are referred to as *bona fide occupational qualifications (BFOQs).*

If a job calls for heavy lifting, for example, is it a BFOQ for men only? Not necessarily. There are women who have the capacity to do the job, and there are men who may not have the required strength. This can be determined by requiring that all applicants—both men and women—pass a weight-lifting test.

And that's not all. Suppose a job calls for driving a forklift truck, and the operator is occasionally required to do heavy lifting. A woman applicant

Words to Work By

A **bona fide occupational qualification** (**BFOQ**) exists when the gender of the employee is essential to performing the job. Some wags have commented that the only undisputed bona fide occupational qualifications are a wet nurse (for a woman) and a sperm donor (for a man).

may be able to drive the truck but not do the lifting. If the lifting is only a small part of the job, you cannot reject her. She is capable of performing the majority of the work, and other people can be assigned to handle the lifting.

Suppose you have always had an attractive woman as your receptionist, and the job is now open. Is this a BFOQ for a woman? Of course not. There's no reason that a man—with the personality for the position—cannot be just as effective.

Employers often claim that their policies on hiring women are not based on prejudice but on sound business reasons. Women often have children at home and can't travel, can't work overtime, and stay home every time a kid is sick. The law does not recognize these as legitimate reasons. Many of the questions usually asked of female applicants concern their family responsibilities. Despite the laws, employers still ask women about these matters. In Chapter 4, you will learn what questions you may not ask and how to get the information you need lawfully.

The sex discrimination provisions of the equal employment laws also cover maternity and pregnancy. Although this was implied in the Civil Rights Act of 1964, it was clarified and strengthened by the Pregnancy Discrimination Act of 1978.

The basic principal of this law is that women who are pregnant must be treated the same as other applicants and employees. In screening a pregnant applicant, she must be judged on her ability to perform the job for which she applies without regard to her current condition.

You may be concerned that, if you hire her, she will have to take time off for delivery and care of the infant and perhaps will not even return to work. Under this law, you must assume that she will only be away from the job for a relatively short period of time. The law says that pregnancy should be considered the same as a temporary disability. There's no question that it's temporary, and in most cases, it will be only a minor inconvenience to the company.

The law applies not only to applicants who might be rejected because of pregnancy but to current employees who may be terminated, denied benefits, or otherwise penalized on the basis of her pregnancy or maternity.

There are some jobs in which working conditions such as exposure to certain chemicals might be dangerous to unborn children. Many companies used to have fetal protection policies that excluded pregnant women and sometimes all women of childbearing age from these jobs. The U.S. Supreme Court ruled that such policies were illegal, and women could not be barred from these jobs.

Lawyers specializing in employment law strongly recommend that, when a woman is hired or later assigned to work in such a position, she be carefully informed about the workplace risks and be asked to sign a release. Because recent studies show that certain workplace substances can affect the male reproductive system, men hired or assigned to such jobs should also be informed of the risk, and releases should be obtained.

The Age Discrimination in Employment Act of 1967

The Age Discrimination in Employment Act of 1967 (ADEA), as amended, prohibits discrimination against individuals 40 years of age or older. Some state laws cover all persons over the age of 18.

Unlike the Civil Rights Act of 1964, which covers all employers with 15 or more employees, the ADEA applies to organizations with 20 or more employees.

The original law only protected people between the ages of 40 and 65. Companies could legally refuse to hire people over 65, but that was changed by later amendments. Now there is no maximum age. You cannot refuse to hire an applicant as long as he or she is otherwise qualified, even if that person is 100 years old. The law also prohibits mandatory retirement at any age with a few exceptions (for example, companies may require senior executives to retire at a specified age).

Note that the law does not apply to people under 40. Theoretically, you can turn down a 35-year-old applicant as being too old for your "trainee" job—but don't try it. Many states cover everybody over the age of 18. Even if your state has not reduced the age, you can get into trouble.

Hiring Hints

When you interview older applicants, avoid the stereotypes that may keep you from hiring highly qualified people for the wrong reason.

A few years ago, a company rejected a 30-something applicant and told her they wanted a younger person for that position. She was advised that, since she was under 40, she couldn't file a complaint of age discrimination under federal law or in that state. Here's what happened: The State Job Service sent a 43-year-old applicant for an interview and, when she was rejected, filed an age-discrimination charge against the firm.

Even though most company application forms don't ask for a person's age or date of birth and most people omit that information from their resumés, it's still easy to guess an applicant's age range within a few years. A team leader who prefers that young people join his or her team may overlook, just because of age, potential members who could be of great value to the team.

The Applicant Is Overqualified

The term "overqualified" is often a euphemism for "too old." Some people may have more know-how or experience than a job requires, but that doesn't necessarily mean they won't be productive. Discuss the details of the work with the applicant. It may be an opportunity for the person to learn new things. He or she may be able to contribute to the job some expertise that makes it more challenging. Judge the person as an individual, not as a member of an age group.

The Applicant Made More Money in the Last Job

You note that on the application form, the candidate has indicated that his/her current or most recent salary is higher than you can offer. People with many years of experience often earn more money than those with less experience. If this is a factor in your hiring decision, discuss it with the applicant. He or she should be the one to determine whether the salary is satisfactory. You may worry that, if a better paying job comes along, the new member will jump to it. That may happen, of course, but a younger person would probably do the same.

Employment Enigmas

Everybody on your team need not be in the same age group. Being of different age levels isn't necessarily a barrier to cooperation and collaboration. Make that determination on the basis of the candidate's personality, not based on his or her age.

This Is a Trainee Position

Just because the job calls for training does not qualify it as a BFOQ. The old concept that you can't teach an old dog new tricks is not true. People can be trained at any age. Companies worry that, after extensive training at great cost, the older person will not be around long enough to have it pay off. Nonsense. Studies show that, once older workers have mastered a job, they are likely to remain for more years than their younger counterparts.

Our Benefits Plan Won't Cover Older Employees

The law requires that your benefits plan cover *all* workers. In 1990, Congress passed the Older Workers Benefits Protection Act (OWBPA), which requires employers to provide older workers with benefits equal to those provided for younger workers. However, if the cost of providing equal benefits is higher for the older worker than the younger, the employer can provide reduced benefits as long as the payment made or the cost incurred on behalf of the older worker is the same as for the younger worker. This eliminates the excuse for refusing employment to an older person because benefits will cost more.

The Americans with Disabilities Act

The newest and probably least-understood civil rights law is the Americans with Disabilities Act (ADA). This section discusses some of the highlights of the law and how it applies to you as a manager. Your company must adhere to this law if it has 15 or more employees.

What You Can Do—What You Don't Have to Do

The ADA makes it illegal to discriminate in hiring, in job assignments, and in the treatment of employees because of a disability. Employers must make reasonable accommodation so that these people can perform the essential duties of their jobs.

This accommodation can vary from building access ramps for wheelchair users to providing special equipment for people who are seeing- or hearing-challenged, unless this type of accommodation is an undue hardship for the company. Undue hardship is usually defined in monetary terms. If an applicant who uses a wheelchair applies for a job with a small company, the cost of building an elevator or a ramp to give access to the floor on which the job is located may be a financial hardship. If it is not possible to provide a less expensive accommodation, the company could reject the applicant. If the same applicant applied for a job in a more affluent company, however, it may not be considered undue hardship to do the necessary construction.

Accommodation doesn't always require expensive construction. The hypothetical examples in this list examine some other ways to meet this requirement:

➤ The small company you work for wants to hire an accountant who uses a wheelchair, but the accounting department is on the second floor of your building. The building has no elevator or ramp, and providing one would cost more than the company can afford. Must you do it? No. That would be an undue hardship for your company. There may be other ways to accommodate this person, however. Use your imagination. Why not let him work on the ground floor? His work could be brought to him. It may be an inconvenience, but it would qualify as reasonable accommodation, and it would enable you to hire a particularly competent accountant.

➤ A highly skilled word processor operator is legally blind and walks with the aid of a white cane. She can transcribe from dictated material faster and more accurately than many sighted people can. You want to hire her, but you're concerned that in the case of a fire or another emergency she would be a danger to herself and others. The accommodation you can make is to assign someone to escort her in case of an emergency.

➤ An applicant for an assembler in a factory had been badly injured in an automobile accident. The job requires him to stand at a workbench all day. He is unable to stand for long periods. Is this a legitimate reason to reject him? Accommodations can be made. Perhaps a high

Employment Enigmas

If you suspect that an employee cannot perform a job because of alcohol or drug abuse, have the person tested. Employees should be made aware that this policy will be followed, and it should be clearly stated in the company's policy manual.

stool could be provided so the employee could reach the workbench without having to stand. If that option isn't feasible, the job structure could be changed so he could work part time on that job and do other work that didn't require standing for long portions of the day.

What About Alcoholics and Drug Users?

Alcohol and drug users are considered disabled under the ADA. If a person can perform a job satisfactorily, a previous record of alcoholism or drug addiction is not reason enough to refuse hiring. If an applicant is still addicted, however, and it resulted in poor attendance or poor performance in his or her previous job, you can reject the person—not because of the addiction but because of poor work habits.

Attitude of Other Employees

Resentment of other workers when special consideration is given to a disabled person because of accommodation is not an excuse to refuse to employ him or her.

The mechanics at the Tool Machinery Co. spent about 80 percent of their work time in the shop fixing and adjusting various pieces of equipment. About 20 percent of their work required going out to the factory floor and installing, fixing, or adjusting equipment that couldn't be brought to the shop. Because this work was more strenuous and often physically uncomfortable, the mechanics referred to it as "dirty work," and they took turns when such assignments came up.

When an opening occurred in the department, the best-qualified applicant was Chad, a master mechanic with an excellent employment record. However, Chad was unable to walk without the aid of two canes. It was no problem for him to get to the shop, but he could not maneuver through the plant and was unable to go through the physical contortions necessary to reach inside and around the machinery.

To accommodate for this disability, it was arranged that all of Chad's work would be at the workbench. The outside work would have to be distributed among the other people. This meant that each would have a larger share of the "dirty work." When Tom, the supervisor, notified them about this situation, they objected. "Why should we have to spend more time on these tough jobs and he doesn't? Hire somebody who can do it all."

What would you do if you were the supervisor? You cannot legally refuse to hire Chad. You don't want the current mechanics to be unhappy. Tom could have just said, "It's the law; we must hire him." Instead, Tom appealed to their nobler motives. "Chad is a great guy. His old company went out of business, and his former boss told me he had 'magic hands'—could fix anything and had a great creative mind that enabled all of his co-workers to benefit from his ideas. Despite his handicap, he has mastered a tough job. It means, at the most, one or two hours extra time each week out on the floor. You're not going to let a little inconvenience prevent Chad from utilizing his talents and making a living."

Result: Chad got the job and, within a few weeks, had overcome the initial resentment and was accepted as one of the guys.

The Plus Side

On the positive side, you can utilize the talents of physically and mentally challenged people. Even in this day of computers and technological sophistication, many types of work are still routine and repetitious, resulting in high turnover among workers who are assigned to that work.

Many companies have found that people who are mentally challenged can do this work and are not bored by it. These people are often capable of learning much more than you might expect. It takes more patience, and some tasks may have to be simplified, but trainees who master these tasks retain the skills and often improve on them. Coaches who are specially trained to work with people who are mentally challenged are available in many communities. Your local mental health association can tell you whether this type of help is available in your area.

Hiring Hints

When you interview a candidate for a new job or consider someone for a promotion, don't focus on disabilities. Concentrate on that person's *abilities*.

Equal Pay Act of 1963

The Equal Pay Act 1963 requires that an employee's gender not be considered in determining salary (equal pay for equal work).

Because this act is an amendment to the Fair Labor Standards Act, all employers engaged in interstate commerce are covered no matter how many employees they have. The law was passed to counter a common practice of paying women less than men who were doing similar work.

For example, a male "porter" on the cleaning crew was paid more than a female "maid." Often this was justified by claiming that the porter had heavier work such as climbing ladders and lifting heavy loads. However, this often represented a minuscule part of his work. Most was the same as that of his female counterpart.

In the olden days, it was assumed that men should be paid more because they supported a family, and women only worked if they were single and had to support just themselves. If a married woman worked, it was to earn "pin money" to supplement her husband's income. Now, of course, we don't accept these myths, but the practice of paying less to women persists. According to the latest figures, women in the workplace paid on an hourly basis earn only 73.2 percent of what men earn, women paid on a weekly basis make 76.3 percent, and women paid on an annual basis make 81.8 percent.

Comparable worth goes beyond the concept of equal pay for equal work, in which male and female employees performing the same work must be paid at the same rate. Comparable worth extends this concept. Employees performing completely different jobs should receive equal wages if the jobs are of approximately comparable value to the employer.

For example, a company employs administrative assistants who are primarily female and electricians who are predominantly male. The admins are paid at a rate of about 80 percent of the salary paid to the electricians. Under the comparable worth theory, a point system is created by which all jobs are measured. Points are based on job analyses and include such factors as education or training required, degree of responsibility, contribution to the profitability of the organization, and so on. Although the two jobs are entirely different, they can be measured in the same manner. If, hypothetically, the analysis of the administrative assistant job and the electrician job result in the same number of points, their salaries should be at the same rate.

This is still a work-in-progress. Although some companies are rating jobs in this manner and several government agencies have adopted it, most private sector organizations have not taken this step.

Hiring Hints

One way to overcome concerns about comparable worth is to eliminate sex-segregated jobs. Make every job open to qualified candidates of both sexes and establish training programs to train women to qualify for previously male-dominated positions.

The Immigration Reform and Control Act of 1986

You're worried. You continually read about companies that get into trouble for hiring undocumented aliens (no, not Martians—people from foreign countries). You're almost afraid to hire anyone who has a foreign accent. Not hiring someone because of this fear is illegal.

It's Up to You to Find Out

You cannot discriminate against a person because he or she isn't an American, but you must make sure an applicant is legally allowed to work in this country.

In Chapter 5, "More on Employment Laws," you will learn how to prevent your company from inadvertently running afoul of immigration laws.

The National Labor Relations Act

Long before the civil rights laws were passed, Congress enacted the Wagner Act in 1935. It prohibited employers from discriminating against workers on the basis of union membership or activity. The Taft-Hartley Act amended this law in 1948, and it is still in effect.

Discriminating Against Union Members

These laws cover a variety of matters relating to employer-union relations, some of which apply to the hiring process. It is illegal to discriminate against a person because he or she is a member of a union. You may not even inquire whether an applicant is a union member.

Before the passage of the Taft-Hartley Act, many management-union contracts called for a *closed shop*. The company was required to hire people who were members of the union—often through the unions hiring halls. This was outlawed by Taft-Hartley. However, contracts may call for a *union shop* in which nonunion members may be hired, but they must join the union within a specified period of time after employment.

What About "Right to Work" Laws?

One of the major areas of contention in the debates in Congress when the Taft Hartley Act was proposed was the rights of workers to decide whether they wanted to join a union. If the contract called for a union shop, employees of that company would be compelled to join the union whether they liked it or not. A compromise was reached on this point. Instead of outlawing union shops nationally, the decision was delegated to the states.

Several states passed "right to work" laws, which prohibit a company or union from requiring that employees join a union as a condition of employment.

Most states have fair-employment laws. Because some state laws are stricter than the federal laws, make sure you know what your state requires.

In addition, several presidential executive orders require that certain government contractors and other organizations receiving funds from the federal government institute affirmative-action programs to bring more minorities and women into the workplace (see Chapter 5).

Words to Work By

In a **closed shop**, a company is required to hire *only* members of the union with which it has a contract. In a **union shop,** a company may hire nonunion members, but they must join the union within a specified time after being hired.

Employment Enigmas

Don't ask applicants if they are members of a union, even if your contract calls for a union shop. Bring up the subject of union membership only after you've made a job offer.

It's important to remember that an employer isn't obligated to hire an applicant just because he or she is in a protected category (such as a person covered by the ADA). An employer can still hire another, better-qualified candidate. The employer cannot use discriminatory information, however, to *exclude* a candidate who otherwise is the most qualified for a job or a promotion. Managers, therefore, must avoid doing, asking, or saying anything that could possibly be construed as discriminatory or be misinterpreted regardless of whether it was a factor in a hiring or promotion decision.

The Least You Need to Know

➤ The Civil Rights Act of 1964 prohibits discrimination in employment based on race, color, religion, national origin, or sex.

➤ Women who are pregnant must be treated the same as other applicants and employees. In screening a pregnant applicant, she must be judged on her ability to perform the job for which she applies without regard to her current condition.

➤ The Age Discrimination in Employment Act of 1967 (ADEA), as amended, prohibits discrimination against individuals 40 years of age or older. Some state laws cover all persons over the age of 18.

➤ The Americans with Disabilities Act makes it illegal to discriminate in hiring, in job assignments, and in the treatment of employees because of a disability. Employers must make reasonable accommodation so that these people can perform the essential duties of their jobs.

➤ You cannot discriminate against a person because he or she isn't an American, but you must ensure that an applicant is legally allowed to work in this country.

➤ You cannot refuse to hire a person because he or she is a member of a labor union.

Chapter 4

Watch Your Language

> **In This Chapter**
>
> ➤ Determining your knowledge of the equal employment laws
>
> ➤ Writing and placing want ads that comply with the law
>
> ➤ Knowing which questions can and cannot be asked at an interview
>
> ➤ Designing an application form that complies with the law

In the preceding chapter, you learned what laws must be taken into consideration during the hiring process. This chapter tackles some of the pragmatic problems in applying the law. First we'll discuss the terminology used in job specifications, help-wanted ads, and job orders given to employment agencies or other recruiting sources. Then we'll examine questions that can be asked of applicants in an application form and in an interview.

Testing Your Knowledge of the EEO Laws

To function as a manager today, you must be thoroughly familiar with various state and federal laws concerning equal employment opportunity. To help you measure your knowledge of these laws, take the following quiz. It covers only a few of the key factors in the laws, but it should give you some insight into understanding this important area.

The Questions

In answering the quiz, don't write your answers in the book but on a separate sheet of paper. Then give the quiz to other members of your staff.

On an application form or in an interview, is it legal for you to ask the following? (Answer **Yes** or **No**.)

_____ 1. What are the names of your nearest of kin?

_____ 2. Do you have a permanent immigration visa?

_____ 3. Have you ever been arrested?

Are the following help-wanted ads legal?

_____ 4. Management trainees: College degree; top 10 percent of class only.

_____ 5. Accountant: Part-time opportunity for retiree.

_____ 6. Sales: Recent college graduate preferred.

Other areas:

_____ 7. Companies may give tests to applicants to measure intelligence or personality as long as the publisher of the test guarantees that it is nondiscriminatory.

_____ 8. A company may refuse to employ applicants because they are over 70.

_____ 9. A company may refuse to employ an applicant if she is pregnant.

_____ 10. A company may ask whether a woman has small children at home.

A company may indicate an age preference if …

_____ 11. It is for a training program.

_____ 12. Older people cannot qualify for the company pension program.

_____ 13. The job calls for considerable travel.

Miscellaneous questions:

_____ 14. A company may specify that it requires a man for a job if the job calls for considerable travel.

_____ 15. A company may specify that it requires an attractive woman to greet customers and visitors.

The Answers

The following answers are based on federal law. Some states have interpreted the laws somewhat differently. In addition, because new laws, administrative rulings, and judicial interpretations are promulgated from time to time, the reasoning on which these answers are based may change. Keep in mind the job-relatedness of the questions and the kind of effect they will have when asked of ethnic minorities or women. These are key factors in determining the legitimacy of the questions.

1. **No.** You cannot ask about next of kin because the response may indicate national origin if the name differs from the applicant's. You may not even ask whom to notify in case of emergency until after you hire an applicant.

2. **Yes.** Immigration laws require that legal aliens working in the United States have a permanent immigration visa (green card).

3. **No.** Courts have ruled that because ethnic minorities are more likely than nonminorities to be arrested for slight minor causes, asking about an arrest record is discriminatory. You *can* ask about convictions for felonies (see the section "Criminal Records" later in this chapter).

   Employment Enigmas

   Watch your language. Don't use terms or phrases that can be interpreted as subtle discrimination. Companies have been accused of discrimination against men by advertising that a receptionist needs to be "attractive" and against women by specifying that a warehouse employee needs to be "strong."

4. **No.** Unless you can substantiate that students from the top 10 percent of their class have performed significantly better than students with lower grades, this ad isn't job-related.

5. **No.** Because most retirees are over the age of 60, specifying a "retiree" implies that persons between the ages of 40 and 60 are not welcome. The Age Discrimination in Employment Act protects persons older than 40 against discrimination because of their age.

6. **No.** The phrase "recent college graduate" implies youth. As noted, even the implication of "youth" violates the terms of the ADEA.

7. **No.** The Supreme Court, in *Griggs vs. Duke Power Co.,* upheld the EEOC's requirement that intelligence and personality tests must have a direct relationship to effectiveness on the job for the specific job for which the test is used. Because only the company using the test can verify this relationship, it must be validated against each company's experience.

   Hiring Hints

   A good way to keep out of trouble on equal employment matters is to require all people who do any interviewing at all to attend an annual—or even better, a semi-annual—program that will keep them aware of the laws and any changes made in them and keep them alert to their responsibilities.

8. **No.** The Age Discrimination in Employment Act prohibits discrimination against people who are 40 years or older. There is no top age limit.

9. **No.** Pregnant women may not be refused employment. Employers cannot ask an applicant whether she is pregnant or comment that the company doesn't hire pregnant women. If a pregnant woman is rejected, she has to prove that the reason for the rejection was her pregnancy.

10. **No.** Because men aren't usually asked whether they have small children at home, it has been interpreted as a means of discriminating against women.

11. **No.** Training programs may not be limited to young people.

12. **No.** Participation in a pension program is not an acceptable reason for age discrimination.

13. **No.** Ability to travel is not related to age.

14. **No.** Ability to travel is not related to gender.

15. **No.** A company's desire to have an attractive woman as a receptionist doesn't make it a bona fide occupational qualification (see Chapter 3, "What the Laws on Employment Cover").

Every manager who hires people should, ideally, score 100 percent on this quiz. Failure to comply with any one of these rules may result in complaints, investigations, hearings, and penalties.

Now let's look at some of the specific problems you may face in applying these laws in your hiring practices.

Job Specifications

When a vacancy occurred on Ken Bradley's team, he wrote a memo to the human resources department giving them the specs for the position. He accompanied it with the following memo:

> "We're an aggressive, hard-hitting bunch of young guys. Get me a sharp, up-and-coming recent college grad. Most of my boys are Ivy Leaguers, so that will be an asset. And, oh yes, no hippies—get me a clean-living churchgoer."

This job specification has several violations of the equal employment laws. Let's see why:

➤ The phrase "young guys" violates the prohibition of both age and sex discrimination. Avoid terms that even hint at gender such as "guys" or "boys."

➤ The phrase "recent college grad" violates the law because "recent" usually means "young." Of course, some people graduate from college in their 40s or older, but they're still the exceptions to the norm.

➤ "Ivy Leaguer" discriminates against people who, because of their race or religion, have chosen to attend primarily minority colleges or religion-sponsored schools. Also, because minorities are likely to be less affluent and attend less expensive schools, hiring only "Ivy Leaguers" has the effect of discriminating against minorities.

➤ The term "churchgoer" violates the prohibition against religious discrimination. It can be interpreted as discriminating against people who choose not to belong to any organized religion or interpreted as "Christian only" because members of other religions may not attend "church."

Words to Work By

Diversity in the workplace means a culture in which people from a variety of different racial, ethnic, religious, and gender groups work together to achieve common goals.

In seeking new team members, it not only is unlawful to give preference to people with backgrounds similar to other team members and to discriminate against those who differ, it's also not good business. Each team member brings his or her individuality to the team. Often, these differences result in obtaining fresh views and creative approaches to the team's activities. This helps promote *diversity in the workplace*.

Help-Wanted Ads

Before the civil rights laws were passed, want ads frequently included factors that are now illegal. Most newspapers listed jobs for men and jobs for women in separate sections. Ads listed restrictions or preferences based on race, or religion, or nationality. In my research for this book, I scanned the want ads in the New York Times in the 1930s. Here are some typical ads from that period:

Chef, French, for prestigious restaurant. Experienced in haute-cuisine.

You cannot require that the chef be French. You can require experience in French cuisine, but this can be acquired anywhere in the world.

Secretary. Steno 130 wpm; typing 70 wpm. Prefer Catholic.

Even though "Catholic" is listed as a preference rather than as a requirement, it is still illegal.

Salesman—Sell candy to retail outlets. Good opportunity for Negro.

The preceding ad was placed in the "Help Wanted—Male" section. The job title specified "salesman." Today, it would be probably be titled "Sales" and be placed with all the other sales positions with no indication of sex. Even though this job is seeking a member of a minority group, it still is illegal because it discriminates against all other racial groups. However, if applicable, you could indicate: "Sell to retail outlets in Harlem."

> Draftsman—Experience in mechanical design. Must be U.S. citizen.

It is illegal to discriminate against noncitizens. As noted in the preceding chapter, noncitizens cannot be barred from employment if they have the legal right to work in the U.S. If this job requires security clearance, that fact can be stated in the ad. Although it's much easier for a U.S. citizen to obtain security clearance, noncitizens are eligible.

Where the ad is placed can also determine it legality. The owner of a large machine shop in Milwaukee had an opening for a tool and die maker. Some of his best workers had received their training as apprentices in Germany. To attract prospects with a similar background, he placed an ad in the German-language newspaper. Result: He was cited by the State Civil Rights agency for discrimination on the grounds that, by placing the ad only in a German-language publication, he discriminated against African Americans, Hispanics, and people from non-German ethnic groups. He was advised that it was okay to advertise in a foreign-language paper, but to comply with the law, he had to also run the ad in one or more of the local newspapers.

Things You'd Like to Know But Can't Ask

In your desire to obtain as much information as you can about an applicant so you'll make the right hiring decision, you may ask questions that seem to be important but that violate equal employment opportunity laws. There are lawful ways to obtain important information and not violate the laws. Let's see how this can be done.

Marriage and Children

The most frequently asked illegal questions relate to marriage and child care. "But this stuff is important," you might say. "I *need* to know."

Suppose your group puts in a great deal of overtime—often on short notice. One applicant is a married woman (you noticed the ring on her finger), and you think you have to know whether she has children at home. Your reason is that "everyone knows" women with children have to pick them up at daycare and can't work overtime. Another applicant isn't wearing a ring. Maybe she's divorced. Maybe she has children. You have to find out to know her availability, right?

Wrong in both cases. Of course it's important to know whether applicants can work overtime on short notice, but you cannot assume their availability to work based on their responsibility for child care. In many families, the father or another relative picks up a couple's children from a daycare facility. The woman may have made arrangements with the school or a center to handle this. It's not an assumption you can make.

The inability to work overtime isn't limited to child-care matters. Anyone—single or married, man or woman—may not be able to work overtime for all kinds of reasons.

How do you deal with this issue? You tell both men and women applicants about the overtime and then ask whether that will be a problem.

Here's a good rule of thumb: Don't ask questions of one gender that you wouldn't ask of the other. "Okay," you think. "I'll ask both men and women about their children, and then I'll be safe." Nope, even this method can be interpreted as discrimination.

If you ask a male applicant how many children he has and he says he has four, your reaction may be, "Good, here's a stable family man. He'll work hard to support his family."

If you ask a woman applicant the same question and she gives the same answer, do you have the same reaction? Usually not. Managers often think that a woman will stay home from work every time one of her children gets sick, but such assumptions are unfair. In many families, both spouses share childcare responsibilities or make arrangements for it.

Here's another good rule of thumb: Don't ask applicants any questions about marriage or family. Period. These types of questions elicit information that may be used to discriminate against women.

> **Hiring Hints**
>
> In choosing interview questions, ask yourself whether knowing the answer to each question is necessary to determine whether applicants can do the jobs for which they have applied. Steer clear of questions that even hint at relating to a person's race, religion, national origin, gender, age, or disabilities.

Criminal Records

You cannot ask applicants whether they have ever been arrested. Surprised? You shouldn't be. In our judicial system, after all, a person is innocent until proven guilty. Because police are often tougher and more likely to make arrests in minority neighborhoods, asking about arrests has an adverse effect on some minority groups.

You can ask about convictions for a felony; however, you cannot refuse to hire a person solely on the basis of a conviction—unless it's job-related. You might, for example, disqualify an applicant from a cashier's position if he was convicted for theft but not if he was convicted for disorderly conduct.

Lie-Detector Tests

Employees handle cash or confidential information in many companies, so employers want to do their best to weed out dishonest people. For years, companies used polygraphs to screen applicants for these sensitive jobs but no more! A federal law now restricts the use of these lie-detector tests.

Exempt from this law are government agencies, defense contractors, companies providing armed security guards, and a few others.

Although lie-detector tests are not legal in the hiring process, they can still be used as part of an investigation for theft, embezzlement, industrial espionage, and similar offenses. Before using polygraphs for any purpose, check with your attorney to ensure compliance with all applicable federal, state, and local laws.

Legal and Illegal Preemployment Questions

Although the civil rights laws vary somewhat from state to state, federal laws govern all organizations doing business in the United States. The following list is a general guideline that is applicable under federal law and in most states. However, to ensure that you are in compliance with the legal requirements and interpretations in the state(s) in which your organization operates, check with local authorities and/or an attorney specializing in this field. This chart applies to questions asked on application or other preemployment forms, in interviews, and in checking references.

Hiring Hints

Polygraph tests records changes in heartbeat, blood pressure, and respiration and are used to detect whether a person is telling the truth.

Keep in mind that some inquiries that would otherwise be considered lawful may be deemed as evidence of unlawful discrimination when the inquiry seeks to elicit information about an aspect of the applicant's background that is not job related or has a disproportionate negative effect on members of minority groups. For example, asking if an applicant owns an automobile—when a vehicle is not necessary for the job—is unlawful because members of some minority groups are less likely to afford car ownership.

The following are some examples of lawful and unlawful questions:

Race or color

    Lawful: None.

    Unlawful: Inquiry regarding complexion or skin coloring.

Religion

    Lawful: None.

    Unlawful: Inquiry into an applicant's religious denomination, religious affiliations, parish, pastor, or the religious holidays observed.

    Applicant may not be told, "This is a (Catholic, Protestant, Jewish, and so on) company."

National Origin

> **Lawful**: None.
>
> **Unlawful**: Inquiry into applicant's lineage, ancestry, national origin, descent, or parentage.
>
> Inquiry into the nationality of the applicant's parents or spouse.
>
> "What is your native tongue?"

Sex

> **Lawful**: None.
>
> **Unlawful**: Inquiry into gender.
>
> "Do you wish to be addressed as Mr., Mrs., Miss, or Ms.?"

Marital Status

> **Lawful**: None.
>
> **Unlawful**: "Are you married, single, divorced, or separated?"
>
> "Where does your spouse work?"
>
> "How many children do you have?"
>
> "What are the ages of your children?"

Birth Control

> **Lawful**: None.
>
> **Unlawful**: Inquiry into capacity to reproduce, advocacy of any form of birth control, or family planning.

Age

> **Lawful**: "Are you 18 years or older? If not, state your age."
>
> **Unlawful**: "How old are you?"
>
> "What is your date of birth?"
>
> "What year did you graduate?"
>
> Requiring applicants to submit proof of age in the form of a birth certificate or baptismal record. If proof of age is required for benefits or other reasons, the applicant should be told to present it when he or she reports to work.

Birthplace

> **Lawful**: None.
>
> **Unlawful**: Inquiry into the birthplace of the applicant, applicant's parents, spouse, or other close relatives.

Disability

Lawful: "Do you have any impairment—physical, mental, or medical—that would interfere with your ability to perform the job for which you have applied?"

"Do you require any special accommodation to perform the job for which you apply?"

Unlawful: "Do you have a disability?"

"Have you ever been treated for any of the following diseases ...?"

Arrest Record

Lawful: "Have you ever been convicted of a crime? Please give details."

Unlawful: "Have you ever been arrested?"

Name

Lawful: "Have you ever worked for this company under a different name?"

"Is any additional information relative to a change of name or the use of an assumed name or nickname necessary to enable a check on your work record?"

Unlawful: Inquiry into the original name of an applicant whose name as been changed by court order or otherwise.

Inquiry into the maiden name of a married woman.

Photographs

Lawful: None.

Unlawful: Requiring or providing the option for applicants to affix a photograph to an employment form at any time before hiring.

Taking a photograph of applicant prior to hiring or a video of the interview.

Citizenship

Lawful: "Are you a citizen of the United States?"

"If not a citizen of the United States, do you intend to become a citizen of the United States?"

"If you are not a citizen of the United States, have you the legal right to remain permanently in the United States?

"Do you intend to remain permanently in the United States?"

(See the discussion of hiring noncitizens in Chapter 3.)

Unlawful: "Of what country are you a citizen?"

Inquiry into whether an applicant is a naturalized or native-born citizen. Inquiry into the date when parents or a spouse obtained citizenship.

Requesting proof of citizenship or immigration documents prior to employment.

Language

Lawful: "What languages do you speak and write fluently?"

Unlawful: "What is your native language?"

"How did you acquire the ability to speak and write a foreign language?"

Education

Lawful: Inquiry into the applicant's academic, vocational, or professional education and the public and private schools attended.

Unlawful: Inquiry into the dates attended or graduated.

Experience

Lawful: Inquiry into work experience.

Unlawful: None.

Relatives

Lawful: Inquiry into the name of an applicant's relatives other than spouse already employed by the company.

Unlawful: Inquiry into names, addresses, ages, number, or other information concerning an applicant's spouse, children, or other relatives not employed by the company.

Notify in Case of Emergency

Legal: None.

Unlawful: Inquiry into next of kin.

Inquiry into the name and address of the person to be notified in case of emergency. This may be asked only after an employee is hired.

Military Experience

Lawful: Inquiry into an applicant's military experience in the armed forces of the United States or a state militia.

Unlawful: Inquiry into an applicant's general military experience, which might include serving in another country's armed forces.

Organizations

Lawful: Inquiry into an applicant's membership in organizations that the applicant considers relevant to his or her ability to perform the job.

Unlawful: "List all clubs, societies, and lodges to which you belong."

Driver's License

Lawful: "Do you possess a valid driver's license?"

Unlawful: Requiring that an applicant produce a driver's license prior to employment.

Does Your Application Form Comply?

Like every aspect of the hiring process, an application form must comply with equal employment laws. In today's litigious society, you'd think most companies would be conscious of this situation and have these forms reviewed carefully by legal experts.

Frequently Found Violations on Application Forms

As a consultant, I have had the opportunity to see countless company application forms. I'm amazed that even now—30 years after the EEO laws went into effect—errors like the following are found on these documents:

➤ Age or date of birth

➤ Marital status

➤ Number of children or ages of children

➤ Year of graduation or dates of attendance at schools

➤ Arrest records

➤ Maiden name

➤ Person to notify in case of emergency or next of kin

➤ Ownership of automobile

➤ Health-related questions

Sample Application Form

If your form includes any unlawful questions, it should be discarded immediately, and a new form should be designed. The sample application form shown here is typical of those used by many companies, and it may give you some guidelines. In addition to the questions asked in the sample, companies often add questions that are of particular concern to them.

Application for Employment

Date: _____

Name: _____

Social Security Number: _____

Address: _____

City, State, ZIP: _____

Phone: _____

Position sought: _____

Salary desired: _____

Education

Level: _____

School/Location: _____

Course: _____

Number of years: _____

Degree or diploma: _____

College: _____

Other: _____

Employment Record

1. Company/Address: _____

Dates: _____

Salary: _____

Supervisor: _____

Duties: _____

_____

Reason for leaving: _____

_____

2. Company/Address: _____

Dates: _____

Salary: _____

Supervisor: _____

Duties: _____

_____

Reason for leaving: _____

_____

3. Company/Address: _____

Dates: _____

Salary: _____

Supervisor: _____

Duties: _____

_____

Reason for leaving: _____

_____

How were you referred to this company? _____

_____

Are you 18 years of age or older? Yes/No

continues

continued

If you're hired, can you provide written evidence that you are authorized to work in the United States? Yes/No

Is there any other name under which you have worked that we would need in order to check your work record? Yes/No

If Yes, please provide: _____

_____

_____

Applicant's Statement

I understand that the employer follows an "employment at will" policy, in that I or the employer may terminate my employment at any time or for any reason consistent with applicable federal and state laws. This employment-at-will policy cannot be changed verbally or in writing unless authorized specifically by the president or executive vice president of this company. I understand that this application is not a contract of employment. I understand that the federal government prohibits the employment of unauthorized aliens; all persons hired must provide satisfactory proof of employment authorization and identity. Failure to submit such proof will result in denial of employment.

I understand that the employer may investigate my work and personal history and verify all information given on this application, on related papers, and in interviews. I hereby authorize all individuals, schools, and firms named therein, except my current employer (if so noted), to provide any information requested about me and hereby release them from all liability for damage in providing this information.

I certify that all the statements in this form and other information provided by me in applying for this position are true and understand that any falsification or willful omission shall be sufficient cause for dismissal or refusal of employment.

Signature _____ Date _____

An example of an application form.

Of course, you are not limited to asking only the questions on the sample form. It may be important in screening for the jobs in your organization to ask many other questions related to the employee's qualifications. For example, companies hiring technical and professional people often ask about membership in professional societies, awards earned, and papers published. For some jobs, you may want to get more details on certain aspects of education or experience.

Remember that the form should meet your needs while complying with appropriate laws.

The applicant's statement at the end of the application form is included at the advice of attorneys to protect the employer. This will be discussed in Chapter 23, "Making the Job Offer."

The Least You Need to Know

➤ In writing job specs or determining job requirements, concentrate on what is actually needed to perform the job and avoid stereotyping prospects by sex, age, race, or other factors that are not job related.

➤ Before placing a help-wanted ad, review it to make sure it is in compliance with the pertinent laws.

➤ Don't try to evade the laws by asking an employment agency or recruiter to screen out members of a certain gender, race, or religion.

➤ In choosing interview questions, ask yourself whether knowing the answer to each question is necessary to determine whether applicants can do the jobs for which they have applied.

➤ Steer clear of interview questions that even hint at relating to a person's race, religion, national origin, gender, age, or disabilities.

➤ Learn the types of questions you can and cannot ask on an application or in an interview.

More on Employment Laws

In the two preceding chapters, we examined the laws with which you must comply that relate to equal employment opportunity. In this chapter, you will learn about two additional factors in this area. One factor is affirmative action, which is required under certain circumstances. The other factor is the special problems faced when hiring non-U.S. citizens. We'll also discuss the various penalties you may incur for violating any of the civil rights laws and what you should do when you face complaints or charges.

Affirmative Action

Title VII of the Civil Rights Act of 1964 (the Equal Employment Opportunity law) requires that covered organizations should not discriminate in hiring or on the job because of race, religion, national origin, or sex. Nowhere in the law does it even hint that companies should give special preference to a person because of any of these factors.

In fact, the law specifically states that "Nothing contained in this subchapter shall be interpreted to require any employer, employment agency, labor organization ... to give preferential treatment to any individual or to any group because of the race, color, religion, sex, or national origin of such individual or group."

Advocates of stronger measures point out that many discriminatory practices of the past remain so deeply imbedded in basic institutions of society that these practices have an extremely unequal effect on certain groups even when the employer has no conscious intent to discriminate. To help members of these groups catch up with the majority groups, it was suggested that affirmative action programs should be established.

To meet this objective, President Lyndon B. Johnson issued an executive order (#11246) that required not only special preference for certain minority groups but an active program of affirmative action to recruit members of these "protected classes" into companies that held contracts with the government.

Executive Order #11246 (as amended by Executive Order #11375) requires affirmative action programs by all federal contractors and subcontractors that have contracts of more than $50,000 and have 50 or more employees.

Specific requirements for such programs are spelled out in Revised Order #4 issued by the Office of Contract Compliance of the U.S. Department of Labor, which was designated as the administrator of the executive order.

In addition to the organizations covered by executive orders, any company that violates the EEO laws may be required by the EEOC to establish an affirmative action program. (See the discussion of violations later in this chapter in the section "What Happens When Laws Are Violated.")

Words to Work By

An **executive order** is not a law. It is an edict promulgated by the president without being passed by Congress. Executive orders do not apply to the entire population—only to government agencies or organizations that do business with the government. Violation of an executive order can lead to loss of the contract.

The Protected Classes

Although discrimination against all minority groups is illegal, only five groups have been designated as "protected classes." They are ...

➤ **Blacks:** This covers all individuals who are of African American background. In reporting, however, blacks of Hispanic background are listed under Hispanics.

➤ **Hispanics:** This group includes all people who derive from countries in Latin America. People from Spain are not considered Hispanics.

➤ **Asians or Pacific Islanders:** This group includes people who derive from the Asian mainland, Japan, Taiwan, the subcontinent (India, Pakistan, Bangladesh), and all the nonwhite population of the Pacific islands.

➤ **Native Americans or Alaskan Natives:** This group includes people deriving from American Indian and Eskimo tribes. (It is not politically correct to call them Indians or Eskimos. The proper terms are "Native American" and "Alaskan Natives." If you're not worried about PC, use the commonly understood terms. If you are PC conscious, don't elaborate on this category.)

➤ **Women.**

Companies required to engage in affirmative action programs must bring into their companies members of each of these classes in proportion to the population of people in each class in their community. These numbers are based on figures issued by the Department of Labor and can be obtained from the Office of Contract Compliance, U.S. Department of Labor, Washington, D.C., 20010.

Contractors must then make a survey of their current work force to determine the number of employees in each category for each job classification. This helps them set goals to bring into each job classification a representative group of people from all the classes in the community. For example, a company may have a staff consisting of 40 percent black employees in a community where the African American population is 12 percent. But they are not in compliance because all the black employees are in the lowest labor class. To comply, steps must be taken to bring more African Americans into the higher-level jobs.

Employment Enigmas

Even when complying with the AAP requirement to keep a record of all applicants by "protected class," it's illegal to mark on their application form any reference to these factors. One solution is to have applicants complete a separate form for this information and keep it independent from the application form.

Seeking Applicants from Minority Groups

The executive orders require companies to set specific goals and a timetable to bring into their organization members from the protected classes. To do this requires more than just advertising that you are an equal opportunity employer. You must be proactive.

For example, the ABC bank complained that it was unable to hire more African Americans. The reason: They claim members of that group never apply to them for jobs. This may be true, but it's not a good excuse. The reason blacks don't apply is that the bank has a reputation for only hiring a few token blacks—a teller or two and, occasionally, a junior executive to "sit near the door."

If a company wants to correct this image, it must take positive steps in that direction. Try the following:

➤ Advertise in newspapers read by the community you wish to attract. There are newspapers and magazines that cater to African Americans, Spanish-language papers that reach the Hispanic community, and others that are read by Asians and Native Americans. The same is true of radio stations.

➤ Cultivate organizations that work with the group you want to reach. If you seek women in management or professional jobs, contact Catalyst at www.catalystwomen.org or the National Organization for Women (www.now.org.)

➤ Set up job fairs in the communities where people of the group you seek live.

➤ Work with high schools, community colleges, and colleges to engage interns and summer employees.

Making Your AAP Work

The most important measure of an affirmative action program is its results.

Extensive efforts to develop procedures, analyses, data collection systems, report forms, and fine written policy statements are meaningless unless the end product leads to improvement in the hiring, training, and promotion of minorities and women in all parts of the organization.

The essence of your affirmative action program should be as follows:

➤ Establish strong company policy and commitment.

➤ Assign responsibility and authority for the program to a top company official.

➤ Analyze your present work force to identify jobs, departments, and units where minorities and women are underutilized.

➤ Set specific, measurable, attainable hiring and promotion goals with target dates in each area of underutilization.

➤ Make every manager, supervisor, and team leader responsible and accountable for helping to meet these goals.

➤ Reevaluate job descriptions and hiring criteria to ensure that they reflect actual job needs.

Hiring Hints

To determine work force composition, an information report known as EEO-1 must be filled out annually. Employers with 100 or more employees and government contractors and subcontractors with 50 or more employees must complete it.

➤ Actively recruit minorities and women who qualify or can become qualified to fill goals.

➤ Review and revise all employment procedures to ensure that they do not have a discriminatory effect and that they help attain goals.

➤ Focus on getting minorities and women into upward-mobility and relevant-training pipelines where they have not had previous access.

➤ Develop systems to monitor and measure progress regularly. If results are not satisfactory to meet goals, find out why and make necessary changes.

Reverse Discrimination

In their efforts to comply with these executive orders and bring into their organizations more minorities and women, some companies have been accused of reverse discrimination. They give preference to members of protected classes and therefore have discriminated against members of other nonprotected groups. For example, a white man is well-qualified for an open position. A black or Hispanic man whom he believes is less qualified gets hired. The white man may claim that he was discriminated against.

The Supreme Court ruled on this in the case of *United Steelworkers of America vs. Weber* in 1979. In 1974, the Kaiser Aluminum Co. and its union, the United Steel Workers, joined in a voluntary affirmative action program designed to increase the number of African American workers in higher-skill-level (craft) jobs in one of its plants. Prior to the promulgation of this program, craft workers were selected from current employees in the lesser-skilled categories on the basis of seniority. Because the company had not hired blacks until a few years before this agreement, very few blacks had enough seniority to qualify.

The program specified that 50 percent of all new craft trainees would be black regardless of seniority. The plan was to remain in effect until the percentage of blacks in the craft jobs was equal to the percentage of blacks in the local labor market.

One of the white production workers passed over for the training program was Brian Weber. Weber filed suit charging that he was discriminated against because he was white.

The Supreme Court ruled against Weber. The justification: Voluntary affirmative action programs designed to eliminate racial imbalances in traditionally segregated job categories are permissible. This decision did not endorse all AAPs, but it legitimized programs that were designed to correct past racial discrimination.

Employment Enigmas

Failure to obtain documentation of a noncitizen's green card or other authorization to work can lead at the minimum to a loss of production due to deportation of the alien and at the most to fines or imprisonment.

Because of concerns about reverse discrimination, there's a strong movement afoot to eliminate or at least modify affirmative action.

Laws have been passed in several states eliminating affirmative action in college admission and in "set asides" of government contracts to minority contractors. Several more recent court decisions have nullified some affirmative action programs. However, companies covered by the executive orders should continue to develop AAPs and work to make current programs effective.

With the current shortage of job applicants in many categories, more and more companies are employing diverse work forces made up of men and women from many different cultures. The challenge in the future will not be hiring minorities and women but training and promoting them to the higher-level positions that have for so many years been denied them.

Hiring Non-U.S. Citizens

There are two facets involved in the hiring of people who are not citizens of the United States. First, there are the immigrants who come into this country—many legally, many more illegally—looking for work. The greatest percentage of these people seeks lower-level positions as farm hands, factory workers, hospital and nursing-home attendants, taxi drivers, and similar positions. Your main concern here is to make sure the applicant has the proper documentation.

However, there are situations in which an employer may actively recruit men and women from foreign countries for hard-to-fill jobs. Most of these people are professional or highly skilled workers. Hospitals need physicians and nurses, which are in short supply in their communities. Technical organizations need engineers and technicians to staff their teams. In this section, we'll learn what is required to bring these specialists into the United States and onto your payroll.

Examine the Documentation

As noted in Chapter 3, "What the Laws on Employment Cover," noncitizens who work in the United States must have proper documentation. To ensure that you comply with regulations, do the following:

➤ Have all new employees (not just the ones you suspect are foreign) fill out an I-9 form. You can obtain copies from the Immigration and Naturalization Service. This form should not be completed until *after* a person is hired. When a starting date is agreed on, the employee should be advised that he or she must submit proper documentation before being put on the payroll.

➤ Have new employees provide documents to prove their identity. You have to be sure a new employee isn't using someone else's papers. Acceptable documents include a driver's license with photo, a school ID with photo, and similar papers.

➤ Have new employees provide documents to prove citizenship. These documents include a current U.S. passport, a certificate of naturalization, a birth certificate, or a voter-registration card.

➤ Noncitizens must have documents that authorize employment. The most commonly used authorization is Form I-551, usually called a "green card." (It originally was green, but now it's pink.) The employee's photograph is laminated to the card. Other forms are acceptable for students who may work while in school and some other exceptional cases.

No Required Documents

If the person you hire cannot show you the required documents, advise him or her to do everything possible to locate them.

If the documents cannot be located, they should be applied for at once. When the application is completed, the employee must give proof to the employer that the application for the document has been sent. This can be in the form of a receipt from the appropriate agency or certified mail sent to the agency.

These receipts should be photocopied and kept until the documents are received and shown to you. The law requires that the employee must present the documents to the employer within 21 days of starting the job, or that person's employment must be terminated.

When the documents have been examined, notations should be made on the Form I-9 indicating the type of document and identification number (if any). Make photocopies of the documents. The originals should be returned to the employee.

Employers who hire undocumented aliens are subject to fines and, in cases of repeated offenses, imprisonment. If you have any doubts about a document or any questions concerning the law, contact the local office of the Immigration and Naturalization Service.

Hiring Hints

Make photocopies of all documents. If some documents are not provided, get proof that they have been applied for. If not presented within 21 days of starting the job, the employee must be terminated.

Employment Enigmas

The immigration laws do not prohibit you from hiring noncitizens. Refusal to hire a person who is legally permitted to work in this country because of his or her nationality is unlawful under the civil rights laws.

Hiring Foreign Students and Specialists

There are other situations in which you may put foreign nationals on your payroll:

➤ Foreign students come to the United States to study a field in which practical training is desirable. The student's university can apply for a practical training (F1) visa. This will allow the student to work for one year in his or her field of study. If the person you want to hire has this visa, you can hire that person immediately, and you need not take any further action. But remember, the visa expires one year after it is issued, and that person can no longer work in the United States unless some other visa is attained. If you are interested in hiring such students, contact universities who train them for referrals.

➤ Exchange students are students from foreign universities who come here to continue their studies and to pick up practical experience in their fields of expertise. To obtain such students, contact exchange student organizations. One such organization is the International Association for Exchange of Students for Technical Experience (www.aipt.org). They provide leads to foreign students, and arrange for the necessary documentation (J-1 visa). Another organization is the American Field Service (www.afs.org), which brings foreign students to American universities and helps locate part-time jobs for them to enable them to gain experience in their areas of interest.

➤ Nonpermanent work authorization (H-1 visa). There are several different types of visas depending on the kind of work in which the individual engages. For example, registered nurses require form H-1A; technical workers require form H-1B. If you can prove to the INS that the skills needed to fill a job cannot be found among American citizens or permanent residents, you may obtain permission to recruit the needed employee from a foreign country.

Once you locate a suitable candidate, you must apply for the H-1 visa. The process is very complicated, and an attorney or consultant specializing in immigration should be retained. Even if you find a qualified candidate who already is in the United States and has an H-1 visa to work in another company, you will need to apply to the Immigration and Naturalization Service to transfer it. This takes four to eight weeks. How to go about recruiting such candidates will be discussed in Chapter 12, "Recruiting for Tough-to-Fill Jobs."

What Happens When Laws Are Violated

You're in trouble. You interviewed four men and one woman for the sales representative opening, and you chose one of the men. Sally P., the woman applicant, files a complaint against you with the EEOC charging sex discrimination. Let's look at what happens once that charge is filed.

Investigation

If the state in which you are located has a civil rights law that covers the situation, the EEOC refers the complaint to state authorities. They will take it from there. If, however, the state fails to resolve the complaint within 60 days, it is given back to the EEOC for final investigation. The procedure is much the same whether it is done by state or federal agencies, so for this discussion, we'll assume the EEOC has jurisdiction.

A copy of the charges will be sent to you. The investigation is usually started with a telephone call, a letter, or a questionnaire being sent to the complainant and the company requesting details of the case. If you fail to respond, the EEOC can obtain a court subpoena to compel you to turn over the records to them.

An investigator will come to your office to question you and to examine the employment files. He or she may interview employees, talk to applicants who have not been hired, and review the EEO-1 reports that show the racial and ethnic makeup of your work force.

Once a charge is made, you can resolve the case by offering a settlement. You can agree to hire the complainant or make a financial settlement. In cases in which a complainant has been terminated, you can agree to rehire him or her with or without back pay.

Employment Enigmas

If your company is charged with violating state or federal laws, contact your attorney immediately. If not properly handled, it can lead to serious consequences.

Of course, the investigation may clear you of the charges. In the case of Sally, you may prove that the man you hired was significantly more qualified for the position. However, that doesn't necessarily end the case. Sally still has the right to take civil action against you in a federal court if she so desires.

If the investigation finds that there is "reasonable cause" of discrimination, the EEOC will attempt to conciliate the matter between Sally and your company.

The EEOC may also take the initiative to investigate a company even when no specific complaint is made. It may send "testers" to uncover unlawful discrimination. Testers are used by both government agencies and civil rights organizations. For example, in one case, a company advertised for a cost accountant. The agency referred three "applicants" with virtually identical backgrounds. Two were black, one white. Both black applicants received short interviews and were politely rejected. The white applicant was given a lengthy first interview and went on to subsequent interviews. This was prima-facie evidence of discrimination, and the company was so charged.

Penalties

If the conciliation process fails, the EEOC can make a decision and enforce it with a court order. It can compel the employer to hire Sally, to pay her back pay from the time of rejection, and to pay her attorney's fees.

In a similar case, one of my clients was ordered to hire the applicant. Since she already had taken another job, however, my client had to pay the complainant the equivalent of the salary she would have earned from the date of rejection to the time she found and started the other job—in this case, six months' pay.

In addition, if the investigation shows that there has been a pattern of discrimination, the EEOC may require the company to establish an affirmative action program to actively recruit members of the classes that have been discriminated against. The company will be required to keep records of every open job, job orders sent to employment agencies or recruiters, help-wanted ads for these jobs, the name and race or national origin of every applicant, and if not hired, the reason. EEOC representatives will inspect these periodically.

As noted in the previous section, if the company is a government contractor or subcontractor, violations of the law and failure to comply with their own affirmative action program can lead to loss of the contract and being barred from doing business with any government agency.

In cases in which the complainant chooses to sue the company, there is the added penalty of a jury awarding huge sums as punitive damages. Complainants have won multimillion dollar awards for the emotional distress caused by the discrimination.

Hiring Hints

Train your receptionists, security guards, and others who may have first contact with applicants to be aware that the manner in which they deal with applicants reflects the company's policies. *All* applicants should be treated with equal courtesy.

How to Deal with Complaints

Although investigators from government agencies may call for an appointment, they often come in unannounced. Remember that they have not come to have a pleasant conversation. Unless they present you with a subpoena or a search warrant, you do not have to talk to them, turn over any records to them, or let them look at any files. Unless you have already discussed the case with your attorney and have been instructed what to do, politely tell them that you cannot speak to them at the moment and suggest that they set an appointment at a later date.

Your attorney will advise you exactly what to do depending on the matters involved. Here are some general suggestions:

➤ If your attorney is not present, bring in another manager to accompany you. He or she can provide information about company practices and policies to back you up. Caution this person not to comment on the specific case.

➤ Answer the questions honestly, but don't volunteer any additional information.

➤ Take notes. Just as the investigator is noting everything you say, you also should note the questions asked and your answers. If testimony is given at future hearings, the investigator will refer to his or her notes. Be prepared to refer to yours.

➤ Keep your cool. Even if the charges appear to be totally unfounded, don't become upset or appear annoyed.

➤ Don't commit your company to anything at a first meeting. You should discuss the matter with higher-level management and your attorney before agreeing to anything.

➤ Screen all records and files you agree to turn over to make sure only those that are pertinent to the case are presented. Unless original records are subpoenaed, send photocopies. If you must send original records, make copies for yourself.

If you follow these suggestions, you will be less likely to make some of the common errors employers make when dealing with a government agency.

Preventative Maintenance

No matter how good your intentions may be to maintain a discrimination-free environment, violations of the law may occur. This may be because some of the managers or team leaders are unsure of what the law requires or let their own biases influence their actions.

Here are some suggestions to help keep you out of trouble:

➤ Establish policies and procedures that are in total compliance with the law and ensure that all employees at all levels are aware of them and that the company takes them seriously.

➤ Run periodic training sessions on equal employment, especially for people who interview applicants.

➤ Use recruiting sources that will reach applicants from all groups in the community.

➤ Develop a standardized interviewing program so that all applicants for the same type of position will be asked similar questions. This will be discussed in Chapter 16, "Planning the Interview."

➤ Keep accurate notes about each applicant and note immediately after the interview any reasons the applicant was being considered or was rejected.

Keeping Alert to EEO Responsibilities

Follow this acrostic to keep alert to your EEO responsibilities:

Go along with the spirit as well as the letter of the law.

Offer women and minorities opportunities that were previously denied to them.

Open training programs to minorities, women, and the physically challenged and encourage them, by offering counseling and support, to complete these programs.

Discipline should be administered equitably and should be carefully documented.

Be aware of your own biases and work to overcome any influence they may have on your job decisions.

Use everyone's abilities optimally. Don't base your views about a person's abilities on age, sex, or race. Don't judge people on what they cannot do but on what they can do.

Set realistic performance standards based on what a job really calls for. Do not specify, for example, that a job calls for heavy lifting when most of the lifting is done mechanically.

Ignore stereotypes and judge people by their individual abilities, strengths, and weaknesses.

Never use racial epithets or slurs—even in jest.

Encourage all people to deal with their coworkers as human beings whether they're black or white; Hispanic, Asian, or Anglo; men or women; physically challenged or able-bodied. Mold them into a team.

Sex life and job life must be kept separate.

Support your company's equal-employment and affirmative-action programs fully in every aspect of your job.

If you follow these guidelines, it will add up to **GOOD BUSINESS.**

The Least You Need to Know

➤ Executive Order #11246 requires companies that hold contracts with the government to institute an active program of affirmative action to recruit members of the "protected classes"—African Americans, Hispanics, Asians and Pacific Islanders, Native Americans, Alaskan Natives, and women.

➤ The challenge in the future will not be hiring minorities and women but training and promoting them to the higher-level positions that have for so many years been denied them.

➤ Noncitizens who work in the United States must have proper documentation. Make photocopies of all documents. If some documents are not provided, get proof that they have been applied for. If not presented within 21 days of starting a job, the employee must be terminated.

➤ If an investigation is started, get legal advice immediately.

Part 3

Sources for Candidates

There are jobs to fill, but where are the people to fill them? It is never easy to fill jobs—and in this age of full employment—locating candidates and selecting from them the best possible employees is a major challenge to managers everywhere.

For some jobs, the person who can do the job best might be working right in your own company and you don't even know it. For other jobs, you may have to seek candidates from far and near and spend hundreds, or perhaps thousands of dollars in your search—and then you're not sure if you made the right decision.

There's no easy way to fill those job openings. In this part, we'll look at some tried and true means of hiring people and also at some new and radical approaches to staffing your organization.

Chapter 6

Your Best Bet May Be Close By

In This Chapter

➤ Using current employees as a primary source—good or bad?

➤ Identifying candidates who have what you need

➤ Moving staff members up the ladder

➤ Encouraging referrals

Some companies rarely look outside their own ranks to fill a higher-level job. They promote or transfer current employees and only go outside to fill jobs at the lowest levels. Most companies today understand that this is not always possible and, as a matter of fact, not always desirable. However, never overlook the resources already in your organization. You may have some staff members with skills that are not being utilized or people who have potential that is not being fulfilled.

This chapter examines the advantages and limitations of using your current staff as a resource for filling open positions. You'll also learn some techniques that will enable you to tap these resources.

Internal Transfers and Promotions

When a change of job involves a promotion, most people are delighted to welcome the opportunity. Although not every transfer is a promotion, it's often an opportunity for someone to learn, gain experience, and take a step forward in preparing for career advancement.

Let's Look at the Advantages

Seeking to fill a vacancy from within the company has many advantages:

➤ People who already work in your company know the "lay of the land." They're familiar with your company's rules and regulations, customs and culture, and practices and idiosyncrasies. Hiring these people rather than someone from outside your company saves time in orientation and minimizes the risks of dissatisfaction with your company.

➤ You know more about these people than you could possibly learn about outsiders. You may have worked directly with a certain person or observed him or her in action. You can get detailed and honest information about a candidate from previous supervisors and company records.

➤ Offering opportunities to current employees boosts morale and serves as an incentive for them to perform at their highest level.

➤ An important side effect is that it creates a positive image of your company in the industry and in your community. This image encourages good people to apply when jobs for outsiders become available.

It Has Its Share of Problems

Although the advantages of internal promotion usually outweigh the limitations, there are disadvantages to consider:

Employment Enigmas

The practice of restricting promotions to current employees tends to perpetuate the racial, ethnic, and gender makeup of your staff. Companies whose employees are predominantly white and male and who rarely seek outside personnel have been charged with discrimination against African Americans, other minorities, and women.

➤ The job may require skills not found in your company.

➤ If you promote only from within, you limit the sources from which to draw candidates, and you may be restricted to promoting a person significantly less qualified than someone from outside your company.

➤ People who have worked in other companies bring with them new and different ideas and know-how that can benefit your team.

➤ Outsiders look at your activities with a fresh view and are not tainted by overfamiliarity.

Most companies use a judicious mixture that combines internal promotion and transfers with outside recruitment to get and keep the best candidates for their openings.

One of the major problems of interdepartmental transfers is the reluctance of department heads to release efficient and productive workers to other departments. One of the first actions of a company planning to implement a policy of internal recruitment is to notify all department heads and team leaders that it will overrule any attempts to keep people who could be more valuable to the organization by transfer to another position. It should also be mentioned that people who are passed over for better positions in other departments are unlikely to remain with the company and probably will seek another job elsewhere—so both the department and the company will lose a valuable employee.

Finding the Right Candidate from Within the Company

Many organizations have developed training programs that provide a steady stream of trained people for their expanding job needs. In some companies, there's a plethora of talent from which to choose.

At times, however, there are no obvious candidates for a vacant job. You may have people in the company who are qualified to do the job—and you don't know it. What can you do?

Search the Personnel Files

If properly maintained, personnel records can be a major resource. Examination of these records may uncover people working in jobs below their education or skill level. It may also reveal people who have had additional training since they were employed.

Any training given by the company, whether internal or outside seminars or programs, should be noted. If the company has a tuition-reimbursement policy, any courses falling into this category should be noted. Employees should be encouraged to inform the human resources department of other courses, programs, or outside training they may have completed.

Personnel records can be an important means of locating people urgently needed by a company. A major aerospace firm recently spent several thousand dollars advertising for specialized engineers needed for a new project in one division of the company. The recruiters were shocked to receive letters replying to the ad from engineers in another division of the same company. The engineers claimed that their specialized knowledge was not

Hiring Hints

Send periodic questionnaires to all employees to bring personnel records up to date. Ask about new skills or knowledge acquired during annual reviews. All this should be incorporated in the personnel records.

being used in their current jobs, and they were seeking a position in which it would be. Had the HR department known about them, it would have saved the company money and time.

Ask the Supervisors

Supervisors and team leaders know a good deal about their associates. Take advantage of this. Let them know what jobs are open in other departments. They may have associates who are qualified.

There are two dangers here. One is that team leaders may be reluctant to lose a good worker, even if the transfer would be advantageous to both the worker and the company. It's not easy to overcome this. The company must have a strict policy on this as previously noted in the section "It Has Its Share of Problems."

The other danger is that the team leader may refer someone he or she wants to get rid of. Give the same careful screening to applicants referred by their team leaders as you would to every other candidate for the job.

Job Banks

To systematize internal searches, many firms have established databases listing all the skills, talents, experience, education, and other backgrounds of all its employees. These are usually referred to as *job banks*, sometimes called *skill banks*.

For example, under "Lotus 123" are the names of all persons who have worked with this program at any time in their careers, whether or not they are currently using this skill. If a need for a team member with this background occurs in Unit A, and the bank lists a person in Unit B who has had this experience but is currently employed in another capacity, he or she may be approached about transferring to Unit A.

As new skills are acquired, internal training programs are completed, and outside training is reported, they are added to the database.

Words to Work By

A **job bank** or **skill bank** is a database listing all the skills, education, experience factors, and other background of all employees. It can be searched to match job openings against the current work force.

Job Posting

Many companies make a practice of posting job openings on bulletin boards or listing them in company newsletters so that any employee who believes he or she is qualified can apply. Indeed, many union contracts require that job openings be posted.

Posting a job opening encourages current employees to apply, especially those who may qualify for the job but are not known to the manager or team leader seeking to fill the job. Sandra L. worked in the order-processing department, but her career goal was in sales. Everybody told her she had a "sales personality," and she had some part-time selling experience. When an opening for a sales trainee was posted, she applied. The Sales Manager interviewed her and recognized her talent. She was transferred into the sales-training program and, in time, became one of the company's star sales reps. Had the job not been posted, Sandra would not have known there was an opening, the sales manager would not have known about Sandra, and the company would have missed a high-potential employee.

There are still companies in which minority and women employees are not usually considered for certain jobs. Job posting enables members of these groups to apply and be given serious consideration. For this reason, many compliance agreements with the EEOC include a requirement that all jobs be posted.

However, there's a downside to posting jobs. When a current employee applies for a posted job and is rejected, you have a disgruntled employee. Some may quit, causing the loss of a good employee. Some who stay lose self-confidence and make little effort to build up their competence. Some go back to work and bad-mouth the company to their co-workers, leading to low morale.

When rejecting an employee for an internal transfer or promotion, take the time to explain in detail why he or she did not qualify. Point out any areas that need improvement so that next time this type of job is posted, he or she will be better equipped to handle it and will have a good chance of getting it. Suggest what additional training the individual needs and, if pertinent, what the company will do to help the person attain that training.

Promotion Policies

Advancement within an organization is an ideal way to fill higher-level jobs. Although there are many people who are not career oriented and shun moving into positions demanding responsibility, a great number of men and women look for advancement as a means of career growth. If they cannot advance in your company, they'll move to another company in which they can. Successful companies recognize this and provide opportunities for their best staff members. Let's look at some commonly followed policies.

Hiring Hints

Post jobs on the company intranet—the internal variation of the Internet that can only be accessed by company employees.

Employment Enigmas

When several employees apply for a posted job—and there is only one opening—assure the unsuccessful candidates that they were seriously considered and, if true, that there will be future opportunities for which they will be considered. Guide them as to what they can do to improve their chances in the future.

The Einstein Theory of Promotion—Relativity

If you're a relative of the boss, you get the promotion. *Nepotism* has been a factor in promotion since ancient times. Popes and kings appointed nephews and cousins to cushy jobs. In the world of business, parents "hire" their sons or daughters as vice presidents. Even distant relatives get preference over strangers.

Words to Work By

Nepotism is preference shown in promotion or treatment on the job by higher-level managers to relatives or close friends.

In family-owned businesses—and there are thousands of them all over the world—it is expected that management will be in the hands of the family. This poses two challenges to the owner: (1) ensuring that the heir-apparent and other relatives are capable of doing the jobs to which they are appointed, and (2) attracting and retaining qualified nonfamily members who accept being limited in advancement by nepotistic policy.

In my consulting practice, I have worked with many family-owned businesses to help them deal with both of these problems.

Here are some guidelines I have recommended:

➤ Carefully plan the succession of management. If your heir-apparent is a son, daughter, or other relative, make sure he or she is capable of handling the job and really wants to become part of the family firm. Discuss the business with your prospective heirs early in their lives. Have them work in the firm after school and during summers. When they are ready for full-time work, have them start in lower-level positions and test their capability on the job. Don't let your love for them affect an honest evaluation of their assets and liabilities. Train them to reinforce their strengths and to build up their weaknesses. Promote them only when they are ready to take on the duties and responsibilities of the higher position.

➤ Build up a team of managers from both family and nonfamily members. Avoid giving preference to your family. Give the nonfamily members opportunity to express and implement their ideas. Reward them financially and with recognition. Make them an integral part of management. Your heirs will need their support when their turn comes to take over the firm. By building up a culture of cooperation and collaboration within the management team during your tenure, you will most likely ensure its continuation in the future.

➤ For heirs-apparent: You have both a blessing and a curse. Being the son or daughter of the boss puts you in the position of having first crack at promotion and eventually a top-level position in the firm. On the other side of this coin, you are expected to be a superior worker. You are being watched not only by your parent, the boss, but by the nonfamily managers, other employees, and perhaps customers and financial analysts. You will have to prove to them that you are capable of managing the firm when your turn comes. Unless you earn their respect, you will not receive the support from them that is essential to your success and the company's survival.

➤ For nonfamily members who work for family firms: Don't assume that, because you are not a member of the family, you are destined to be restricted in growth. True, you may never be the CEO (although there are many instances in which this has occurred), but as the company grows and as you prove your worth, you can grow with it and move into significant, well-paid, and challenging positions.

If You Don't Quit or Die, You're Promoted

In many companies, promotions are based on seniority. When an opening occurs, the most senior member of the department or team moves up.

Fair? After all, doesn't a person who has served long and loyally deserves promotion? Not necessarily. A long-term, loyal employment record is commendable, but it doesn't necessarily qualify the member for the higher level. The position often requires skills not used at the lower level. Not only may specific educational or professional experience be needed, leadership skills also may be essential to the job.

When a position develops at any level, it should be analyzed to determine what the person who will perform the job should bring to it in terms of education, training, experience, and personality. If the most senior person in the group falls short in any of these areas, somebody else should be considered. You may have to select a person from the group with lesser seniority, transfer somebody from another part of the company, or hire an outsider.

Telling the senior member that he or she is not getting the promotion must be done with sensitivity. The person bypassed has most likely been a productive worker who may have been waiting for years for this opportunity. Don't surprise him or her with the public announcement of the appointment. Explain as best you can why the decision was made before it is announced to the other employees.

The Best Worker Gets the Promotion

When promotion by seniority is not mandated, employers can select the best worker for the job. The best mechanic is promoted to master mechanic, the best accountant to controller, the best sales rep to district manager.

This is an excellent way to choose a person for a higher-level technical position such as moving a programmer up to a systems analyst, but if the job is at the management level, it is not enough.

Promotion resulting from competence is an incentive for team members to work hard and smart with the carrot of promotion dangling in front of them. But the best worker may not necessarily be the best leader or manager. It takes additional and often different skills to be successful in the higher-level job.

Employment Enigmas

Your best worker may not be your best bet for promotion to team leader or supervisor. More important than technical competence are leadership ability, communication skills, and superior interpersonal relations.

This doesn't mean that good performance should be ignored. Doing good work certainly should be a factor in making the decision, but as pointed out before, it is only one of the facets of succeeding in a leadership position.

To qualify for any position, the candidate must meet a variety of qualifications as determined in the job specification (see Chapter 2, "Do You Know What You're Looking For?"). To determine whether the person you are considering is qualified, you must undertake the same procedures that you would if you were screening outside applicants. Indeed, you can obtain much more information about internal candidates than you can about outsiders. The techniques that can be used in this process will be discussed in Part 5, "Making the Interview More Meaningful."

Career Pathing—A Proactive Approach to Promotion

When Kevin K. was hired by Southeast Utilities, he went through a series of evaluations and was assigned to a training program. When the program was completed, he was assigned to a team in the technical support department. During the first few years, he was given progressively more responsible assignments and did very well in each of them.

At his third annual performance review, he was informed that, because of his excellent record, he was chosen to participate in the company's *career pathing* program. To ensure that the expanding needs of the company continued to be met, several men and women were selected each year to be assessed and trained to move up the corporate ladder.

The first step in this process was to report to an "assessment center," where he was given a series of tests and interviews and participated in interactive exercises with other participants. (How assessment centers are conducted will be discussed in Chapter 19, "Special Types of Interviews.")

After the results were analyzed, he met with the Career Pathing Team of the human resources department to discuss their findings, his own ambitions, and the opportunities available in the company.

Kevin was told that there were many opportunities for a person with his talents in the organization, and the team suggested several areas he should consider for his career path. They pointed out that, to become better equipped for growth within the company, he should acquire more knowledge in the information technology areas and develop managerial skills.

To start the ball rolling, he was advised to sign up for an advanced computer-training program; when completed successfully, he would be transferred to a position in the IT department where he could hone these skills. In addition, to prepare him for eventual promotion to management, he was advised to enroll in an MBA program at the local university under the company's tuition-reimbursement plan.

This career pathing program was not just an altruistic action to help Kevin grow in his career. It created within the company a core of well-trained, highly motivated employees to fill the ever-growing need for technicians and managers.

Words to Work By

To promote the careers of their employees, many companies have instituted **career pathing** programs. Employees are assessed to determine their potential and what steps they must take to move up into positions that will be of greatest value to both the company and themselves.

Using Current Employees as a Recruiting Source

The men and women who work for you are an excellent source for getting people like themselves. Many of them have friends from school or from previous jobs who have similar backgrounds and who may be prospects for your open positions. Programs to encourage referrals by employees have been instituted in many companies.

This has not always been the case. In fact, many companies had policies to refuse employment to friends and relatives of current employees. Before the EEO laws banned such questions, application forms often inquired whether the applicant had relatives or friends within the company.

One reason for this policy was the fear that, if friends or relatives worked together, they might form cliques that would disrupt the smooth flow of operations. Over the years, labor shortages, better understanding of group dynamics, and greater decentralization of business functions have made this fear less valid.

Employment Enigmas

The morale and attitudes of the people in a company can make or break a referral campaign. If employees are discontented, it's unlikely they will refer friends even if the rewards offered are substantial.

Encouraging Employee Referrals

The most important factor is developing a program of employee referrals is company morale. The morale and attitudes of the people in a company can make or break a referral campaign. If employees are discontented, it's unlikely they will refer friends.

Managers often kid themselves into thinking their organization is "one big, happy family," when under the surface it is seething with discontent. Periodic employee-attitude surveys or evaluations by outside consultants can bring out the true status of morale. If it is not satisfactory, the referral program will not work until steps are taken to correct the problems that cause the poor morale.

Some programs may be limited to occasional suggestions made by team leaders and others in management that friends are welcome to apply for jobs. Others may involve formal campaigns with prizes, rewards, and publicity.

An effective program requires considerable planning. A typical employee-referral campaign includes announcements in the company publication, colorful wall posters, notices on bulletin boards, announcements over the public address system, special team or department meetings, and letters to the homes of each employee.

Hiring Hints

To get the attention of your employees with regard to your referral program, play up the benefits to the referrer in your announcements. Publicize it with colorful wall posters, notices on bulletin boards, announcements over the public address system, special team or department meetings, and letters to the homes of each employee.

Reward Programs for Successful Referrals

Prizes or bonuses sometimes are offered for each person employed through the program—usually contingent on the new employee remaining with the firm for a specified period of time. The amount of the award varies from company to company and usually depends on the difficulty of locating qualified candidates. Most company rewards range from a set fee such as $100 for referring a semiskilled factory worker or an office clerk to several thousand dollars for technicians, engineers, and professional staff members.

Some firms conduct contests in which the team or department that makes the most referrals over a period of time is given a prize in addition to the rewards paid to the men and women who make the referrals.

Publicizing the awards in the company newsletter, by making a presentation at a meeting or luncheon, and by sending press releases to local newspapers encourages other employees to make the effort to seek people they can refer.

Advantages and Limitation of Internal Referrals

The following are some of the many advantages of internal referrals:

➤ The relatively low cost compared to paying for advertising, employment agency or recruiter fees, or the high expenses of field recruiting.

➤ The high quality of employee referrals. Most people are reluctant to refer someone who will not be a credit to them.

➤ The spirit of cooperation and collaboration that ensues when staff members become part of the hiring process.

However, there are some limitations:

➤ When companies rely on referrals as their major source of recruitment, they tend to perpetuate the racial and ethnic makeup of their workforce. This may impede affirmative action programs.

➤ If referred candidates are rejected, the referring employees may resent the decision, and this may be reflected in their work.

➤ If many of the referred candidates are rejected, employees may be discouraged from making referrals. They think, "What's the point. They'll turn 'em down anyway."

The last two problems may be alleviated by carefully writing the job specs so that referring employees know just what is required. You also should take the time to explain to the referrer why the person referred was not accepted.

> **Hiring Hints**
>
> When paying a bonus for referring a hired applicant, give the winner the award in cash and hand it to him or her in new, crisp $100 bills. Make it even more meaningful by picking up the tab for the added income tax.

Former Employees

People who previously worked for the company are known quantities and may be logical candidates for rehire when new vacancies occur.

Laid Off or Downsized Employees

Workers who have been laid off usually have a high priority in returning for rehire. They are a logical first source for filling vacancies.

In most union contracts, it is specified that laid-off workers must be rehired before outsiders are even considered. This makes sense when the new job is the same as the one previously held, but this is not always the case.

When a company downsizes, entire categories of work are often eliminated, and the new jobs require different skills. However, many of the downsized workers may have the aptitude to be retrained in the new skills, and often it is faster and less expensive to rehire and train these people than to spend the time, energy, and money to seek people with these skills from the outside.

Retirees

Retired workers often are interested in returning to work—either on a part-time basis or as independent contractors. In this way, they can retain their pensions and still put in several hours a week on the job.

Hiring Hints

When an employee with skills and experience that are in short supply retires, offer him or her the opportunity to work part time after retirement. You'll be amazed at how many will accept.

When Dan D., a chemical engineer, retired from his job, he was given the option to work as a consultant on a three-days-a-week basis. He politely refused, saying he'd looked forward to retiring for years and had plans to travel, play golf, and spend time with his grandchildren. His boss wished him well and told him the offer would remain open if he changed his mind. Three months later, Dan called. He'd taken a month's trip to Europe and had spent the next two months playing golf every day and lolling around. He was getting bored, and three days of work a week would enable him to have as much free time as he really wanted. He returned as a consultant, contributing his expertise to the company and still enjoying a partial retirement.

Job Sharing

Words to Work By

In a **job sharing** situation, two employees share one job. Work time is scheduled so that the position is always covered. Each is paid at the same rate but only for the time they work.

A relatively new phenomenon in the workplace is having two people share one job, known as *job sharing*. Lisa L. and Debra D. represent a good example of how this works. Both women worked in the customer service section of the company, took maternity leave to have their children, and returned to work. After Lisa's second child was born, she wanted to leave the job to give more time to her children, but she needed the money and losing her benefits would cause her great hardship. Her boss suggested that she and Debra, who was in a similar situation, share the job. Each would work half-time on a mutually acceptable schedule. They would be paid on the basis of the actual hours they worked, but the company would continue to provide full benefits. (Plans differ from company to company; some pay reduced benefits to job-sharers.)

The women and their boss worked out a mutually acceptable schedule. The job was covered on a full-time basis. The two women met or communicated by e-mail or telephone to fill each other in on pending matters. In this way, the company retained the services of two experienced, competent workers and saved the time and expense of recruiting and training a new person to fill that position.

At one of my client's companies, a husband and wife shared one job. Both were laboratory technicians and had met on the job. When they had their first child, they chose to share both the job and child care, and the company agreed to a job-sharing arrangement. So far, it is working very well for both the company and the couple.

Former Employees

Don't overlook people who left your company if you were sorry to lose them. If the circumstances that caused them to leave have changed, they might be persuaded to return.

Claudia M., the human resources manager of her company, made a practice of keeping in touch with former employees. Some had been downsized when their departments were eliminated; others had left the company for better-paying jobs or job advancement that was not available to them when they left.

When a job opened for which a former employee might qualify, Claudia contacted the person to discuss the job. Some, of course, were interested in returning, and they were invited for further discussion.

If the person left because of opportunities that were not available at the time of his or her departure, but now there were such opportunities, she would point this out and suggest they come by to discuss it. This often involved some tough selling, but it often led to rehiring a high-potential person.

Ask for Referrals

This was not the only reason for Claudia's call. If the former employee was happily employed, she would ask if the person knew of someone who might be qualified and interested. This often led to a referral.

People who formerly worked for your company know a good deal about the work you do and the kind of skills needed. If they left with a good feeling about your organization, they can be an excellent source for referrals.

The Least You Need to Know

➤ People who already work in your company are familiar with your company's customs and culture. You already know a lot about them. Filling jobs with these people saves time in orientation and minimizes the risks of dissatisfaction with your company.

➤ Posting a job opening encourages current employees to apply, especially those who may qualify for the job but are not known to the manager or team leader seeking to fill the job.

➤ When a position develops at any level, it should be analyzed to determine what the person who will perform the job should bring to it in terms of education, training, experience, and personality.

➤ Career pathing enables companies to work with high-potential workers in developing their skills for growth within the organization.

➤ Rewards and bonuses for referring applicants who are hired should be commensurate with the difficulty level of filling the job.

Writing Employment Advertising

Most companies use some form of advertising to attract applicants for open jobs. Millions of dollars are spent each year in employment advertising.

Ads range from a few lines in the local newspaper's help-wanted section to full-page ads in national publications and technical journals. It's expensive to run these ads, and the results vary considerably. Of course, the number of responses to an ad is closely linked to the availability of applicants in that field. The shorter the supply of candidates, the more thought must be given to where the ad is place, how it is designed, and what it says. To get the person(s) you want, you have to make your ad stand out.

This chapter covers how to write ads that won't just draw a batch of resumés; they'll attract qualified applicants for your openings.

Recruiting Residuals

According to a survey conducted in 1999 by the William Olsten Center for Workforce Strategies, the companies surveyed said that 43 percent of new hires were recruited through classified advertising, 13 percent through employee referrals, 12 percent through employment agencies and recruiting firms, and only 5 percent through Web sites and other Internet postings. The balance came from miscellaneous sources.

Where to Place Your Ad

The selection of the most effective medium depends on the type of position being advertised. If the job is one that most likely will be filled by a local resident, the logical source is a local newspaper; if you are willing to relocate a candidate, your best bet is to utilize media that the type person you are seeking will be most likely to encounter.

Local Newspapers

For most positions in the lower salary levels, local papers are the way to go. If you are seeking factory help, restaurant workers, retail sales associates, clerical staff, and similar jobs, it isn't necessary to go beyond the local population to fill the jobs.

Most communities today usually have only one or two newspapers. Study the ads currently running in the paper. For example, you may find that only the morning paper has an abundance of help-wanted ads, and the evening paper only has a few specialized ads. Obviously, the best paper to use would be the morning paper; most job seekers will be looking there.

If the job hard to fill and you feel the person who can fill it is probably currently employed and not likely to be reading want ads, don't place your ad in the help-wanted section. Choose another section of the paper.

You'll often find jobs for financial and managerial positions placed as display ads in the business pages of the paper. People with the desired background will usually read the business pages, and your ad may attract them even though they may not be actively searching for a new job.

Hiring Hints

If more than one newspaper in your community carries help-wanted ads, use the one that contains the most ads for the type of job you are advertising. That's where the applicants are looking.

Companies have found that ads in the sports section are effective in attracting applicants for sales jobs. Some newspapers have special help-wanted columns in sections that contain articles related to the field. For example, *The New York Times* has many ads for teachers and school administrators in its education section and ads for health care workers on the pages devoted to health and medicine.

One of my clients opened a branch office in a shopping center in a newly developed suburb. He staffed the entire office through an ad in the local "shopper"—a free newspaper distributed throughout the area primarily carrying advertising from the local merchants.

Out-of-Town or National Newspapers

When the candidates for your job are not likely to be in your vicinity, you have to search for them wherever they are. With the tremendous growth in the computer field, people with the skills needed have become extremely difficult to find. Everybody knows that many of these IT specialists are congregated in Silicon Valley in California. The newspapers in the cities that make up this area are flooded with ads offering opportunities all over the country for people who may want to relocate.

When a major aerospace company on Long Island in New York closed its doors a few years ago, the local newspaper contained ads from aerospace firms in several states, seeking people who were being let go.

For some jobs, it may be best to advertise in a national publication, but only a few newspapers have a national circulation. Among them are *The Wall Street Journal, USA Today,* and the national editions of *The New York Times, The Los Angeles Times,* and *The Chicago Tribune.* Advertising in any of these publications is expensive and usually is used when seeking a senior executive, a hard-to-find specialist, or a person with national or global expertise.

Hiring Hints

If you learn that a competitor or a company that is likely to employ people with the skills you need is downsizing or going out of business, advertise in the papers in their area.

Employment Enigmas

Don't pay for more than you need. You can limit your expenses in advertising in national publications. Most have regional editions, and ads can be placed in only the regions you desire.

Trade or Professional Magazines

Almost all industries have publications that cover their particular field. Magazines like *Chemical Engineering* run articles about developments and activities in companies in the chemical and related industries. *Women's Wear Daily* covers the garment industry;

The American Banker covers the banking industry. There are similar publications for hospitals, the hospitality industry, retailing, insurance, metalworking, and most every type of business. In addition, professional organizations have magazines devoted to their special needs. They are often published by the professional association. For example, there are publications for accountants, various disciplines of engineering, human resources professionals, IT specialists, and many others.

Advertising in these media may help locate specialists more effectively than using local papers or national publications of more general interest. They circulate in a wide geographic area and are read by the very people you are seeking.

The main problem with trade-paper advertising is that there is usually a long lead time between the insertion of the ad and the publication of the magazine. Most trade publications are monthly, and copy must be submitted two to five weeks before publication. This delay makes these media less effective in filling positions in which there is an immediate need. Some publications of this sort are daily, weekly, or bimonthly and have shorter lead times.

If you have a continuing need for certain types of personnel, trade magazine is an excellent resource. Running your ad in every issue or in several issues each year will keep your name and needs in front of the readers; when they are ready to seek a new job, they are likely to contact you.

Hiring Hints

When advertising on radio, particularly during "drive-time," provide a toll-free telephone number and repeat it several times in the ad. Remember, most drivers can't write while driving. Repetition will help them remember the number.

Radio and Television

A great source for advertising aimed at local people is "drive-time" radio. You have a captive audience. While riding in their cars and listening to their favorite stations, you hit them with your ad. If your ad sounds exciting enough, they'll contact you when they get home—or even immediately from their cell phones.

Network television is much more expensive and probably is not as effective. The audience is too broad, and your ad competes with advertising for products and services. However, some national companies like General Electric have included announcements about job openings in some of their TV advertising.

Cable TV is a better bet. In many communities, local cable channels have programs about jobs and careers. Advertising for personnel on these programs will reach active and potential job seekers. On some of these programs, companies may list job openings at no cost.

Billboards

A highly effective medium for attracting factory help is the plant-gate billboard. If a plant is located along a busy street or highway or can be seen from a freeway, workers passing on foot, by car, or on public transportation will see it regularly. Companies using such signs find that they bring in a large number of applicants. Some companies use regular commercial billboards in various part of the community to advertise for personnel.

To make your billboard more enticing, have it designed professionally rather than just posting a list of openings. Change the copy periodically to maintain reader interest.

Hiring Hints

Try advertising in movie theaters. It's relatively inexpensive ($24 per screen per week). Target ads to run during movies that likely job prospects will watch. The National Cinema Network in Kansas City, Missouri, is the largest cinema marketing company.

Recruiting Residuals

One company in Kansas used the old Burma Shave formula to advertise for machinists. The first sign read: "Why work far? You can work near." The second sign read: "Skilled machinists, come in; work here." The third sign was the company name and an arrow pointing to the entrance to the parking lot.

Choosing the Format

Most help-wanted ads are placed in the classified columns of the newspaper. This is the best location for routine jobs.

If a job is hard to fill, however, it may be more effective to run a display ad—that is, a larger ad that can be placed anywhere in the paper.

When Classified Ads Are Appropriate

Most job openings are for relatively routine jobs. The company needs operators for its machine or assembly lines, a clerk for the office, packers for the warehouse, servers and cooks for a fast-food restaurant, sales clerks for a retail store, and similar positions. The applicants must come from the community because it doesn't pay to relocate them. People who are actively looking for a job will read the want ads.

There are many restrictions in placing classified ads. Most newspapers do not allow the use of art work or photographs and only allow the use of one type style. Because the ad cannot be made more attractive by using art or a variety of fonts, it's difficult to make your ad stand out against the competing ads. Later in this chapter, you'll learn how to make your ad stand out within these restrictions.

Classified ads are usually listed alphabetically by job title. You must choose the appropriate job title, even if it may differ from the title used by your company. For example, your title for the open job is "Engineering Associate," but the job does not call for an engineering education; it's a clerical position that keeps engineering records. If you used the company title, it would appear under "Engineers," and you would not get the type of candidate desired. Study the help-wanted column. What title used there best describes the job? You may find that similar jobs are listed under "Admin. Asst.—Engineering." Use that title for the ad.

Later in this chapter, you'll find guidelines on writing effective classified ads.

Words to Work By

Classified ads are ads placed in a special section of the paper containing the help-wanted ads. Format is usually limited to a specific typeface and allows no artwork. **Display ads** may be placed anywhere in the paper. Display ads can be designed with borders, artwork, photos, and a variety of typefaces.

Display Ads

Display advertising is usually used for positions that are more difficult to fill such as engineers, information technology specialists, professional staff, managers, and executives. Because these ads cost considerably more than classified ads, a company does not use them unless it feels the prospects for such a job will not usually read the classified section of the newspaper.

As previously noted, display ads can be placed in any section of the paper, although most of these ads appear on the business pages. Some newspapers place some display ads in the classified section.

Unlike with classified ads, which are restricted by limited typefaces, in a display ad, you can use a variety of typefaces or specially designed layouts. Because most human resource managers are not familiar with the nuances of display advertising, assistance in writing these ads should be obtained from the company's advertising department or ad agency. Or, as discussed later in this chapter, the company may use an ad agency that specializes in recruitment advertising.

Later in this chapter, you'll find examples of display ads.

Signed vs. Blind Ads

Although many classified and display ads identify the company seeking the candidates, a great number of ads are *blind ads*. Instead of listing the company's name, they use a box number.

Many factors must be considered in deciding whether to use a signed or blind ad. These factors should be weighed carefully for each ad, and the decision should be appropriate to the particular position and the circumstances involved.

If the company is well-known, the name alone will attract people. Nothing is more effective in recruiting personnel than a good name—a company people want to work for and be associated with.

Words to Work By

Blind ads are employment ads in which the name of the company is not listed. Applicants reply to a box number.

On the other hand, there are many good reasons a company may not wish to divulge its identity. There are occasions when it is desirable to keep a certain opening confidential from its own staff or its competitors. In this case, a blind ad is advantageous.

Another reason for not identifying the company is that, if it runs a signed ad, it is often swamped with unqualified applicants who phone or visit the employment office without appointments. More embarrassing are the phone calls to company officials from friends, vendors, and customers recommending people for the job. These people—usually unqualified for the openings—must be interviewed to maintain good relations with the referrer. This is a waste of valuable time, and when the applicant is rejected, tactful explanations are required.

The use of a blind ad avoids some of these problems. A box number hides the company's name, but it creates other problems. First, the value of the company's reputation is lost. Even more important, currently employed persons may be reluctant to answer blind ads. They don't know to whom they are writing, and they may fear it's their own firm or one related to it. Because some of the best-qualified candidates are currently employed, a company may lose these applicants by not identifying itself.

There are some ways to overcome this problem. One way is to list a phone number without identifying the company. Callers can be screened on the phone, and those who sound qualified can be invited for interviews. Neither applicants nor companies need to identify themselves until they are satisfied that there is mutual interest.

Another technique used by companies, particularly for senior positions, is a third-party ad. In this case, an employment agency or an executive recruiter will run the ad under its name. It will screen all inquiries, eliminating the time-consuming chores of reading letters and resumés and interviewing people who are of no interest. Because the agency name is usually known to the public and because agencies and consultants depend on maintaining confidence to stay in business, currently employed people are more likely to answer the ad.

Hiring Hints

If you list a telephone number in your help-wanted ad, use a dedicated phone—one not used for any other purpose. This will prevent the switchboard or direct lines used for regular business from being tied up with job inquiries.

Making the Ad Stand Out

You ad will be placed in the paper with many other ads seeking to fill similar jobs. Why should an applicant answer your ad rather than one of the others? Of course, a person desperately seeking a job will probably answer any and all ads that sound promising. But the best applicants are often currently employed and are reading the help-wanted ads to see if a job that appeals to them is listed. They may scan the columns, read only ads that stand out, and answer just those that appeal to them. These are the people you want to attract. You have to get them to notice your ad and respond to it.

The Four Principles of Good Advertising

Advertising specialists have formulated a four-point guide for writing good ads. These principles apply whether you are advertising a product or service or seeking personnel.

Attention

You must first attract attention to the ad. It must be seen to be read. One way to get the reader's eye in a display ad is by its design. The use of photos or artwork and fancy borders or typefaces is designed to get the reader to read the ad. The most effective attention-getter is the headline—usually the job title.

In display advertising, the ads are not placed in any special manner. They appear among news items and other ads. If you advertise for a financial executive, unless a job title such as "VP—Finance" or "Manager Financial Analysis" or "Corporate Controller" heads the ad, no matter how pretty the ad is, the person you want will not bother to read it. You can find some excellent examples of display ads in most editions of The Wall Street Journal and in the Sunday editions of the New York Times, and the other major newspapers listed earlier in this chapter.

In classified ads, getting the reader's attention is more difficult. Because of the restrictions on design and typeface, you are limited in using attention-getting gimmicks. The best way to attract attention to your ad is the judicious use of white space.

Sample Classified Ads

Can you determine which ads stand out?

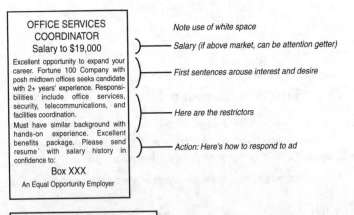

OFFICE SERVICES COORDINATOR
Salary to $19,000

Excellent opportunity to expand your career. Fortune 100 Company with posh midtown offices seeks candidate with 2+ years' experience. Responsibilities include office services, security, telecommunications, and facilities coordination.

Must have similar background with hands-on experience. Excellent benefits package. Please send resume' with salary history in confidence to:

Box XXX

An Equal Opportunity Employer

Note use of white space
Salary (if above market, can be attention getter)
First sentences arouse interest and desire
Here are the restrictors
Action: Here's how to respond to ad

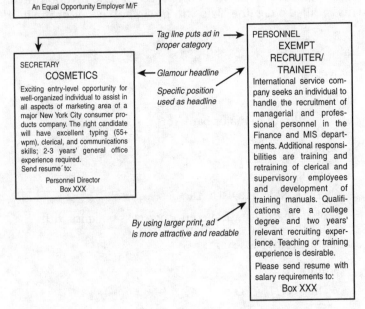

OFFICE MANAGER

Full-time position with New York City-based sales/service office. We are seeking a sharp, bright individual to supervise a small staff (under 5 persons) and manage office. Must be highly organized, good customer communicator, and have current experience in office administration. Excellent salary + 100% company-paid benefits for you and your dependents. Please send resume', including salary requirements, to: PO Box XXX

An Equal Opportunity Employer M/F

This ad seeks a similar candidate, but note how crowded it is. It is difficult to read and does not draw attention because of a lack of white space or an attractive headline.

Tag line puts ad in proper category
Glamour headline
Specific position used as headline

SECRETARY
COSMETICS

Exciting entry-level opportunity for well-organized individual to assist in all aspects of marketing area of a major New York City consumer products company. The right candidate will have excellent typing (55+ wpm), clerical, and communications skills; 2-3 years' general office experience required.

Send resume' to:

Personnel Director
Box XXX

By using larger print, ad is more attractive and readable

PERSONNEL
EXEMPT RECRUITER/ TRAINER

International service company seeks an individual to handle the recruitment of managerial and professional personnel in the Finance and MIS departments. Additional responsibilities are training and retraining of clerical and supervisory employees and development of training manuals. Qualifications are a college degree and two years' relevant recruiting experience. Teaching or training experience is desirable.

Please send resume with salary requirements to:

Box XXX

The closely spaced ads seem to merge into each other; those with white space above, below, and within the copy are easy to see and read. You pay for white space at the same rate as the lineage, but it's well worth the cost.

101

Recruiting Residuals

Over the past few years, many companies have started advertising open jobs on their Web sites. Responses are requested via e-mail. Some companies report good returns. (You'll learn more about this in Chapter 11, "Using the Internet as a Recruiting Source.")

You will want to write an attractive headline that will attract attention to your classified ads. Many employers use the job title as a headline because the ads are usually listed by job category in alphabetic order, This isn't necessary, write an exciting headline so that the ad will attract more applicants than other ads in the column in the same job category.

Because most papers list the jobs by job title, the first word of the ad should be the title, but the first word doesn't have to be the headline. You can state the job title in small print at the top. This is called a tag line. Below it, in larger type, print the headline followed by the text.

Here is a sample ad for trainees:

(tag line)	Trainee
(headline)	LEARN
(text)	Opportunity in major bank for …

Here is a sample ad for a chemist:

(tag line)	Chemist
(headline)	CREATE NEW PRODUCTS
(text)	Global pharmaceutical company seeks chemist with …

Here is a sample ad for an administrative assistant:

(tag line)	Admin. Asst.
(headline)	WORK WITH CEO
(text)	Growing company seeks college graduate with computer skills …

The headline should be concise and have pulling power. A list of such words and phrases is provided later in this chapter.

Interest

Once the eye has been attracted to the ad, it is essential to develop interest in the job. The job content itself may be the best interest factor. You might write, for example, "Work on new product research," "The latest high-tech equipment," or similar advantages. Salary and benefits are certainly interest factors. Other factors may include special advantages, opportunity for advancement, the chance to learn the newest developments in a field, or an especially desirable geographic area. Refer to the list of ideas that attract interest later in this chapter.

Desire

The appetite has been whetted, interest has been awakened, and now the ad must create the desire to answer it. Amplification of the interest factors plus the extras offered by the job in terms of growth, job satisfaction, and personal value help create this desire. Appeals to family needs such as health insurance, telecommuting, and daycare assistance attract family-oriented candidates. Tuition-refund programs and nearby graduate schools appeal to education-oriented people.

Ads should be written with readers in mind. Advertising specialists call this the YOU approach. Readers are more interested in themselves than anything else. Write the ad to appeal to them—not to satisfy your own ego. To develop desire, the readers must identify with the ad. Each has to say "This is for me" for the ad to be a success.

Action

Not only must the ad be appealing, it should instigate action. Readers have been attracted to the ad, their interests have been aroused, their desires have been catered to, and now they must be told what to do to satisfy this desire. The most effective way to capitalize on this is to make the action as easy as possible. Ask applicants to phone, write, or visit the company. If immediate action is desired, request that they telephone. List the name of the person to call, the phone number, and the time to call. If more detailed preliminary screening is requested, have them fax, mail, or e-mail a letter or resume. For certain jobs, the company may prefer to have the candidates come directly to the office. If so, give good directions in the ad.

Employment Enigmas

In your ads, only key job requirements should be noted. By listing preferential or minor specifications, you might eliminate people who are well-qualified for the job but who lack some minor attribute that could be acquired on the job.

Targeting the Candidates You Want

These four points will make candidates want to apply to the company, but attracting people is only part of the process. You don't want to be deluged with unqualified people. The ad must also provide details about what qualifications the applicants must have.

List the job specifications that are essential for the job. If you know many possible candidates are available, you should make the specs as detailed as possible so you won't be deluged with unqualified or semiqualified applicants. If the job is hard to fill, make the specs broader. You may get some candidates who are not as close as you'd like, but they may have potential for consideration.

The following are some phrases that can "glamorize" your ads:

➤ **Describing your company**

Major company

Blue chip

Global

High Tech (Internet, e-based)

Glamour product (TV network, ad agency, fashion)

Location (Sunbelt, Suburban, near home)

Expanding organization

Fortune 500

Modern facilities

Campus-like atmosphere

Local assets (school system, recreational facilities)

➤ **Describing job advantages**

"Assistant to Top Executive"

New plant or facility

Ground-floor opportunity

Rapid advancement

Grow with the company

Company car

Profit sharing

Stock options

Employee discounts

Learn

Challenge

➤ **Action**

Phone today

Fax your resumé

E-mail us now

Will respond within 24 hours

Working with Ad Agencies

If you only place a few help-wanted ads a year, you can place them by phoning them in to the classified advertising department of the newspaper. The department will provide you with the guidelines and rules required. If you place a large number of classified ads or even just one display ad, however, you are better off using an ad agency.

Using an ad agency has many advantages and very few disadvantages:

➤ Because these agencies know a great deal about the various media, they can quickly lead you to the best source for advertising for the type of personnel you need.

➤ They can help you design the ad to make the most of the space you buy.

➤ Because of their ongoing contacts with newspapers, they have a better chance of getting your display ads placed in desirable locations than you would on your own.

➤ They don't charge you anything for placing your ads. Their fees are paid by the media. However, if they do special work for you such as designing a display ad, they may charge for that service.

> **Hiring Hints**
>
> You can save money if you advertise in the classified sections on a regular basis. Check to see if the papers in which you do most of your advertising offer annual contracts. By guaranteeing to purchase a specified amount of advertising space each year, the cost per line may be reduced considerably.

Choosing the Right Agency

The ad agency your firm uses to place product advertising is probably not the one to use for employment advertising. This is a specialized field, and there are agencies in every city that deal with this.

The best way to locate such an agency is to ask the classified advertising manager of your local paper for suggestions. You also can ask the employment managers of other companies in your community who they use.

Visit the agency and discuss your needs with the manager. Have him or her show you some of the ads the agency designed. Let him or her know the types of personnel for which you advertise.

Working with the Ad Agency

The ad agency will appoint one of its staff members to deal with your account. Get to know this person. Invite him or her to see your facility. The more the account

executive knows about your jobs, the culture of your company, and your likes and dislikes about advertising, the more helpful the agency can be.

If there is enough lead time between writing your ad and its appearance in the paper, have the account executive fax you a proof of the ad. This will enable you to study it, correct errors, and make changes before it gets into the paper.

After the ads have been published, keep a record of the returns (see the next section) and discuss it with the account executive. For some hard-to-fill jobs, you may have to repeat the ad several times to attract viable candidates. In other cases, if returns have been unsatisfactory in terms of either the number of responses or the quality of the applicants, rather than repeating the same ad, all or some of the content should be changed, or it may be better to place it in a different publication.

Employment Enigmas

To ensure accuracy of content and to approve style of presentation, print proofs of all display ads. Whenever possible, classified ads should be checked carefully by an HR staff member, the leader of the department in which the job exists, and an advertising specialist.

Measuring the Effectiveness of Your Ad

Since advertising is a major source of recruiting, it makes sense for the human resources department to keep records of the responses received.

Response Logs

Some companies keep careful records of the results of each ad. They want to know which ads bring results and which do not. This also enables them to repeat the ads when similar positions have to be advertised again. These records also serve as a control sheet for checking advertising invoices from the newspaper or the ad agency.

One simple way to keep these records is in a standard desk diary. Paste each day's ads on the proper page. Next to it, indicate the cost of the ad and the number of responses.

You could also use a special form for this. An example of such a form is shown in the newspaper advertising log in the next section.

Evaluating the Responses

The number of responses received is not as important as the quality of the responses. Did the ad bring in the kind of applicants you seek? This can be determined by the number of respondents you invited in for interviews.

If most of the respondents were not worthy of an interview, you should rewrite the ad with more restrictions.

One of my clients ran this ad:

> ASST. TO PRESIDENT
>
> Great opportunity for college grad to join growing Internet company. Computer background. MBA desirable. Good salary + benefits. Send resumé to P.O. Box XXXX.

Good ad? Too good. It drew a mailbag full of replies, most of them only marginally qualified. Just to read the resumés took hours and hours of valuable time.

The ad was rewritten with much more specific job requirements. The response was much smaller but more targeted to what the company sought.

Of course, if an ad doesn't draw enough respondents, it may be because of a dearth of applicants for that job type. But it may be that the ad was not attractive enough. Try rewriting it with more of the AIDA concepts.

The following is a sample newspaper advertising log:

Job _____

Department _____

Number of openings _____

Dates inserted _____

Newspaper or magazine _____

Number of responses _____

Number of interviews _____

Number of hires _____

Cost of ad _____

(Paste ad here)

Recruiting Residuals

TelServe, Inc. has developed an Internet program called Ad Manager that enables employers to select, place, track, and measure the performance of recruitment ads. To learn more about this, call 1–800–906–0101.

The Least You Need to Know

➤ When placing ads, if the job most likely will be filled by a local resident, the logical source is a local newspaper; if you are willing to relocate a candidate, your best bet is to utilize media that the type person you are seeking will be most likely to encounter.

➤ If the job is hard to fill and you feel the person who can fill it is probably currently employed and not likely to be reading want ads, don't place your ad in the help-wanted section. Choose another section of the paper.

➤ To attract factory help, advertise on a billboard at the plant site that can be seen by workers passing on foot, in cars, or on public transportation.

➤ The AIDA formula summarizes the four principles on which good ads are built: Attention—Interest—Desire—Action.

➤ Keep a log recording the results of each ad. This will enable you to check each ad's effectiveness. It also serves as a control sheet for checking advertising invoices from the newspaper or the ad agency.

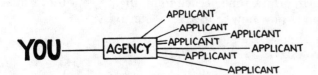

Chapter 8

Employment Agencies

In This Chapter

➤ Advantages and problems in using employment agencies

➤ What does it cost and is it worth it?

➤ Finding the agency that can best help you

➤ Getting the best service from agencies

➤ Dealing with public employment services

➤ Using temps as fill-ins or try-outs

➤ Don't hire them, lease them

One of the most effective sources for filling your job vacancies is using employment agencies. Human resources managers are in general agreement that these specialized services save them considerable time in locating people and greatly augment their own recruiting resources.

In this chapter, you'll learn how to select and work effectively with private employment agencies and the costs involved. You'll also learn about government-sponsored job services and other not-for-profit job-referral units.

Job openings often occur in which part-time or temporary help can do the job. Temps are used to fill in for people who are out ill, on vacation, or on assignments away from the office. Some companies use temps to fill a job while they seek a permanent employee. Some hire a candidate in whom they have serious interest through a temp agency to try the individual out before making a formal offer.

A relatively recent approach to filling personnel needs is to lease employees, just as one might lease a car or a piece of equipment. Instead of putting employee on its payroll, a company contracts with a leasing company to supply the people, who may work on the company's premises or, in some cases, in a separate facility.

Should You Use an Employment Agency?

Your objective is to fill an open job as rapidly as possible with the best-qualified applicant at the lowest cost. Unless you are exclusively engaged in hiring, you probably have many other duties that may have to be neglected while searching for personnel. Employment agencies can cut down on the time needed to fill the job, but they can be a waste of your time if you don't know how to use them effectively.

What They Can Do

Employment agencies will not necessarily solve all your hiring problems, but they often can make the process less time consuming, costly, and frustrating. Some of the advantages of using employment agencies are …

➤ They can save you money. Hiring is costly. Ads cost money. The time used in interviewing applicants costs money. Going out of town to interview applicants or bringing them to your facility costs money. And of course, using agencies usually—but not always—costs money (see the section "What It Costs You" later in this chapter).

➤ Employment agencies can save you time. Agencies often have files of qualified applicants who can be referred to you immediately.

➤ If your job opening is in a specialized field, agencies that deal heavily with people in that field have resources to reach top-level candidates who may be interested.

➤ They prescreen candidates and refer only those who are close to your specs. This saves you the time and energy of reading countless resumés and interviewing unqualified applicants.

➤ They can keep your company name confidential until you are ready to interview the applicant.

➤ If you develop an ongoing relationship with an agency, it will inform you about highly qualified people who become available even when you don't have an immediate opening. It may be worthwhile to create an opening for a high-potential individual.

Employment Enigmas

Even greater than the direct costs of hiring (advertising, agency fees, and travel) are the indirect costs: the salaries for the time spent by people engaged in the hiring process (reading resumes, interviewing applicants, checking references, and related work).

What They Cannot Do

Some companies have made the mistake of turning over the entire hiring process to an agency. This doesn't work.

Agencies are not substitutes for a company's employment department. They don't know the inner workings of your company and the subtleties of your corporate culture.

It's up to you to develop job specs and convey them to the agency. The agency's job is to locate possible candidates, to do preliminary screening, and to refer the candidates closest to your requirements to you. Don't rely on any outsiders to make final decisions as to whom you will or will not hire.

Agencies cannot be used to shield you from charges of discrimination. Some companies "hint" to agencies about the type of person they want referred to them. If a charge is then lodged against you, you cannot use the defense that "The agency didn't send me any women or blacks or whatever."

What It Costs You

It may cost you nothing. Although most private agencies are paid for their services by the employer, some agencies charge the fee to the applicant. Whether the agency charges the company or the applicant often depends on the job market. When jobs are hard to find, the applicant is more likely to be charged; when jobs are plentiful and applicants are hard to find, the burden of payment shifts to the employer.

In most states, fees charged to applicants are regulated by the state, but fees charged to companies usually are not. The reason for this is that the laws were passed because some unscrupulous agencies exploited poor and sometimes desperate job seekers with unreasonable fees. However, agencies were free to negotiate fees with companies.

Even today, particularly in smaller communities where there are not too many jobs available for clerical and certain other routine jobs, the agencies will still charge the applicant.

Agencies work on a contingency. There are no up-front costs. You only pay a fee if a person referred by the agency comes to work for your company. Fees vary. The fee for most agencies is based on a percentage of the annual salary paid to the employee. The percentage charged often rises with the salary paid. Here are some fee structures as taken from the fee schedules of agencies in major cities.

Agency #1: This is the most commonly used fee schedule. For jobs paying $10,000 or less, the fee is 10 percent of the annual salary.

For jobs paying $10,000 to $30,000, a sliding scale is put into effect: 1 percent for each $1,000 of salary. For example, for a $12,000 job, the fee is 12 percent; for an $18,000 job, the fee is 18 percent.

For jobs paying more than $30,000, the fee is 30 percent.

Agency #2: For jobs paying $10,000 to $15,000, the fee is 15 percent. For jobs paying $15,000 to $20,000, the fee is 20 percent. For jobs paying more than $20,000, the fee is 30 percent.

Agency #3: For jobs paying less than $20,000, the fee is 15 percent.

For jobs paying $20,000 to $30,000, the fee is 25 percent; for jobs paying more than $30,000, the fee is 30 percent.

Agency #4: For IT, engineering, and other high-tech jobs with salaries up to $25,000, the fee is 25 percent. For these jobs paying more than $25,000, the fee is 30 percent. For all other jobs, a sliding scale is used up to a maximum of 30 percent for jobs paying more than $30,000.

Why would a company pay such high fees? Companies have found that, unless they are very lucky and find a suitable candidate rapidly, the cost of continuing advertising, screening, and interviewing many applicants can come to an even higher figure than the agency fee. By presenting only viable applicants, money and time are saved making it a cost-effective process.

Suppose that, after you pay the fee, the employee doesn't work out. He quits after a few months, or she doesn't perform as well as expected and you discharge her.

Most agencies will refund part or all of the fee. Like the fees, refund policies vary. The agency might say, "We did our job by finding her for you. You made the final decision on hiring. It's your mistake. No refund." Or the agency might guarantee that, if the employee leaves or is terminated within one year, the full fee is refunded. Most agencies take a middle ground. Here are some examples.

If the employee leaves …

➤ During first month on the job, the refund is 100 percent.

➤ During second or third month, the refund is 75 percent.

➤ During fourth, fifth, or sixth month, the refund is 50 percent.

➤ After sixth month, no refund is given.

Employment Enigmas

What happens if the person hired through an agency quits or is terminated for not being able to do the job or for another reason? Before dealing with an employment agency, get a written statement regarding its policy for refunding all or part of the fee or replacing the employee at no extra charge under these circumstances.

Hiring Hints

When jobs are scarce and applicants are plentiful, agencies are more likely to be amenable to reducing their fees. But you have to ask for it—so negotiate for the best deal you can get.

Some agencies do not make cash refunds; instead, they may guarantee that, if the employee leaves for any reason during a specified period of time (six months or a year, for example), they will place another person in the job at no additional fee.

Don't assume that an agency you have not dealt with before has the same policy as the ones you currently work with. Before dealing with a new agency, have someone send you a written statement of the fee and refund schedules so there won't be any misunderstandings later on.

Picking the Right Agency

In small communities, there probably are only a few agencies from which to choose. In larger cities, there may be dozens or even hundreds of agencies. Which ones are best for you?

Where to Look

One logical source is recommendations from other companies in the area. Ask the human resources people or managers who do hiring in other firms who they use and about their experience.

Another source is the local newspapers. In large cities, most agencies advertise the job openings on which they are currently working. Many newspapers have a separate section in the help-wanted columns for agencies to list their jobs. Studying these ads will show you which agencies have a significant number of openings in each category. Also scan the regular help-wanted ads in the categories in which you are interested. An agency may have placed several ads for jobs of that type.

Let's say your company has a need for a cost accountant. You note that the XYZ agency has several similar openings. This indicates that the agency most likely understands the job requirements for cost accountants, and they probably have applicants with that background registered with them.

You also note that the XYZ agency has listings for sales reps, clerks, secretaries, and bookkeepers but none for programmers, engineers, chemists, or any jobs in the management areas. This agency may be a good source for some of your openings, but it would be a waste of time to use it for others.

Hiring Hints

Peruse the agency listings for several days (including the Sunday paper) to get a good idea of each local agency's capacities and specialties.

Another source for locating agencies is an agency's own initiative. It may send direct-mail advertising or solicit business by telephone or by a personal visit. This will give you insight into what the agency can and cannot do for you.

How to Make Preliminary Choices

Once agencies are located and identified, analyze them to determine whether they will meet the standards you expect of your resources. Because no agency can be better

113

than the people on its staff, the makeup of the staff should be examined. What is the level of their education and experience? Do they have the qualifications to understand your job requirements? Some agencies may have specialists with direct backgrounds in the areas for which they screen personnel. Although this is helpful, it's not necessary for an agency counselor who recruits engineers to be an engineer. He or she should, however, have enough knowledge to evaluate the experience and backgrounds of applicants for engineering positions.

Check with other firms who have used this agency. Be prepared to ask them good questions about their experience. Learn what each firm feels the strengths and weaknesses of the agency are. Find out what they have done to develop a good relationship with the agency.

In cases in which you may require more than the usual services, determine whether the agency can provide it. You may want the agency to test applicants for clerical jobs to determine their typing or word-processing skills. If so, learn what tests are used and how they are processed.

Hiring Hints

Ask other firms about their experience with an agency before deciding to use it.

Hiring Hints

For a list of agencies by location and by the types of jobs in which they deal, purchase the National Directory of Personnel Services ($30) from NAPS, 3133 Mt. Vernon Ave., Alexandria, VA 22305.

If your company needs to tap resources in other parts of the country for some hard-to-fill jobs, determine whether this agency has such contacts. Many agencies have national connections. Some are branches of national chains and can call on branches in cities where the applicants you are seeking are likely to be found. Other agencies belong to cooperative groups of agencies that interchange jobs and applicants. Selecting an agency with this facility is especially important if your searches must be broader than the local market.

If the candidates you need are likely in cities other than your own, make sure the employment agencies you use are part of a national chain or members of an interchange association.

Get Off Your Duff and Visit Them

If your preliminary investigation indicates that the agency is a possible source, it's worth the time to visit it. Meet with the owner or manager and speak with the counselors who will work with you. Observe them at work. Listen in, if you can, to how they interview applicants.

Look over their facility. Is it comfortable? Is it a professional atmosphere? Do they use computers? Faxes? Any other equipment?

If you are satisfied that the agency can help you, give it a few jobs to work on. You can learn much about its value from how it handles them.

Working Effectively with the Agency

Working with an agency means more than just calling in a job order and waiting for the agency to refer applicants to you. Remember that you are not the only client serviced by the agency. To ensure that you obtain the best possible service, you must make an overt effort to develop a close relationship with the agency counselors who work on your job openings.

Make Sure the Counselor Understands Your Specs

No agency can help fill a company's requirements unless it is given full job descriptions and specifications. It should know the technical requirements as well as the personality factors that will influence the selection of a candidate. It must be told the relative importance of each job spec. This is particularly important because the ideal candidate rarely appears. For example, the job specification may call for a person who has six qualifications, but only two may be critical. To send a candidate with only four of the requirements sounds reasonable, unless the missing ones are the critical factors. Be sure the counselor not only has the formal job description but also understands the priorities of the qualifications.

Invite the counselor to your facility. Have him or her observe the jobs he or she will be working on. Introduce the counselor to the team leaders and department heads so he or she can get a concept of the personalities involved. That way, he or she also can learn what the person who will be the new employee's supervisor really wants in a new employee.

Hiring Hints

Agencies refer to the staff members who take job orders, interview applicants, and make referrals by various names. Among them are counselor, consultant, and account executive.

Communicate—The Importance of Feedback

After every interview with a candidate referred by an agency, review with the counselor your reaction to the applicant. If the person is rejected, go over the reasons why so the counselor can make a better selection next time.

This feedback is essential—especially when dealing with a new agency or counselor. It helps the person focus on exactly what is needed. If the applicant is to be given further consideration, let the counselor know why you felt he or she was a good candidate and explain what the next step will be. Be sure to indicate whether you wish to see additional candidates before making your final decision.

Many HR managers keep records of the number of referrals made by each agency and the number of people employed from these referrals. If there are relatively few referrals or a disproportionate rate between referrals and hires, the relationship should be reevaluated. Perhaps the agency did not really understand the job specifications.

Clearer communications may be in order. Perhaps this agency is not the right one to use for this particular type of job. It may have been great in recruiting clerical help but a poor source for technical people.

These figures should not be looked at in a vacuum. They should be adjusted by an analysis of the job market. If the agency has not produced, the problem may not be with the agency. There may just be a general shortage of people in that field.

Another factor to be considered is the number of applicants referred by the agency who were offered employment but did not accept. This may be due to a variety of factors that are not the fault of the agency, and it should not be charged against it.

Hiring Hints

Once a relationship has been established with an agency, it's good business to evaluate periodically how effective the agency has been as a recruiting source.

Your Obligation to the Agency

It is your responsibility to ensure that, once an applicant is referred by an agency, the agency is given full credit for the placement. In cases in which more than one agency refers the same applicant to a company, the credit for placement goes to the first agency who called this person to the attention of the company. To protect agencies against this type of conflict, date-stamp incoming resumés and applications. The referring agency is noted, and any subsequent referral by another agency or another source is returned, noting that there was a prior referral.

Occasionally, employers will, as a favor, send an applicant referred to them to another company that they know has a similar opening. In such cases, the agency has no claim to a fee from either of the companies. The ethical way to handle this is to call the agency and suggest that someone contact the other company to make a referral.

There are advantages to giving an agency an exclusive listing, but you are under no obligation to do so. Some agencies will request or even require that you give a job order only to them. If you have an ongoing relationship with the agency and know from past experience that the counselors work hard to fill your jobs and have a good record of success in doing so, it makes sense to give them the opportunity to work on the job order without competition from other agencies. It motivates them to give your job order preference over other firms seeking similar types of people. However, no agency can guarantee that they will fill a job. To protect yourself, put a time limit on any exclusive arrangements. For example, you may give the agency exclusivity for several weeks; if the job is not filled, you can then try other agencies or advertise on your own.

Government Job Services

Every state has its own job service that's aided and coordinated by the United States Employment Service (U.S.E.S.), a division of the U.S. Department of Labor.

When created in the depression years of the 1930s, the primary function of the state services was to help find jobs for the unemployed. The same agencies were usually responsible for administering unemployment insurance plans.

An unemployed person is still required to register with the state job service to qualify for unemployment benefits. As a result, these offices are usually referred to by the public as "unemployment offices."

The Upside of Using State Job Services

The state job services have always been a major source for hiring blue-collar help. They usually know the needs of the companies in their areas and can serve them rapidly and effectively. If there are shortages of certain types of labor in one part of the state, they can recruit from other parts of the state and occasionally from other states through the U.S.E.S.

The state job services test applicants for certain skills and aptitudes. They work with employers to assist them in planning for job searches, and when large numbers of workers are needed, they have the facility to recruit statewide or even from other states. And, of course, there is no fee for their services.

The Downside of Using State Job Services

Many employers have found fault with the quality of referrals from the state job services. People not really interested in working accept referrals to maintain their unemployment benefits—a waste of time for the company interviewing them.

Generally, the state job services have not been a good source for higher-level positions. Despite government efforts to upgrade the image, employers are reluctant to entrust their more complex job specs to the state services. Currently, employed applicants seeking better professional, technical, administrative, and managerial jobs will usually not register with state services.

The Future: One-Stop Career Centers

The federal government recognizes these problems and has taken steps over the years to correct them. In 1998, Congress passed the Workforce Investment Act, which initiated a system of One-Stop Career Centers that combine training, education, and employment programs in a single location. More than 30 states already have these one-stop systems in place. There is no charge to employers or the candidates for this service. The service offers the following:

➤ Recruitment and prescreening of applicants

➤ Posted job listings on America's Job Bank, a data bank operated by the U.S. Department of Labor

➤ Wage and labor market information

➤ Compliance advice on federal laws

➤ Interviewing facilities for employers

➤ Training in various types of job skills

➤ English-language classes

➤ Aptitude testing

For more information about how this program can be of value to your company, contact the job service in your state or log on to the Department of Labor's Employment and Training Administration Web site at www.ttrc.doleta.gov/onestop/.

Not-For-Profit Agencies

In addition to government-sponsored job services, there are some other sources that may be of help in locating personnel.

Trade Schools

Most trade schools have placement services to place graduates in the fields for which they have been trained. If your company has jobs in fields for which such trade schools exist, they can be a good source for trainees in these areas. Because these schools train people specifically needed in an industry, they have a higher than average placement rate. Most trade-school placement services do not charge a fee for placements, although some may charge a nominal fee to cover expenses.

Occasionally, a trade-school placement service will be able to help you find experienced people in a particular field by referring alumni. Former students who have several years of experience may register with the school's placement services when seeking a new job.

Professional and Technical Associations

Most professional associations have informal placement services for their members. Members seeking jobs send their resumés to the placement committee. When companies list jobs with the association, appropriate resumés are referred to them. The problem here is that the services or committees often are run by volunteers. In some organizations, the committee meets once a month or less, resulting in a loss of time in sending out the resumés. And since the members are not trained in employment screening, they may refer unqualified candidates, wasting the employer's time.

Some organizations do have full-time professionals doing the placement. When contacting a professional association for referrals, learn how they are organized and operate.

Team Members Who Are Not on Your Payroll

You don't have to hire people to have them work for you. Almost all companies have used *temps*—people who work on the company's premises but are on the payroll of a temporary-staffing or employee-leasing service—at some time during each year.

Using Temp Agencies

According to a survey conducted by the American Staffing Association, 90 percent of all companies in America use temporary help services.

Temporary services differ from employment agencies in that they don't place people in jobs; they hire people themselves and "lease" them to employers who require either full-time or part-time workers for short periods of time. These jobs range from simple clerical or low-skill laborers all the way to professional and executive positions.

The temp services charge a fee to the company based on the skill level and the number of hours worked by the people they supply. Because the workers are not on your payroll, you pay no benefits or payroll taxes. You are free from the burden of withholding income taxes. They accrue no sick leave or vacation time. If they are absent, the temp service will send another person to do the work. If you are not satisfied, the service will replace them. You don't have the hassle of hiring, disciplining, and perhaps firing people.

Some companies use temps as a means of trying out employees before hiring them onto their own staffs. If the person works out satisfactorily over a period of time, the company may offer him or her a regular position with all the benefits that entails. In such cases, the temp agency will usually charge the company an additional fee for the placement.

Most temp services have a reservoir of trained people for the jobs they fill. To ensure the quality of their people, they provide training programs in clerical and computer skills as well as in other areas commonly needed by their clients.

Words to Work By

Temps (temporary personnel) are people who do work for the company but are not employed by the company. They are on the payroll of a temporary-staffing or employee-leasing service. Usually they are used for short-term assignments such as filling in for absent employees or augmenting permanent staff when needed.

By developing an ongoing relationship with one or more temp services in your community, you can be assured of a continuing flow of people to help keep the work going during rush periods. It also alleviates pressure on your regular staff during times when there are vacancies in your teams or departments.

Rent-a-Worker

Some business executives have a dream—to run a company without the problems of hiring, administering, and dealing with employees. Believe it or not, it can be done. Instead of hiring people, you can lease them just as you would a car or a piece of equipment.

This is not a totally new concept. Companies have existed in the engineering field for decades that provide engineers to work on clients' projects. Referred to as "job shops," they service construction or technical firms that need engineering work done on a project. Rather than hiring their own engineers for relatively short-term projects, they farm it out to a job shop.

Over the past few years, this concept has spread. Some companies now only maintain a core group of key personnel and have most of their work done by leased employees. Many of the leading temp services have expanded into this field.

In many cases, leased employees work on company premises. They may even be downsized company employees who were hired by the staffing service and then leased to their former employer.

The advantage of leasing employees is that the company is relieved of having to recruit staff and dealing with all the administrative headaches.

However, there are many drawbacks to leasing people. When you lease a car, you're still responsible for maintaining it. When you lease personnel, you still have to train them and direct their work. They may not be your employees, but they are your associates. It's up to you to keep them motivated. This is not easy when you have no control over their compensation. It's tough to build up a sense of loyalty and ownership when the team member doesn't identify with the company.

Outsourcing

Cutting payroll to a minimum was one of the results of the downsizing trend of the 1980s and early '90s. Companies "reengineered" their processes and found that it was often more economical to outsource activities that previously had been done in-house. Whole departments were eliminated, and the work was subcontracted to outside vendors.

Some companies encouraged laid-off workers to form their own companies and become the subcontractors. For example, one of my clients eliminated its traffic department. The CEO told the traffic manager to open a traffic-consulting business and agreed to retain it to handle its traffic activities. With this as a basis for starting up the new business, the traffic manager had no trouble raising the necessary capital. Today, he serves not only his former employer but many other companies in his community.

The Least You Need to Know

➤ Agencies work on a contingency. You only pay a fee if a person referred by the agency is hired to work for your company. Before dealing with an agency, have someone send you a written statement of the fee and refund schedules.

➤ To ensure that you obtain the best possible service, you must make an overt effort to develop a close relationship with the agency counselors who work on your job openings.

➤ After every interview with a candidate referred by an agency, review with the counselor your reaction to the applicant.

➤ Keep in touch with your favorite agencies even when you have no job openings. This will motivate them to give your jobs special attention when you do have openings and to let you know about high-potential people even when you have no current openings.

➤ Government and not-for-profit job services are another source for hiring people.

➤ Temporary services differ from employment agencies in that they don't place people in jobs; they hire people themselves and "lease" them to employers who require either full-time or part-time workers for short periods of time.

Headhunters

Headhunters? Sounds barbarous. No, these are not savage tribes that cut off the heads of their enemies. "Headhunter" is a nickname for a special type of recruiter who aggressively goes after candidates for his or her clients rather than waiting for applicants to come to him or her. The people in this field are not happy about being called headhunters; they prefer the more professional title "executive recruiters."

Executive recruiters, in their present form, have been a major source for locating senior managers and hard-to-locate technical and professional people for about 40 years. They have helped some of the major corporations in this country and abroad fill their top-level positions.

As jobs become harder and harder to fill, the use of these recruiters has proliferated. Worldwide search revenues of executive-search firms have nearly tripled of late from $3 billion in 1993 to an estimated $8.3 billion in 2000, according to Greenwich (Conn.) based search-industry consultant Hunt-Scanlon Advisors.

Agencies vs. Headhunters

Many people think of executive-recruiting firms as just another type of employment agency. Although there are some similarities and, indeed, some employment agencies will do proactive searches for clients, they generally operate in a different fashion.

Method of Operation

Employment agencies obtain applicants primarily through advertising, their reputations, and referrals. Most people who register with an employment agency are active job seekers. They either are not currently employed or, for whatever reason, have chosen to seek a job while still employed.

The agency will usually interview the applicant and check his or her background against the current list of job openings. If there is a match, the agency refers the applicant to the client. As pointed out in Chapter 8, "Employment Agencies," some agencies also will test applicants and check references.

When agencies receive a job order, they will send several resumés to the employer who will choose which people should be invited for interviews.

If no open jobs fit the applicant's qualifications, the agency will retain the applicant's information in its files. When new job orders develop, the agency will search these files to locate qualified candidates. One advantage of using an agency is that they have such files.

Some agencies will market an applicant. If they don't have an available position, they will contact companies that are likely to employ personnel with the applicant's background to explore possible interest in him or her.

Executive recruiters work quite differently. The focus of the recruiter's activity is the employer—not the applicant. The recruiter spends time with the client studying the job that needs to be filled, researching to determine in what companies the target person is probably working, identifying possible candidates, and then contacting them to sell them on looking at the job.

When a candidate expresses interest, the recruiter will meet with him or her for an informal interview. Usually the name of the employer is kept confidential until an interview with the employer is arranged. If there is mutual interest, the candidate will be invited for a more detailed interview, references will be checked, and then the recruiter will discuss the candidate's background with the client. Unlike an agency, the executive recruiter does not send a batch of resumés from which the employer selects people to be

Hiring Hints

Use executive-search firms for jobs in which it is more likely that the person you are seeking is not actively looking for a job.

interviewed. All the screening is done by the recruiter who presents a select few candidates for consideration by the employer.

Later in this chapter, we'll follow an executive search from start to finish to see how a headhunter operates.

Who Uses Headhunters?

Executive-search firms are not always the most cost-effective way to find the candidates for your open jobs. They are expensive (see the next section) and often take lots of time (see the section "A Case Study" later in this chapter).

Using headhunters pays off when the job you need to fill is a top-level executive position or a very hard-to-fill job.

Unlike the more populist staffing firms—which fill large numbers of low-end jobs—big-name search firms use their vast network of contacts to place middle- and upper-level executives. Although they start with jobs that pay upwards of $100,000, the real money comes from filling senior-level jobs from the $250,000-a-year Senior Vice President to the CEO. Search firm powerhouses such as Spencer Stuart's Thomas J. Neff and Heidrick & Struggles' Gerard R. Roche have filled some of corporate America's most prominent CEO openings.

The Cost of Using Headhunters

It's not cheap. Fee structures vary somewhat in the field. Be sure to get a full understanding of what it will cost before engaging an executive recruiter.

The Typical Fee Formula

Most search firms base their fees on the salary paid to the person hired. The most common percentage is one-third of the salary. If the compensation package also includes bonuses or stock options, some search firms factor their estimated value into the fee.

Unlike employment agencies, executive recruiters usually receive a nonrefundable retainer before they start the assignment. This retainer is usually one-third of the estimated fee. When the job is filled, the fee is recalculated based on the actual salary less what has already been paid. If the job is not filled, there is no additional fee.

Employment Enigmas

To keep recruiting costs under control, specify that any out-of-pocket expenses incurred by a recruiter must be approved in advance.

In addition to the fee, the employer agrees to pay expenses incurred in the search. This includes travel costs of the recruiter, travel costs of candidates, telephone costs, and other expenses directly involved in the search.

Other Formulas for Setting Rates

Can you get a better deal? Probably. There are many good search firms that will offer you lower rates or a different formula. It depends on the difficulty of filling the job and the competitive situation among search firms in your area.

Some firms charge as follows:

➤ **Hourly fees.** Just as lawyers charge their clients on the basis of billable hours, some search firms use a similar formula. They set an hourly rate with a maximum fee of one-third the annual salary paid to the successful candidate. The fee will be calculated both ways, and the client pays whichever is lower. If the job is filled rapidly, you may save money.

➤ **Flat fees.** Some search firms, particularly those associated with the management-consulting divisions of the major accounting firms, charge a flat fee that is paid whether or not the job is filled. These fees are usually lower than the contingency fees; however, you take the risk that they may not find a suitable candidate.

➤ **Payment in equity.** Some recruiters dealing with high-tech companies have worked out deals to accept part of the fee in company stock. This way, the company benefits by conserving its current cash position, and the recruiters benefit by what they hope will be the growing value of the stock.

Most executive recruiters do not refund fees if the selected candidate doesn't work out. However, they will usually seek a replacement at no additional fee other than reimbursement of expenses.

Is It Worth the Cost?

Vacant jobs cost money. The higher the level of the vacant job, the more it costs the company. In the high-tech companies of California's Silicon Valley, according to top headhunters, there are currently about 500 vacant CEO positions. Many of these are in startup firms in which the creator/inventor of the product or service is desperately in need of an experienced management leader to move the organization into the mainstream. A survey conduced by A.T. Kearney and Joint Venture Silicon Valley Network suggests that empty posts like this cost those firms $3 billion to $14 billion annually.

Most readers of this book will not be searching for CEOs, but the loss of income to a company when any senior job is not filled is tremendous in terms of lost productivity, lost direction, and the added burden of work for the existing staff.

Experienced recruiters have a proven record of filling jobs relatively rapidly and with more chance of success than most other sources. They are worth the fees they charge.

Choosing the Right Recruiter

There are many excellent recruiters available, but a firm that is excellent for one company may not be for another. Some search firms concentrate on one industry such as banking, automobiles, or high tech; some focus on a job classifications such as financial, marketing, or manufacturing executives.

Hiring Hints

To obtain a list of executive recruiters and their specialties, contact the Association of Executive Search Consultants, 500 Fifth Ave., New York, NY 10110 (Phone: 212-398-9556) or consult the organization's Web site (www.aesc.org).

Ask for Recommendations

As in identifying vendors of any product or service, your first source should be recommendations from satisfied customers. Ask colleagues in other companies who they have used. If you are a member of a trade association, ask for recommendations from other members.

Industry Specialists—Pros and Cons

When selecting a recruiter, it is advantageous if the firm has lots of contacts in your industry. One of the main reasons for using a headhunter is to reach executives who are experienced in dealing with the kind of problems you face—and they are probably employed now by a competitor or a company doing related work. If the search firm has serviced such companies, it probably knows the field and can do a good job for you.

Makes sense, right? But not always. It's an unwritten law among search firms that they will not contact employees of a current or recent client when searching for candidates. For example, if you're looking for an executive with a background in designing computer chips, your best candidate may be currently working at Intel. But if the search firm you are using has Intel as a client, it can't touch any Intel employees. You'd be better off selecting another search firm.

A Case Study

To give you a clearer idea of just how a search is conducted by an executive recruiter, let's take a case from the very beginning to the final steps in hiring. We'll call the company Sweet Sixteen Cosmetics, a New York City–based manufacturer and marketer of beauty products aimed at teenage girls. The company is seeking a marketing manager.

Understanding the Job

Dave and Diane Dunne founded the company in 1988. Their products are marketed chiefly through chain drug stores and department stores. Dave, the "inside boss," handles manufacturing, finance, and distribution. When they started the company, Diane was its only sales person; over the years as sales manager, built up a sales force of 15 people covering the northeast area and 30 independent sales reps covering the rest of the country.

Sales grew to $20 million by 1996 but have leveled off since then. Diane noted that the teen market was growing, but they were not. She recognized her own limitations and decided that in order to move ahead, the company needed a marketing executive who could develop and implement a strategy for growth. They contacted Marketing Searchers to conduct the search.

Employment Enigmas

It's not smart or economical to give a job order to more than one executive recruiter. For positions worth retaining head-hunters, there are only a limited number of prospects. A good recruiter should be able to reach them all.

Marketing Searchers assigned Arthur Roberts to head up the search team. At his first meeting with the Dunnes, they described how they envisioned the new job. Roberts' first question was whether this was a new job or a replacement for Diane's current position. Diane made it clear that she was to continue as sales manager. The need was for a marketing executive, not a sales executive.

Because this job had not previously existed, it was necessary to develop a comprehensive job description and job specification for it. In cases in which the assignment is to refill an existing job, on the other hand, the first step is to study the current job description and then discuss with the principals what, if any, changes they want to make.

Hiring Hints

Make sure the recruiter understands not only your job specifications, but the personal characteristics of the people with whom the person hired will work closely.

It was determined that the position would be at the vice presidential level and would chiefly involve analyzing the market for their products, planning how to penetrate that market more deeply, identifying additional markets, suggesting added products that could be sold to these markets, developing marketing strategies, and working with Diane in gradually converting the sales force from primarily using independent representatives to a company-employed sales staff.

Roberts carefully observed the personalities of the Dunnes. He knew that the person they hired must have the personal traits needed to work with a husband-wife team and must be comfortable with their style of managing.

After the first meeting, Roberts asked the Dunnes to draw up a tentative job description and specification based on their conversation. At their next meeting, this was discussed and modified. It was decided that the person they sought was probably currently a marketing executive in a company that marketed products sold to drug, food, or low-end department or discount stores. Experience in the teen market would be helpful but was not essential. A salary range of $100,000 to $125,000 with performance bonus was set.

A retainer of $11,000 was paid to Marketing Searchers (one-third of a prospective fee of 33 percent of $100,000.) The balance was to be paid upon completion of the search and would be adjusted based on the salary actually agreed upon.

Employment Enigmas

Give the recruiter some leeway in selecting sources. Don't insist that the candidate come only from your competitors or even your industry. Put the emphasis on what is needed to meet your objectives.

The Search Begins

Roberts' first move was to identify the companies in which the person they wanted was probably now employed. His staff compiled a list of consumer-products firms that sell merchandise in the approximate price range of Sweet Sixteen's lines. This list was broken down into three categories:

➤ Health and beauty aids (known in the trade as HBA)

➤ Low-end fashion items

➤ Others in related markets

The research staff of Marketing Searchers listed the companies in each group by sales volume. Since Sweet Sixteen was at the $20 million level, the ideal candidate would come from a company or a division of a company with sales of at least $30 million and probably not more than $100 million. A person working for too small a company would not have the necessary know-how, and someone from too large a company would probably be accustomed to working with large marketing staffs—and this was to be a one-person job with a minimum of support staff.

After the companies were listed, the researchers identified the names of the marketing managers, assistant marketing managers, and where pertinent, product managers.

Roberts perused the lists and chose the people he would telephone. Let's listen in on a typical conversation:

"Mr. S., I called you because I know you've been engaged in HBA marketing for several years, and I need some help in finding a candidate for a marketing job for one of my clients. Perhaps you know somebody who might be interested in an opportunity to start up and run a marketing program."

He'd then briefly describe the job. Mr. S. may politely decline: "No, I really don't know anybody." He may express interest: "Tell me more." Or he may say: "Let me think about this. Can I call you back?"

Quite often, when people are interested, they don't want to discuss it from their office. They will suggest that you call them at home, or they will phone you later.

Roberts might make dozens of calls before getting a positive response. Occasionally, the person called will actually suggest the name of a possible candidate, but most often, the response is "I might be interested myself."

The Follow-Up

From this first go-around, 12 people expressed some interest in the position. Roberts spoke to each of them at length on the telephone. Only two of these prospects were close enough to the specs to be seriously considered.

He continued his telephone contacts and, over the next few weeks, generated several more positive responses from which three more good prospects were culled.

He was now ready to meet with these five prospects; two were located in the East so he invited each of them to come to New York and meet with him for lunch at his club. Two were in California. Rather than bring them across the country, Roberts chose to fly to Los Angeles and interview them there.

At these informal interviews, he was able to obtain more information about each candidate, tell them a little more about the job, and get a personal impression. As a result, four of the prospects were eliminated. The surviving candidate would be processed further (see the following section).

Over the next month, he continued the search, followed the same procedure, and came up with three more viable prospects.

During the search, Roberts kept his clients informed of the progress, telling them about the candidates he had seen and his reaction to them.

The Decision

After interviewing 14 candidates, Roberts chose six for serious consideration. Each of these people were given in-depth interviews by Roberts and were evaluated by a psychologist; two more of the prospects were eliminated. A careful check was made of the backgrounds of the remaining four. All checked out well.

The recruiter never makes the final decision. This must be made by the client. Roberts discussed each candidate with the Dunnes and pointed out that, on the basis of the screening, any one of them could be successful in the job. However, due to the differences in their specific backgrounds, each offered different capabilities. It was up to the Dunnes to decide which of them best fit their needs and, most important, which one they felt they could best work with.

Each prospect was invited to the Sweet Sixteen office, was given a tour of the facility, was interviewed by the Dunnes at the office and over lunch.

After much thought and discussion between Dave and Diane and some consultation with Arthur Roberts, they chose Donna Tellesole, currently the divisional marketing manager of the teenage products division of a women's fashion house.

The Negotiation

Throughout the interview process, Roberts had established the salary requirements of each candidate and all the finalists were in the range. Specific negotiation as to the compensation package now took place.

Hiring Hints

Negotiations on compensation should be conducted by a company executive—not the recruiter. However, no candidate should be referred unless the recruiter has ascertained that their compensation requirements are in line with what the client has budgeted for the position.

Although some recruiters offer to handle this delicate subject, most clients prefer to do this themselves. Dave met with Donna and worked out a mutually acceptable deal. Donna agreed to a salary of $110,000 plus a bonus based on increased sales. The Dunnes and Donna reviewed the job description and were happy to accept several of Donna's ideas for making it even more effective. A starting date was set.

The day Donna started the job, Roberts was notified. Marketing Searchers sent a bill for the balance due, now calculated at 33 percent of the starting salary of $110,000 less the $11,000 retainer. Expenses had been billed as they incurred.

The Least You Need to Know

➤ Executive recruiters differ from employment agencies in that agencies generally work from their files or advertise to attract applicants. Recruiters proactively go out to identify and contact prospects.

➤ Using headhunters pays off when the job you need to fill is a top-level executive position or a very hard-to-fill job.

➤ In selecting a recruiter, it is advantageous if the firm has lots of contacts in your industry. One of the main reasons for using a headhunter is to reach executives who are experienced in dealing with the kind of problems you face.

➤ It's an unwritten law among search firms that they will not contact employees of a current or recent client when searching for candidates. This may keep them from contacting the best person for your job. Ask the recruiter about current clients.

➤ Make sure the recruiter understands not only your job specifications but the personal characteristics of the people with whom the person hired will work closely.

➤ Negotiations pertaining to compensation should be conducted by a company executive—not the recruiter.

Chapter 10

Other Sources

In This Chapter

➤ Hiring newly minted college grads

➤ Utilizing trade schools and community colleges

➤ Making and keeping contacts—the art of networking

➤ Going from customers to employees

➤ Recruiting from the military services

➤ Dealing with unsolicited applicants

In addition to using ads, agencies, and recruiters to fill your job openings, other sources can be used to recruit members for your teams. A significant source for people with little or no experience that have the potential for development are colleges and universities.

College recruiters, sometimes called campus recruiters, are specialized members of the human resources department whose major function is contacting and visiting colleges all over the country to seek graduates to fill their companies' ever-growing demand for college-trained people. Many firms send recruiters to several colleges each year to interview and select new graduates for their training programs. For some jobs in which college is not necessary, applicants can be obtained from trade schools and community colleges.

This chapter looks at how to build and use a network of people to refer the types of applicants you seek, how to convert customers into employees, and why to consider people leaving the military services for your job openings. We'll also explore all of these sources so you can determine how to use them to help you fill your job requirements.

Recruiting at Colleges

Almost all major companies recruit at colleges and universities. There is a highly competitive market for college-educated men and women. Companies, government agencies, and even the armed forces are constantly and actively seeking to attract the best students. Because more and more students have gone on to graduate schools in the past several years, college recruiting has become a multiphase operation with recruiters calling on both graduate and undergraduate school-placement offices.

Hiring Hints

All members of your technical or other departmental staffs who are called upon to assist in college recruiting should be given special training in interviewing techniques.

Most companies look to the college campus because they wish to train and develop their own people and provide formal management-training programs. Some of these programs are of a general nature in which trainees are exposed to all phases of the company's operations. Other firms hire graduates for specific types of jobs such as engineering, marketing, information technology, or finance.

Set Clear Objectives

To do the best job of recruiting, companies must have clear objectives and a system geared toward implementing them. Here is an example of one company's objectives:

➤ **Develop sound working relationships with the academic world.** This requires more than just an occasional campus visit. Contacts must be made and continued over a period of time. Get to know professors who often motivate students to become interested in specific companies. This involves cooperation with the college in research projects, summer internship program for students, using faculty members as consultants, and participation in technical societies on campus.

➤ **Satisfy both immediate and long-range personnel objectives on a continuing basis.** To do this, you must maintain a regular flow of campus interviews, even in years when immediate needs are smaller than usual. If a company skips a year, it may take several more years to regain the loss of rapport caused by the lapse.

➤ **Centralize the program within the human resources department, yet maintain participation of team leaders and department managers.** HR staffers should control the program, but specialists in the fields in which recruits are needed should be involved in the process.

➤ **Be economical.** Plan campus visits so there is a minimal waste of time and expertise. If several divisions of a company want to visit the same campus, plan so they don't conflict.

➤ **HR staffers should always be available to participate in career days and other campus activities.** They should make it their business to cultivate the college-placement officers and faculty in schools in which they do significant amounts of recruiting.

Choosing the Colleges

Picking the appropriate colleges is key to the success of the program. One factor is location. Is the school near the company headquarters or one of its facilities? Nearby schools are a good source because they are likely to produce prospects who know the company and would like to work for it. It's also economical.

Size also is an important factor. Small schools often don't have a sufficiently diverse body of students to warrant a recruiting trip. However, there's usually less competition from other campus recruiters at small colleges, and those who visit have a better chance of attracting top students. If a company has specialized needs for which students are being trained in certain smaller schools, these certainly should be visited.

The standards of the school are important. Higher standards mean better students. Some companies insist on limiting consideration to just the top 10 or 20 percent of the class. This might be shortsighted. Assuming that academic record alone is a good indicator of success—and there is much dispute over this—the standards of many schools differ. A student who just barely passed at MIT may have graduated in the top third of the class at another school. If academic standing is a factor in selection, the standards of the school should govern the level at which the cut-off percentile is set.

Another criterion in selecting schools is the academic calendar. Schools that are on trimesters graduate potential employees three times a year. This is useful because new hires can be absorbed throughout the year rather than being concentrated in June.

Companies should evaluate previous results at each school. If the recruiting sessions were fruitful, the school should be visited regularly. If not, it's wise to evaluate the reasons before dropping the school from the itinerary. A university from which the company has had poor results might be providing a competitor with several graduates each year. Recruiting may be unsuccessful for one company due to poor coordination or bad campus relationships; quite the opposite may be true for your competitor. It's better to work out the problems and salvage a good potential source than to drop the college.

Planning the Visit

The date of the visit is important, and it varies from school to school. Avoid a date that might conflict with the school's social or sports calendar. The day before the big game or after the prom is a poor time for recruiting.

Let the placement director know what sort of jobs the company has open and what type of candidate is most likely to qualify. The director can save the company a lot of time by preselecting students who have the basic requirements and are interested in the available jobs. Send along a brochure with a description of the company, the opportunities it offers, what the jobs entail, and other assets that will sell the company to the students.

Characteristics of a Good Campus Recruiter

The one real key to the success of a college recruiting program is probably the recruiter. Some of the characteristics of a good recruiter are ...

➤ Personal flexibility and maturity that engenders immediate rapport with the candidates.

➤ The ability to make objective decisions about applicants free of bias or prejudice.

➤ Empathy but not sympathy so that rejections of candidates who don't meet company needs are not a problem.

➤ The ability to communicate easily with all types of people both within the company and at the colleges.

➤ A high level of energy. Must be able to cope with a heavy travel schedule, detail work, and the stress incumbent to the job.

➤ The ability to handle large volumes of paperwork and administrative detail. Should be able to work rapidly so that good candidates will not be lost because of red tape.

➤ The ability to adjust to and cope with frequent changes in schedule.

➤ Confidence in self and enthusiasm for the company.

Hiring Hints

One of the most effective ways to sell a company on campus is to provide summer internships. Not only do the interns often return as full-time employees after graduation, they also become the company's greatest boosters on campus during the following year.

Preparing the Campaign

Several months before the visit, copies of literature and a list of available jobs should be sent to the college placement office. It's also good business to send copies of the brochures and job specs to the heads of the various technical or business departments of particular interest to the company. Letters should be written to people known to the company from previous contacts or through recommendations of who might be able to refer students to the recruiter.

An unusual but effective approach has been used by Texas Instruments to attract students to the company. They offer a free career-counseling service on their Web site for college seniors. It lets students test their ability to do certain jobs, matches skills and opportunities, and provides advice on writing resumés and taking interviews. Students who use the service are informed about jobs at Texas Instruments and are told when recruiters will be at their campus.

Prior to leaving for the college, the human resources department should check with the college to verify the number of students to be interviewed and to confirm pertinent matters.

The recruiter has a dual job at the campus interview—selecting and attracting applicants. Note that *select* is mentioned first because the recruiter is there to obtain the very best candidates for the company's needs. This must be done in a relatively short interview—usually no more than 30 minutes. Equally important to making good selections is developing interest in the company so the prospect will seriously consider the job. Accomplishing this requires an interview plan that is highly structured yet flexible enough to be adapted to each applicant.

The primary function of a college interview is screening to determine whether a candidate is worthy of further consideration. If the prospect passes this preliminary interview, he or she will be invited to the company for a more thorough screening.

Employment Enigmas

Don't oversell the job. Good college interviewers never use a hard-sell approach. Their enthusiasm for the company and their ability to show how the job meets the students' objectives makes the student recognize the advantages of pursuing the job.

Subsequent Interviews

Invitations to the company offices are extended to candidates in whom there is some interest. During this visit, the prospect meets with HR people, department heads or team leaders in the areas where jobs are open, and others at the facility.

This visit gives the company an opportunity to provide the applicant with more information. More important, it enables the company to evaluate the candidate in an off-campus environment and to probe into areas the recruiter didn't have time to explore at the college.

The company visit should be well planned:

1. The letter of invitation should be warm and friendly but businesslike. It should be made clear that the trip is at the company's expense. Also included should be

details as to travel directions, hotel accommodations, and a general outline of the plans for the day.

2. A member of the HR staff should meet the applicant and act as host. This often is the person who conducted the campus interview. Seeing a familiar face will reduce stress. A plant tour is usually arranged so the applicant can get an overall view of the facility.

3. The interviews should be scheduled to minimize wasted time between interviews.

4. Lunch should be arranged for at the facility or at a nearby restaurant. Often the host will take the candidate to lunch, but it is better to have a young person from the department or team in which the prospect will work accompany him or her to lunch. It provides an opportunity to chat with the employee informally about his or her experience with the company. Having prospects learn about the success stories of their peers is an excellent technique for selling the job to the prospect.

5. Questioning and evaluation of the applicant at the second (and subsequent) interview is more intense and detailed. Matters that were treated superficially at the campus interview can be dealt with in depth. Doubts about motivation, technical skills, and personal traits can be explored.

6. If the applicant passes the screening, an offer should be made as soon as possible. If it can be made at the time of the visit, it should be done. If this isn't possible, inform him or her when a decision can be expected—and do it.

7. Offers may be made orally, but it is usually confirmed by a letter stating the type of position, the salary, the approximate starting date, and any conditions to be met. For example, the letter may state that the offer is subject to passing a medical examination and receiving the degree.

Because an applicant may receive several offers (the average is 6, but in high-tech fields, candidates may get 30 or more offers), the decision must be made within a short period of time or the prospect will be lost.

If an applicant rejects your offer, try to find out the reason. It's the only way the recruiting effort can be evaluated and you can find out where it is failing. Attention to the answers can do much to improve the college recruiting program.

Community Colleges

There are a great many jobs in most companies that do not require college degrees but do require specialized training. This training is often provided by two-year community colleges. There are community colleges in almost every community in the country.

Community colleges offer Associate degrees, usually an Associate in Applied Science (A.A.S.). This prepares the students for many technical jobs in which the four-year Bachelor's degree is not needed. However, many community college graduates do go on to get their Bachelor's or even Master's degree.

Working with Faculty and Administration

It's easy to keep in close touch with the placement office and the faculty of community colleges. Because they're local, you can have an ongoing relationship with them. It's inexpensive since no travel is required.

Many companies have established solid relations with their local community colleges by giving them financial aid, providing special equipment they may need, and encouraging company employees to teach courses there.

Placement officers and faculty members should be invited to visit the company so they can become acquainted with its facilities, its culture, and the working environment.

Company representatives should always participate in college career days and job fairs and should work closely on a one-to-one basis in counseling students on jobs and careers.

Internships

Internship programs are established so that students can work part time at the company while pursuing their Associate degrees at the schools. This not only gives them practical experience, it enables the company to give the school suggestions on the effectiveness of courses and what, if any, changes might be made to improve the training given to the students.

Another advantage of student internships is that the company can observe the interns and can identify whom it may want to hire once they complete the program.

Recruiting Residuals

If you are looking for interns, you can advertise for them on the Internet at little or no cost. Log in to one of these sites: www.internshipprograms.com, www.jobweb.org, or www.studentsearch.com.

Setting Up Special Programs

Community colleges usually offer courses designed to serve the industries in their communities. In South Carolina, for example, where many textile companies are located, community colleges offer courses in various aspects of technologies needed in that industry. In Wichita, Kansas—the home of Lear Jet, Cessna, and a Boeing plant—community colleges train students in aviation-based programs.

If there's shortage of certain types of skills needed by a company, it can request that the community college develop courses to train students in those skills. For example, when a chemical company in western Pennsylvania suffered a shortage of lab technicians, it worked with the local community college to create a series of courses to train technicians. The company donated the necessary equipment to the college and recommended two staff members to teach the courses. Once the program was established, the college trained dozens of students who were hired by the company.

Hiring Hints

One way to draw in candidates for your technical teams is to recruit top graduates of community colleges and offer them tuition-refund programs to continue their studies in the evening sessions of local four-year colleges.

Community colleges are not the only training facility a company may use. Many universities have continuing-education divisions that offer certificate programs in special areas. Some years ago, the Employment Agency Association of New York decided that a formal program to train employment-agency counselors would be valuable. A representative of the association contacted New York University's School of Continuing Education. The association and the school worked together to develop a program that met the needs of the association and the standards of the university.

Trade and Technical Schools

As noted in Chapter 8, "Employment Agencies," most trade and technical schools have placement offices to find jobs for their graduates. In addition to listing your job orders with these schools, you can work with them in much the same way as community colleges. Work with them to create courses to train people in the skills you need; encourage your workers and supervisors to teach courses in their skill areas at the schools.

Hiring Hints

One way to obtain preferential treatment in referrals from colleges, community colleges, or tech schools is to have alumni of these institutions act as liaisons with their alma maters. Happily employed alumni are the best credentials a company can offer a placement officer.

Recruiting Networks

Lots of people have gotten their jobs because of a personal contact. It's a cheap and easy way to obtain employees, yet we can't depend on knowing some-body who knows someone for each job we have to fill.

Creating Your Network

One way to improve your odds on getting recom-mendations is to *network*—to make connections with people who are likely to know people with the skills and experience your company usually hires.

One logical source is people who work for firms who hire the same types of people you do. It's un-likely that your competitors will refer good people to you, but there are lots of noncompeting firms that may be sources. Cultivate them.

> **Words to Work By**
>
> **Networking** is a means of iden-tifying and cultivating people who may be valuable resources for you in obtaining information, developing ideas, suggesting cus-tomers, and referring prospects for your open jobs.

When you go to a trade or technical association meeting, circulate. Meet people from a variety of companies. Exchange business cards. If you meet a person outside of your business ac-tivities whom you believe may be a source, add that person to your network.

Maintaining the Network

Keep a good record of your networking partners. One way to do this is to set up a spe-cial network file. Set up a card file or a computer file with enough information about the contact to easily retrieve the name when needed.

Here is an example of such a card file.

Card File Example

Network Card File (Front)

Name: _____

Title company address: _____

_____

Phone: _____

Fax: _____

E-mail: _____

How known: _____

Job skills used by the company: _____

Comments: _____

_____

continues

Card File Example   (continued)

Network Card File (Back)

Record of contacts

Date   Notes

_____

_____

Working the Network

Networks have many uses other than recruiting. Salespeople use networks to develop leads on customers, human resources people check with their networks to make salary surveys, and technical people use contacts in their network to learn about new developments in their field.

To make the network truly valuable, you have to keep in touch with members even when you don't need their help—especially when you think you can help them.

For example, Richard B, a computer expert, learns of a new piece of equipment or software. He phones or e-mails members of his network whom he feels would like to know about it. Sheila L., an employment manager, interviews a woman with a background in market research. She doesn't fit Sheila's job, but Sheila is impressed with her background and contacts a few members of her network who may be able to hire her.

When you have an opening, tell the members of your network who are likely to know of somebody who may fit the job. Don't expect them to knock themselves out looking for somebody, but if they do know a qualified candidate, they'll usually be happy to let you know.

Of course, if you hire a person referred by a network partner, don't forget to thank the referrer.

Where Else Can You Look?

In addition to these formal sources, there are several other places from which applicants can be sought. The next chapter looks at the Internet as a recruiting source, and Chapter 12, "Recruiting for Tough-to-Fill Jobs," explores special approaches to find candidates for hard-to-fill jobs. There also are a few miscellaneous resources that can be used for many jobs. Let's look at these now.

Customers

Your customers may offer good leads for employees. Indeed, some of them may want to work for you themselves. Many retail stores and fast-food restaurants have signs in their stores announcing job openings and appealing to customers to apply. Einstein Bros., a large chain of bagel stores, moved this approach up a notch. They created a job-recruiting brochure aimed at reaching customers. The gist was "You're already coming here, so why not get paid to do it?" It worked.

Companies that send out monthly billing statements can include enclosures describing job opportunities. Sears is asking its credit card users to consider working in its department stores. Included in Sears' monthly credit card bills to customers is this message: "Good life. Great job. Sears is now hiring for a variety of exciting positions. Apply at a store near you today!"

The manager of a Toys 'R Us store in Ohio reported that 40 percent of his new employees came as the result of in-store advertising for personnel.

The Military Services

Each year, thousands of men and women complete their military service and seek jobs in the private sector. They may be officers who are retiring after many years of service or enlisted personnel who have put in four or more years and are ready to enter the job market. These men and women are well-trained, disciplined, and motivated.

During their service, they may have acquired skills of great value to your company. Many officers have been trained in such fields as administration, training, logistics, and engineering. In the enlisted ranks you may find electricians, mechanics, machinists, and electronic technicians.

The former soldiers, sailors, and airmen bring to the table leadership experience and rigorous training that most recently minted college graduates don't have.

There has been some resistance to hiring former military officers and non commissioned officers such as sergeants because of the concern that they may have a "management by yelling" philosophy. Some people also worry that former officers won't be able to adapt quickly, that they'll be stuck in a rut. The experience of many companies with recent military hires has put these stereotypes largely to rest. Today's military focuses on coaching, mentoring, and training—all management buzzwords of the '90s.

One way to reach this market is to advertise in newspapers in communities with large military installations or in the military posts' newspapers. Ads can also be placed in national newspapers catering to the military such as *Army Times* and *Navy Times*, both published by Army Times Publishing Co., 6883 Commercial Dr., Springfield, VA 22159. The company's Web site can be found at www.armytimes.com.

Several employment agencies specialize in recruiting people who leave the services. Since these agencies generally advertise in the *Army Times* or *Navy Times*, check their ads to see if they deal with the type of personnel you need and contact them. You can also obtain a list of such agencies from the National Association of Personnel Services (see Chapter 8, "Employment Agencies").

Walk-Ins and Write-Ins

To some HR managers, people who come to the office seeking a job or who send in a resumé on the hope that a job may be available are a nuisance. Others consider them a bonus.

The trouble with unsolicited applicants is that they usually reach the company at a time when there is no need for their services. When you need them, they're not around.

Dealing with Walk-Ins

Many firms have a formal procedure to handle walk-ins. All applicants are cordially greeted and are asked what type of job they are seeking. If the company uses that type of personnel, they are given an application even if no job is currently available. In this way, a backlog of applicants can be developed.

It's also good public relations to give a brief interview to all persons applying for a job. It builds up the company's image in the area and attracts people when they are needed. Applicants who cannot be hired are politely told that there are no current openings, but if an opening does occur, they will be considered. If they don't meet the job requirements, tell them why so they won't be waiting for a call that will never come.

When You Receive Unsolicited Resumés

People in professional, technical, sales, and administrative jobs usually mail, fax, or e-mail their resumés to companies in which they have an interest. Large firms receive thousands of these unsolicited letters each year. It often is not feasible to respond to all of them—or even to read them.

It's possible that, among this myriad of paper, there are some good applicants for jobs you have available—and when companies are desperately seeking to fill some jobs, they don't want to miss anybody who might possibly qualify.

Employment Enigmas

You must keep a record of every applicant interviewed, your decision, and the reasons for it. If a charge is made by the applicant that he or she has been discriminated against, your notes about the interview are important evidence of the legitimate reasons for the rejection.

Hiring Hints

For jobs that are tough to fill, keep the application open indefinitely. Sometimes if you contact an applicant who registered even a few years previously, he or she may have renewed interest when you call. If the person is not interested, ask if he or she knows somebody who is.

Some companies will scan all resumés for viable candidates. Most companies will not acknowledge receipt of the resumé to the sender unless there is interest. Others may send a form letter to all mail-ins who are not called for interviews thanking them for their interest.

Setting Up a Job Bank

To make the most of unsolicited applicants, all applications from walk-ins and re-sumés from mail-ins should be classified by job category and placed in a database for reference when jobs open up.

To avoid clutter in the job bank, set a time limit. All applications should be kept for six months, for example, and then be deleted from the job bank. Applicants are told that, if they are still available after six months, they should apply again.

The Least You Need to Know

➤ In choosing which colleges to recruit at, consider size, academic standards, programs in which they specialize, and overall reputation.

➤ Invitations to the company offices should be extended to candidates in whom there is some interest. During this visit, the prospect should meet with HR people, department heads or team leaders in the areas in which jobs are open, and others at the facility.

➤ There are a great many jobs in most companies that do not require college degrees but that do require specialized training. This training is often provided by two-year community colleges.

➤ Networking is a means of identifying and cultivating people who may be valuable resources for you in obtaining information, developing ideas, suggesting customers, and referring prospects for your open jobs.

➤ Don't overlook people leaving the armed services. Many officers have been trained in such fields as administration, training, logistics, and engineering. In the enlisted ranks you may find electricians, mechanics, machinists, and electronic technicians.

➤ To make the most of unsolicited applicants, all applications from walk-ins and resumés from mail-ins should be classified by job category and be placed in a database for reference when jobs open up.

Using the Internet as a Recruiting Source

Everything is now on the Internet. You can purchase all kinds of goods and services just by clicking your mouse. So why not seek to fill your jobs via computer? The applicants you want are probably sitting at their terminals right now surfing the net and—surprise, surprise—looking at what career opportunities are around.

Much of the Internet advertising for open positions is placed in the company's own Web site. In addition, many firms use several Internet referrals services. In this chapter, we'll explore this relatively new medium and discuss how you can use it effectively.

Using Your Web Pages

Most companies today have Web pages on which they describe the company's activities. These pages are designed primarily so that customers or potential investors can learn about the organization. Many firms include in their Web pages announcements of job openings.

A survey of 1,000 corporate recruiters found that 71 percent report spending up to 20 percent of their recruitment budget on the Internet, but this is growing exponentially. Three-quarters of companies responding plan to increase their Internet recruiting advertising in the coming year.

Designing the Web Page

The trouble with many Web pages is that it's not easy to access the information you want rapidly. Some home pages have little on them but a bunch of icons. You have to click several before you locate the appropriate one. Today, more and more companies are improving their sites to make them more user friendly. To attract applicants, design a special recruiting page and put a connecting link on the home page so applicants can easily access it.

Hiring Hints

Make your recruiting page exciting and enticing. Give prospects an intimate look at the company through video clips, vignettes about successful employees, and meaningful job descriptions. Make it easy to contact the company. Provide an e-mail address for submission of resumés.

If you have a continuing need for certain skills, post the positions on your Web site on a regular basis; to keep it sounding fresh, however, change the text periodically. Don't give up if you don't get responses immediately.

The companies that have the most success with Web-page recruiting are the well-known corporations. Job seekers turn first to the Web sites of companies that have reputations for hiring people in their fields.

You don't have to be a Fortune-500 firm to attract Web readers. Companies that are known and respected in their industries will attract people who have worked in that industry—and that can bring to your attention people with the experience you seek.

Creating Separate Recruiting Web Sites

General Web sites are loaded with information about the company that may or may not be of interest to a job seeker. In fact, the typical prospect is only interested in what jobs are available and will skip reading anything not related to the search. They'll go back to the general information only if a serious interest in the company and the job develops.

One way of encouraging job seekers to turn to your Web site is to create a special Web site with its own

Hiring Hints

Another way of guiding prospects to your Web site is to include the Web address in all your help-wanted ads. Even if the reader of the ad doesn't qualify for the job advertised, he or she may bookmark your site for future reference.

address for listing your jobs. This is particularly valuable for companies that have a wide variety of job openings on an ongoing basis.

Have the page designed by a professional. Web-page designers can help plan a format that will stand out and make it easy for applicants to locate the jobs in which they may be interested. Use of links can help the reader obtain more information, submit a resumé, or get in touch with a company representative to discuss specific matters.

Unlike advertising in a newspaper, your ad is not competing side by side with ads from other companies. You have the undivided attention of the reader. You are not limited by space or format protocols. You are free to tell as much as necessary to attract candidates and at the same time restrict respondents to qualified people.

Every listing should include the answers to these questions:

1. What is the nature of the job?
2. On what aspects of the work will the employee spend the most time?
3. What skills will the employee use on the job?
4. What are the key requirements for being considered for this job?
5. What training will the company give the new employee?
6. What is the range of compensation?
7. What are the advantages of working for this company?
8. To whom can I speak for more information?

Employment Enigmas

Don't clutter the job Web page with irrelevant information about the company such as a profile of the CEO or the history of the company. This can be reserved for the general Web site. Keep the focus on the jobs and employment opportunities.

The e-mail, fax, telephone number, and street address should be printed in large print on every Web page. This information can be placed in a box and printed in color or any other format to make it easy to see. A member of the HR department should be assigned the responsibility of reading, screening, and responding to all inquiries in a timely manner.

Once you have established a reputation of having good jobs listed on the site, people seeking jobs in your field will make regular visits to the site. Sooner or later, a job in which they are interested will appear and they'll respond.

Equally important, they'll tell their friends and co-workers about your site.

Hiring Hints

Advertise the Web site in technical and professional journals. Supplement this by sending them press releases about successful hires that resulted from the site.

Using Internet Referral Services

You may be thinking, "Web pages are okay for big companies. My company isn't that well known. Job seekers are not likely to even know about it, let alone hit our Web page."

The solution: Use one of the many Internet job-referral services. These are the cyber-equivalent of the help-wanted pages in newspapers or technical publications.

Choosing the Appropriate Server

There are several Internet referral services currently online, and many more seem to be opening every month. The first and probably still leading global online network for careers, connecting the companies with qualified career-minded individuals, is Monster.com. It is committed to leading the market by offering innovative technology and superior services that give consumers and businesses more control over the recruiting process.

The monster.com network consists of sites in the United States, Canada, the United Kingdom, the Netherlands, Belgium, Australia, and France, with additional sites to launch soon in Germany and Singapore.

Monster.com offers employers cost-effective and efficient recruiting solutions including real-time job postings, complete company profiles, and resumé screening, routing, and searching. Features for members include resumé skills screening, real-time recruiting, and a comprehensive resumé database with more than one million resumés.

The cost of using these services vary depending on the company's needs. Some companies may opt to use the service for short periods of time to deal with a limited number of job openings; others may purchase long-term contracts. Membership includes both posting job openings and accessing applicant listings. There is no extra charge for contacting or hiring applicants. Check the employer information section at each group's Web site for more specific information.

According to Media Matrix, an Internet consulting firm, the top 10 job sites in June 1999 were

1. Monster.com
2. Careerpath.com
3. Careermosaic.com
4. Headhunter.net
5. Jobsearch.org
6. Hotjobs.com
7. Dice.com
8. Careerbuilder.com
9. Nationjob.com
10. Jobs.com

Job Categories

In the early days of Internet recruiting, it was assumed that the people using the sites would be chiefly computer techies and engineers. That's no longer true. You'll find jobs in every category listed.

Careermosaic.com made a list of the most popular searches during the first six months of 1999. Here are the top 10:

1. Management jobs	6. Human resources
2. Sales	7. Administrative and clerical
3. Engineering	8. Finance
4. Accounting	9. Computer
5. Marketing	10. Analyst

This covers a broad spectrum of occupations, and it's an omen of how jobs will be filled in the years to come.

There's lots of competition for the techies you probably are seeking. To make your on-line postings stand out, Peter D. Weddle, publisher of *Weddles: The Newsletter For Successful Online Recruiting* (www.weddles.com), recommends the following 10 secrets for recruiting success:

1. Create intriguing titles.

2. Summarize the job in the first five lines.

3. Include salary in the first five lines.

4. Use focus groups to determine recent hires' key word searches.

5. Use online space fully. Unlike print ads, postings can include up to 1,400 words.

6. Use your community and professional connections. Link to their sites.

7. Provide instructions with a clear, easy way for candidates to respond to your ad.

8. Remember the passive job seeker! Only 26 percent of the workforce seeks a job at any point in time. Make online application forms short and easy.

9. Tell job seekers how to find your posting. With over 45 million sites on the Internet, use magazines and local newspapers to steer candidates to your site.

10. Describe opportunities, not requirements.

Searching the Applicant's Listings

Another source you should not overlook is the postings of individuals seeking jobs on the job-service Web pages. There are literally thousands of applicants posting their backgrounds on one or more of the listing services.

Finding the person you want is not easy. The usual way to search these lists is by key words. Using job titles alone will probably net an unwieldy number of prospects. You have to add key words based on your knockout factors. As pointed out before, this may eliminate good people who didn't use the key word in their resumé.

Unless there are very few available people in the job you seek to fill, you'll have to spend more time scanning the postings than it may be worth. If you are able to narrow the field down to a reasonable number of prospects, however, it will bring to your attention people who fit your needs. A great portion of the postings are from currently employed men and women who are not registered with agencies, are not regular readers of want ads, and are not desperate for a job.

Writing Your Posting

When you are advertising jobs on an *internal referral service*, you are in competition with many other firms looking for the same type of people. Unlike with print advertising, when applicants can spot your ad because of its size, format, attractiveness, or headline, the net surfer doesn't see your listing unless it comes up in a search.

Words to Work By

Internet referral services are the equivalent of classified ads in the newspapers. Companies post job listings, applicants list their backgrounds, and matches can be made.

Just as you use key words when searching the applicant postings, they use key words to find the jobs they want to investigate.

Job titles are okay, but if they are too general, it may result in so many hits that yours gets lost. Use a specific title, not a general one. If you list "Manager," the prospect will find jobs listed for every type of manager from managing a fast-food outlet to running a multiunit division of a giant corporation. Use the title that best describes the job. For example, you might use "Men's Clothing Retail Manager" or "Manager, Small Regional Bank" or similar titles.

Employment Enigmas

Internet postings should be attractive but not too gimmicky. Serious job seekers are turned off by bells and whistles.

It's not even necessary to use a job title. Because jobs are not placed alphabetically by title but are accessed by key word, select a word or phrase that prospects are likely to consider as descriptive of the job wanted. For example, instead of "Computer Scientist", use a more specific phrase such as "Software Designer—Financial Systems."

The prospect finds your ad. As pointed out in Chapter 7, "Writing Employment Advertising," the ad must both restrict the responses to qualified applicants and make those applicants desirous of pursuing the job. Unlike the limits placed on companies when writing ads for print, postings on Internet services usually have no space restriction. You can make it as long or as short as desired. The cost is not based on size. You can tell all you want about the company and the job, but you don't want to turn off a candidate because of a verbose, self-serving posting. You may want your Web designer to help set up the ads. There are many techniques that can be used to make your ad outstanding.

As time goes on and companies have more experience in using the Internet for recruiting, many of these problems will be worked out. It will become easier for applicants to find the jobs they want and for companies to screen the applicants for their vacancies.

Another way to reach applicants on the Internet is through chat rooms. There are chat rooms for most technical areas. By monitoring these chat rooms, you may make contacts that can be useful in getting leads on good applicants. More on using chatrooms in Chapter 15, "Prescreening Applicants."

Futurists say that within the next decade, not only will the Internet be the prime source for recruitment, applicants will be sending video-resumés by e-mail in response to postings, and preliminary interviews will be conducted over the Internet by means of videoconferencing.

The Least You Need to Know

➤ To attract applicants, design a special recruiting Web page and put a connecting link on the home page so applicants can easily access it.

➤ Make your recruiting Web page exciting and enticing. Give prospects an intimate look at the company through video clips, vignettes about successful employees, and meaningful job descriptions.

➤ On a Web page, you are not limited by space or format protocols. You are free to tell as much as necessary to attract candidates and at the same time restrict respondents to qualified people.

➤ In addition to using a Web page for recruiting, use an Internet job-referral service. This is the cyber-equivalent of the help-wanted pages in newspapers or technical publications.

➤ Another source you should not overlook is the postings of individuals seeking jobs on the job-service Web pages.

Chapter 12

Recruiting for Tough-to-Fill Jobs

In This Chapter

➤ Finding and attracting those rare techies

➤ Attending job fairs and open houses

➤ Becoming global recruiters

➤ Finding sales reps who can sell

➤ Filling jobs in the rapidly growing health care field

When jobs are plentiful, companies put up barriers to keep applicants from flooding their employment offices. When jobs are scarce, not only do they pull down the barriers, they also reach out to identify and attract the men and women needed to keep their operations going.

In seeking these rare birds, don't overlook the traditional methods discussed in the previous chapters. They work, but they may not be enough. You have to take a proactive approach to keep your teams fully staffed.

This chapter examines what some companies do to bring applicants to their doors. Of course, we'll explore the areas of obvious shortage: engineers, IT specialists, and other techies. In addition, we'll look at means of getting good sales reps, finding skilled craftsmen, and filling the many types of jobs in the fast-growing health care field.

Hiring Technical Personnel

Recruiters in this field have had to be creative to keep a flow of candidates for the many jobs open in the companies they serve. And once they find these candidates, they need to be able to offer them a deal that is likely to be attractive.

Let's look at some techniques that recruiters have used.

A Silicon Valley recruiter reported that, despite the growth of computer-oriented firms in her area, there still are companies that don't make the grade and go out of business or that are acquired by another firm. When this happens, recruiters swoop down on the company and literally grab the workers in the parking lot to entice them to look into their job openings.

One recruiter reported, "We look like a bunch of ambulance-chasing lawyers pressing the relatives of disaster victims."

She said, "I'm embarrassed to be among them, but it's part of the job—and it does work."

An employment-agency owner who has lived through eras of both job shortages and applicant scarcity told me that, when jobs were scarce, he would peruse the obituary columns and go after the jobs of the deceased. He said, "Now that the situation is reversed, I shifted my reading to the announcement of engagements and marriages. Most of these items note the occupations of the couple. If the man or woman is in one of the tough-to-fill fields, I contact him or her. You'd be amazed at how many people show interest in a career-enhancing opportunity at this time of lives.

Hiring Hints

A few years ago, some companies sweetened their offers by giving new employees a hiring bonus. This *is* no longer much of a sweetener, however, because almost every company now gives hiring bonuses. It's become a standard part of the compensation package for technical and other hard-to-fill positions.

Employment Enigmas

The compensation package is still a major factor in attracting applicants, but it is not necessarily the best. Outbidding competitors for top people has its limits. You cannot always afford the cost. Other attractors that may be considered are flexible hours, shorter work weeks, and more time off.

Job Fairs

One of the most cost effective means of recruiting techies is the job fair. These "flesh markets" started as an informal part of technical society conventions. For example, when engineers attended the convention, they would often spend more time looking for a new job than attending the workshops and technical programs. Companies would set up elaborate hospitality suites at a nearby hotel and invite prospective employees to visit and learn about the opportunities at that firm.

This soon became formalized into the job fair. As an adjunct to the convention, companies could post jobs and applicants could file resumés. Arrangements were made for interviews between companies and applicants.

Today's job fairs are not necessarily tied in with a convention. Recruiters or trade show operators run most independently. Companies rent a booth at the fair and staff it with representatives of the human resources and technical departments. Applicants are provided with a guidebook indicating the companies participating and the types of positions they are seeking to fill.

The sponsor of the job fair advertises in local and trade papers, and quite often participating companies will advertise their jobs in the papers and invite interested applicants to visit their booth.

Users of job fairs have found them to be a relatively inexpensive way to hire people, and many companies participate in job fairs all over the country several times a year.

Hiring Hints

Make your booth at a job fair attractive and comfortable. Don't decorate it with a blow-up photo of the CEO or the plant (unless it is impressive). Show examples of the work candidates will do. Provide comfortable chairs for visitors. Have knowledgeable staff members available to discuss the jobs.

Open Houses

A variation of the job fair is the company open house. Let's see how one of my clients, an electric-components manufacturer from Long Island in New York, conducted his open house.

Facility: The program was held in the company's employee cafeteria on a Saturday and Sunday. The open-house committee decorated the room with colorful posters, balloons, and flowers. Booths were set up for each of the areas in which jobs were open: research, design, contract administration, manufacturing, and so on. Soft drinks, coffee and tea, and snacks were set up on the cafeteria's counter and were available all day. A nearby conference room was set up to show a video about the plant. Other conference rooms were set up for interviews.

Staffing: A welcoming team was appointed to greet and register each visitor. Technical specialists were assigned to each booth and were instructed in how to describe the open jobs and obtain basic information about the applicant.

Promotion: Ads were placed in newspapers within 100 miles of the facility, inviting interested applicants to visit the open house. These were supplemented by commercials on radio stations in the same geographic area, advertising the job fair and referring prospects to the newspaper ads for details about the job openings.

Applicants were given preliminary interviews at the fair; if there was further interest, they were invited for a more detailed interview as soon as possible—preferably during the next week. About 150 people showed up, of which 30 were invited back and 8 were hired.

A variation of the open house is the "no-frills" open house. The company runs an ad on a given Sunday in newspapers across the country listing jobs and giving a toll-free phone number. Job seekers are urged to call immediately. The hotline is staffed all day by recruiters and technical specialists. Questions about the jobs are answered. Applicants are asked a few key questions, and if there is mutual interest, resumés can be faxed. Because the applicant can call on Sunday and not put it off until the next workday, it encourages prospects to take immediate action.

Authors of Technical Articles

You need an expert? It's likely that the expert you need has published articles about the field in which you are engaged in some technical journal.

Recruiting Residuals

Looking for a really good job? Make yourself known to the companies who might hire you by writing articles for publication in trade journals. Not only does it give you prestige, it also increases your credibility in your profession.

I've been on both sides of this equation. When I was a young personnel administrator, I wrote an article about a program I developed for my company. As a result, a much larger company approached me and offered me a much better job.

Some years later, as a consultant seeking an executive to set up a new technical division for a client, I read several professional journals in the field, contacted the authors, and hired one of them. The time taken and the cost of the hire was a fraction of using more traditional approaches.

Hire a Team

Wouldn't it be great if you could hire a team—a group of guys and gals who have worked together and have developed a coordinated, collaborative interrelationship? Sometimes you can. A few years ago when a large electronics company downsized, recruiters knocked down the doors trying to recruit techies. One company, however, took a different approach. They went after teams.

No, it wasn't a stroke of genius that brought this about. It was pure fortuity. When one prospect was made an offer, he said he was interested in the job but that, since he had been working with four other engineers as a team, he hoped the company he chose to work for could hire all five and keep the team together. This led to interviews with the other team members, and the entire team was hired. The company didn't plan to hire five people at that time, but it quickly recognized that, over time, it would need additional engineers. It stretched the company's budget temporarily, but the team became productive almost immediately; in the long run, it paid off for the company.

Hiring Hints

Don't wait until you have an opening to contact authors of articles that impress you. Write them a congratulatory letter. Add them to your network. Call them for information. Make a friend now. When you do have a job for them, they'll be more amenable to your offer.

Cooperate with Competitors

Sound crazy? Desperate for engineers, a group of technical companies in central New York State decided to stop raiding each other for talent and join forces to attract employees collectively. Through a cooperative Web site, they discuss opportunities and lifestyles in the area. Job seekers can apply for openings or ask for more details online. Since it started in 1998, it has logged a monthly average of 370,000 hits and 17,000 job searches resulting in more than 50 new hires.

Train Your Own Specialists

With the increasing shortage of trained people, instead of trying to outbid competitors for the few available candidates, many firms are planning for their future needs by hiring people who have potential and training them.

As noted in Chapter 10, "Other Sources," arrangements can be made with community colleges and trade schools to offer courses that train people for the special needs of a company. This can be augmented by in-house training, internships for students, and cooperative schoolwork programs in which students work part time in the company while taking courses and getting school credits for the work.

Appoint a "Shepherd"

When the HR director of an Atlanta computer-software designer learned that new graduates of his favorite school, Georgia Tech, were receiving six to ten job offers, he came up with a bright idea to increase his company's chances of getting acceptances. He appointed a current employee, who was an alumnus of Georgia Tech, to "shepherd" the student through the hiring process.

Here's how it works. Ben H., a software designer who was hired three years ago, was assigned to guide the student, Harry L., through the procedure. Ben met Harry when he arrived at the facility, showed him around, and introduced him to the various people who were to interview him. He took him to lunch and answered his questions. They found that they had much in common because they both had studied with many of the same professors and were both ardent football fans and team supporters. After Harry received an offer of employment, Ben phoned him to get his reaction, to clarify any problems, and to encourage him to accept it.

By using *shepherds*, the company significantly increased the number of job offers that were accepted.

Hit the Mall

Addecco, an international employment agency based in California, has placed a number of kiosks in shopping malls and on college campuses throughout the country. Each kiosk has a touch screen that enables job seekers to register with Addecco and to obtain information about local jobs as well as jobs in other cities of interest.

Less sophisticated but equally effective is leasing one of the many booths found throughout most malls. Instead of hawking novelties, jewelry, or pretzels, staff it with a recruiter and display descriptions of your open jobs.

Foreign Sources

American universities are not graduating enough students with majors in science, math, information technology, and related fields. One way to find qualified candidates is to look to other countries.

As pointed out in Chapter 5, "More on Employment Laws," however, it's not easy to get visas for these specialists. You must obtain a H1-B visa for tech workers, and Congress has limited the number of these visas to 115,000 a year. This is far below the needed numbers of such specialists.

Although business lobbyists are pushing for expansion of this number, labor unions and some politicians oppose it, proposing instead funding for more training in these fields in the United States.

How does a company go about recruiting people overseas? The easiest way is to retain a recruiter who has contacts in several countries and can do the recruiting for you. Some recruiting firms have established offices in countries with large populations of trained techies. These countries include India, China, and Russia, where there is a plethora of technically trained people and a scarcity of good-paying jobs.

Words to Work By

Foreign nationals who are imported to work in the United States are called **impats (impatriates)**. Americans who work abroad who are called **expats (expatriates)**.

Some large firms have foreign subsidiaries or associates who are good sources for obtaining *impats*. Other firms send staff members on overseas recruiting trips to find needed specialists. Many American firms send people from the States to work in their overseas facilities. These *expats* are good sources for recruiting people in the countries in which they are located for jobs in the company's home offices.

Recruiting Residuals

You think it's tough to import techies to the United States? In Germany, the rules are so strict that even if you want to hire a foreigner who is working for another company in Germany, he risks deportation by changing jobs. When one company wanted to hire a Russian programmer, it purchased the company where he was employed.

One of the best sources for obtaining referrals is the impats currently employed by your company. They usually know people with skills similar to their own. Ask for referrals. Offer rewards.

Hiring Sales Representatives

Good salespeople are hard to find. Very few colleges even offer courses in salesmanship let along provide a major or a degree. Most salespeople choose this field because of their personality and the monetary rewards it offers. Locating men and women with appropriate sales experience is one of the greatest challenges faced by sales managers. Let's look at what can be done to alleviate this situation.

Employment Enigmas

It takes time, money, and endless patience to bring impats into the United States. Don't expect to fill rush jobs this way. Use a specialized recruiter or an immigration attorney to expedite this process.

Broaden the Specs

One of the most common mistakes sales managers make when trying to fill a sales job is insisting that the person they hire come from a direct competitor. The rationalization for this requirement is that, by knowing the product and the market, they will become productive immediately. The implied hope is that they will bring some of their old customers along with them.

Sound sensible? Maybe. However, there are significant flaws in this logic. First, why should a good sales rep leave one job for another? Perhaps he or she wants more money. Since most sales reps are paid on an incentive basis, why can't they make more money where they are? Maybe their compensation deal is inadequate. If this is true, you may have a good lead. Often, however, they seek a package that is unreasonable; to entice them, you would have to pay more than they are really worth.

Another flaw in this logic is that there are countless examples of experienced sales reps in an industry jumping from company to company in that industry, never really making the grade. They're okay. They bring in some business. They weren't stars in their former jobs, and they'll never be stars in your company.

Employment Enigmas

In hiring sales reps, put the emphasis on ability to sell and not product knowledge. In most cases, it takes 30 days to learn a product line, but it takes 30 years to develop sales skills.

Get out of that rut. Instead of limiting your sources for candidates to people who come out of your industry, seek people who have been successes in any industry. Except for some high-tech products, most intelligent salespeople can be taught the product knowledge needed to sell in a relatively short time. It takes a lot longer to train a person with product knowledge how to sell than to teach a good salesperson your product line.

By opening the door to prospects with a record of success in sales rather than in your industry, you'll fill your jobs faster and more effectively.

Salespeople Who Call On You

At a recent seminar I conducted, I asked participants to describe their most successful hiring experience. Jack K., the owner of a Ford dealership, reported, "I was in the market for a new photocopy machine. One of the sales reps who called on me was a woman selling an import that I had never heard of. It was more expensive than Xerox or Canon. My first reaction was to cut short the meeting and politely send her on her way. There was nothing particularly prepossessing about the sales rep. But there was something about the way she made her presentation: her sincerity in the value of her product, her attentive listening to my questions, and her thoughtful responses that riveted my attention. I didn't buy her product, but I was so impressed by her that I offered her a job with my agency. She gracefully declined, but a few months later, when the company she worked for recognized that they couldn't compete against the leaders in their field and closed their U.S. operation, she called and asked if that offer were still open. Betty joined our team three years ago and today is my number-one producer."

When a salesperson calls on you, you have the opportunity to see him or her in action and can make a much better evaluation of the person's sales capability than you could be made from the usual job interviews. If there are no openings at the present time, make a note of this person. He or she may be your best prospect when a job opens.

In your job, you may not get to see salespeople from other firms. The people in your purchasing department, however, see them all the time. It's their main function. Alert them to you needs. Let them know the types of people you want to hire. Encourage them to suggest to people that impress them to look into jobs with your company.

Make Your Own Salespeople Talent Scouts

Sales reps spend a tremendous amount of time waiting to see their customers. They sit in the reception area along with sales reps from other vendors. They read; they do paperwork; they chat with the others.

Hiring Hints

It takes one to know one. Good sales reps can often spot talent in other salespeople. Make it part of their job description to be on the lookout for sales prospects.

Quite often, they'll pick up hints of discontent. One person may comment about a poor compensation plan; another may be unhappy about a change in territory. Still others may appear to be satisfied but may be always on the lookout for a better opportunity.

During some of your regular meetings with your salespeople, let them know what to look for as they chat with their reception-room colleagues. Encourage them to talk about the opportunities in your firm. Set up a reward program for referrals that result in hires.

Other Areas in Short Supply

High tech is not the only field in which personnel shortages exist. People are in short supply to fill many areas, including skilled craftsmen and the less glamorous and much lower paid positions in the food service and health care fields.

Health Care

According to almost every study of where the jobs of the future will be, health care is always listed among the top categories. Jobs in this ever-growing area cover the entire gamut—from medical doctors, registered nurses, and technicians to the low-paid hospital or home-care aide.

Despite the demand for doctors, U.S. medical schools don't turn out enough graduates to serve America's needs. Despite the long and arduous studies required of physicians, there is no shortage of applicants for medical schools; unfortunately, the schools don't have the facilities to accept more than a fraction of those who apply. To compound the problem, after the physicians complete the schooling, internship, and residencies needed to qualify, a great percentage of them opt to practice in affluent communities or large metropolitan medical centers or continue their studies to qualify as specialists. This leaves a dearth of physicians to serve rural communities and inner-cities.

A similar situation exists in recruiting registered nurses. The shortage of nurses is exacerbated by the need for nurses in positions that are less demanding and often more lucrative than hospital work such as staffing doctors' offices, schools, or a company's medical facility.

There are no easy solutions to this problem. It takes years to train physicians, and there are no short cuts. Today, most of the shortage of physicians is met by impats. Hospitals recruit doctors from other countries, particularly India, Pakistan, and Taiwan. Nurses are recruited from the Philippines and more recently from Mexico and other Latin American countries.

Another way hospitals are solving the RN shortage is by restructuring the job. Nurses traditionally have spent a good deal of their time making patient's beds, feeding them, and performing nonmedical care-giving. By assigning these chores to nurses' aides or others, nurses can concentrate on the areas in which their training is more critical. This reduces the need for registered nurses in many hospitals. On the other side of this coin, many Registered Nurses are being trained to take on some of the duties usually performed by medical doctors. These nurse practitioners are able to conduct diagnostic examinations, read and interpret medical reports, and relieve physicians of some of their responsibilities.

Recruiting Residuals

The Bureau of Labor Statistics puts the number of home health care aides financed by Medicare and Medicaid at 697,000 in 1996, a number that also includes paid housekeepers. Tens of thousands of additional home health care workers will be needed in the coming years, experts say, and the number of jobs to be filled is expected to increase by 76 percent between 1996 and 2006.

The health care field, which is growing so fast that it's almost out of control, needs men and women to staff the patient care requirements in hospitals, nursing homes, and at-home care. As the population ages, more and more people will need this type of care. At present, these jobs are among the lowest paid in our economy. Most workers earn slightly above the minimum wage. This results in a high percentage of poorly qualified people performing sensitive and often critical activities. To attract more competent people, wages will have to be raised and training programs instituted.

Skilled Crafts

If you drive past any factory in industrial America today, you'll probably see bulletin boards advertising for machinists, tool and die makers, and other skilled jobs. Unfortunately, many young people are not willing to go through the many years it takes to master these skills.

Computer-based programs will eventually replace some of these jobs. For example, computer-assisted design (CAD) has already made the job of manual draftsman obsolete. Computer-assisted manufacturing (CAM) is replacing some machine operations. However, men and women will always be needed for the countless jobs that must still be performed manually.

In many foreign countries, there are still apprenticeship programs for many of these skills. Of course, you can attempt to recruit skilled craftsmen overseas, but there are many people already in this country who have been trained in other countries. One way of reaching them is to advertise in foreign-language newspapers. An even more effective way to find them is employee referrals. Current employees who were trained abroad are likely to know others from their home countries who have similar skills. Encourage such referrals by publicizing your needs and by sweetening successful referrals with financial rewards.

The Least You Need to Know

➤ One of the most cost effective means of recruiting techies is the job fair.

➤ A variation on the job fair is the company open house. Companies advertise the list of available jobs and invite candidates to come to the facility where they can learn about the company and the jobs.

➤ Read trade and professional journals. The authors of articles in your areas of interest are potential prospects for your job openings. If they're not available themselves, they are good sources for referrals.

➤ Be a global recruiter. The people with the skills you want may be scarce in America but may be available in some other countries. It's worth the red tape and the expense if you can hire the skills you require.

➤ To hire the best sales reps, don't limit your search to people currently selling in your industry. Successful sales experience is more valuable than product knowledge.

➤ To fill the growing number of openings in the health care field, redesign the jobs.

Part 4

Weeding Out the Unqualified

Once you've located the candidates for your open jobs, the next step is to select that person who will best suit your opening.

Interviewing is still the most frequently used technique in choosing a new employee. Interviewing is expensive. It's time consuming. It takes the managers who do the interviewing away from their regular, productive work.

The solution: Get rid of those unqualified applicants before taking the time to interview them. How? Well, you can't just dump their resumés. But by good prescreening you can reserve your valuable time for people who at least are good possibilities.

COMPUTERS,
CALCULATORS,
IT'S ALL
THE SAME

Chapter 13

Resumés—The Applicant's Sales Tool

In This Chapter

➤ Screening for viable candidates

➤ Reading different types of resumés

➤ Detecting phony claims

➤ Using the resumé to prepare for the interview

Everybody has a resumé. If you put an ad in the paper, you may be deluged with resumés. Reading all these responses takes valuable time. You have to know what to look for.

If the person reading the resumé recognizes it for what it is, it will be much more useful as a screening tool. There is no such thing as a standard resumé. Many resumés are badly written by the applicants and may fail to bring out qualities that are important to success on a job. Other resumés may be prepared for applicants by a professional service that may exaggerate a candidate's experience and give an impression of competence that exceeds the reality.

This chapter looks at what the resumé really is and how you can weed out from all the verbiage whether an applicant is worth spending time on.

Skimming Through the Deluge

You can't read every line of every resumé. You don't have the time, and most are probably from people who are not qualified for your job opening. You have to skim, but there's an art to skimming.

Recruiting Residuals

According to a survey conducted by the Society for Human Resources Management (SHRM), 88 percent of respondents indicated that they spend less than three minutes reading a resumé. A decision that may affect the profitability of the company and the life of the applicant is based on these few minutes.

Knockout Factors

Review the job specs. There are certain qualifications that the prospect must possess to even make the first cut; these are called *knockout factors*. For example, a job calls for a degree in electrical engineering. Assuming that there is no flexibility for this requirement, look first at the education section of each resumé for that degree. No EE degree—dump the resumé.

The job calls for experience in designing servomechanisms. The applicant worked for a manufacturer of servos, but the resumé says not a word about designing them. Put this resumé in the second-choice pile. When you complete your first scanning, if relatively few respondents specify this type of experience, you can telephone people in this pile to determine whether they have the requisite background.

Be careful in choosing knockout factors. By making qualifications, which are desirable but not really essential, you may eliminate well-qualified applicants.

In this computer age, software has been designed to screen resumés. The resumés are scanned into the computer and then searched for key words. If the key words are not found, bye-bye resumé. It sure makes it easier for the recruiters.

But as in any of these situations, computers can't use judgment. An applicant may be well-qualified but fail to use that key word in the resumé. A human being reading the resumé could easily see that the respondent has a viable background, but the computer only searches for the words that have been programmed for the job.

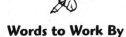

Words to Work By

Knockout factors are certain qualifications that the applicant must have for the job. If the individual doesn't have them, there's no point in spending another second reading that resumé.

Reading Between the Lines

Don't take what you read in the resumé at face value. Read between the lines. Applicants may have hidden negative factors or neglected to note assets that may be of value to your company. Let's look at some of these:

➤ **Gaps in dates.** Many people have had short-duration jobs and leave them out of their resumés. One sign to watch for is specifying years only rather than months and years. For example, 1994–1996 for one job and 1996–2000 for the next. This may mean a short period of unemployment in between jobs in 1996, but it could also hide a short-duration job in 1996 from which the applicant was fired. A variation of this is listing the number of years worked instead of dates of employment. For example, Job A—4 years and Job B—3 years. This may indicate the covering up of unfavorable factors in job history. It could also indicate an emphasis on older background when more recent work experience is not relevant. For example, the job sought is a human resources manager. The applicant did have that experience—10 years ago—but has worked in an entirely different area more recently.

➤ **More space is given to earlier jobs than to more recent ones.** Often this is due to poor judgment on the part of the applicant. He or she "updated" an earlier resumé and added a few lines at the bottom to describe the most recent job. This may not be important in many jobs, but it's a sign of poor planning and possibly laziness. It also may mean that the last job wasn't as important as previous jobs or was held for a much shorter period of time. It's not necessarily a negative factor, but it indicates the need for a more careful look at the applicant.

➤ **Overemphasis on education and nonjob factors.** If a person is out of school for more than five years, the resumé should predominantly indicate work experience. What he or she did in high school or college is secondary to what was accomplished on the job. The

Employment Enigmas

Using key words in screening resumés—whether this is done by computer or by a human being—can cause legal difficulties. If the words chosen are based on a "majority white male culture," they may knock out proportionally more minorities and women.

Employment Enigmas

An applicant who plays up college athletic accomplishments or who still brags about being elected prom queen years after graduation may still be living in the past.

applicant who gives details on current nonwork aspects of his or her life, such as hobbies or volunteer work, may be subconsciously showing where his or her interests really lie.

None of the above is a knockout factor. It simply suggests further exploration in the interview. If the resumé gives you any indication that problems may exist, note them so that, when you interview the applicant, they can be brought out and discussed.

Resumé Styles

One of the reasons a resumé can be misleading is the style in which it is formatted. Applicants can select the style they believe will do the most good, and sometimes this can hide negatives in their backgrounds or overemphasize the aspects they want you to know about. Let's look at two of the most commonly used styles: *chronological resumés* and *functional resumés*.

> **Words to Work By**
>
> **Chronological resumés** present an applicant's background by listing jobs by dates of employment. **Functional resumés** present an applicant's background by listing duties, responsibilities, or accomplishments without regard to the job or company in which they were performed.

Chronological Resumés

This is the most frequently used style. Typically, it starts with education and then lists work experience by dates starting with the most recent job.

> **Nancy Noname**
>
> **Eleventh St.**
>
> **Yourtown, USA**

Education: B.A., New York University, 1992

Major: Economics

Certificate in Human Resources Management, University College for Continuing Education, Hofstra University, 1998

Experience:

Sept. 1994–current, Asst. Director of Human Resources, ABC Co.
(description of duties)

Sept. 1992 to July 1994, XYZ Company, Employment Interviewer
(description of duties)

This is easiest for the employer to read. It provides a clear overview of the education and work history of the applicant. It parallels the typical company application form; however, since there are no space limitations, it gives the writer freedom to expand on job activities. A well-constructed resumé will describe each major phase of the job in enough detail to make it meaningful to the reader. Duties, responsibilities and achievements should be discussed for each job held. Unfortunately, too many resumés are not well-constructed and give little information other than job title.

Functional Resumés

The functional resumé gives an applicant the opportunity to play up job duties rather than the duration of a job. This enables the reader to readily note what the candidate has done. It's a more effective sales tool for the applicant, but it can be used to mislead the reader. Let's see how Nancy Noname's resumé would look in functional form.

Nancy Noname

111 Eleventh St.

Yourtown, USA

Experience in Human Resources Management:

Recruiting: (description of recruiting experience and accomplishments)

Interviewing: (description)

Administration: (description)

Training: (description)

> **Hiring Hints**
>
> When reading a functional resumé, place it side by side with the candidate's completed application form to compare job history with functions indicated on the resumé.

Names of employers and dates of employment may be listed separately or, in some cases, omitted. Education and any other information may be listed at the end of the resumé.

Functional resumés are excellent ways to highlight the background of a person who has done similar work with more than one company, alleviating the need to repeat the same information for each job. They're often used, however, to mask frequent job changes or to give the impression that the candidate has worked much longer in the highlighted functions than he or she has.

Resumé experts recommend a combination of the chronological and functional resumés. This gives the applicant an opportunity to describe each job more fully, and it gives the employer more information than is usually obtained from the traditional chronological resumé. Here's an example:

> **Employment Enigmas**
>
> A functional resumé usually gives the reader much more complete information about what the applicant has accomplished than a chronological resumé, but it has the stigma of possibly being misleading. By having the candidate complete a standard application form, you can obtain the missing information.

Nancy Noname
Eleventh St.
Yourtown, USA

Education: B.A., New York University, 1992

Major: Economics

Certificate in Human Resources Management, University College for Continuing Education, Hofstra University, 1998

Experience:

Sept. 1994–current, Asst. Director of Human Resources, ABC Co.

Administration: (description of administrative duties and accomplishments)

Employment: (description)

Training: (description)

Sept. 1992 to July 1994, XYZ Company, Employment Interviewer

Recruiting: (description)

Interviewing: (description)

Job Analysis: (description)

Gimmicky Resumés

To get your attention, some applicants will send you a cute resumé. Companies have received resumés in the form of poems, fairy tales, greeting cards, fancy brochures, audio- or videotapes, and all kinds of gimmicks created by computers.

If the job is for a person who has creative talents, this may be an asset. It shows creativity. However, for most jobs, it should be looked at as a gimmick and be judged on its content, not its style.

Recruitment Residuals

Companies are beginning to report receiving gimmicky resumés via the Internet. Often included in e-mail are a variety of fancy formats, attached scanned photos, and even voice messages.

Evaluating a Resumé

The resumé can provide a great wealth of information, or it can be a lot of sizzle but no steak. By carefully evaluating the resumé, you can save yourself much time by eliminating people who really are not worth seeing and by preparing good questions for the ones you invite for interviews.

What to Look For

In reading a resumé, here are some suggestions to help you seek important information about the applicant:

➤ **Study the job specifications.** Prepare a list of the significant qualifications the applicant must have. This is a much more detailed list than the knockout factors noted earlier in this chapter. Does the applicant have experience in all or a good portion of these qualifications? If yes, has this experience or training been acquired in a setting comparable to your organization? (For example, systems analysis in a bank is much different from systems analysis in a manufacturing company.)

➤ **Missing qualifications:** If the applicant does not indicate experience in one of your qualifications, it doesn't necessarily mean he or she does not have it. Often a person may overlook an important factor of experience in writing a resumé or omit it to keep the resumé brief. If the applicant has much of what you need but omits a key qualification, phone him or her for more details.

➤ **Depth of experience:** The resumé indicates experience in a desired area, but you can't tell from the description how deep the experience is. Make a note to probe for more details when you interview this candidate.

➤ **Size of the company:** The type of experience a person has often is conditioned by the size of the companies in which it was obtained. For example, a person working in a large department of a large company may do only a specialized aspect of a job. Patti J.'s first job was as a marketing analyst for a large food company. However, all she did was compile sales statistics. On the other side of this coin, Jeffrey R. worked as a marketing assistant in a small housewares company. He performed a variety of marketing functions, but since the company was very small, it didn't have to tools or techniques he might have acquired in a larger organization. In interviewing these candidates, ask good questions about what they actually have done and learned in their current or previous jobs.

➤ **Look for accomplishments.** What makes the applicant stand out in competition with others who have similar experience? Many applicants describe their jobs by echoing the company's job description. This is fine up to a point, but by adding some of the specific results this particular person achieved doing this job, you get an answer to this question.

The "Paper Person"

In reading a resumé, always keep in mind that the piece of paper in front of you cannot completely describe the applicant. The resumé is just a one-dimensional sketch of a multidimensional individual. Yet, the key decision often is made from this "paper person." If you choose *not* to see the applicant based on the resumé, you'll lose this prospect forever—and he or she might have been the best applicant. It's easy to discard a resumé.

Before putting it in the discard file, ask yourself these questions:

➤ Is the rejection based on the applicant's lack of qualifications or a lack of information on the resumé?

➤ If the latter, on the basis of the types of jobs the applicant has held, is it likely that the experience may be there even though it's not specified? If so, it may pay to telephone the applicant to obtain the missing information before making a decision.

➤ Is the reason for rejection a poorly written or poorly presented resumé? If the position calls for communicative skills, this is a valid reason for rejection. On the other hand, eliminating the resumé of a master mechanic because it is poorly written may deprive the firm of a highly skilled potential employee.

Hiring Hints

If an applicant brags in his resumé about routine or superficial achievements, this may indicate a low set of standards.

When in doubt, it pays to obtain further information before making the final rejection. If there is time, you might mail the applicant an application form to complete and return. If not, the telephone is your best bet for determining whether to invite the candidate for an interview.

Losing a qualified person because the resumé is unsatisfactory is not fair to the applicant or to your company.

Detecting Resumé Fraud

Everybody expects resumés to exaggerate a little. Candidates present themselves in as favorable a light as possible, and if they stretch the truth a little, we can pick it up by good interviewing.

But real resumé fraud is a much deeper problem. There have been numerous cases in which candidates lied about key factors such as the level of education completed, degrees or licenses received, companies where they never worked, and similar misrepresentations.

Educational Background

Lots of people claim degrees they don't have. They may have attended the university for a year or two but claim to have a degree. A few years ago, I interviewed a man who claimed an MBA from a university where I was an adjunct professor. After a few questions, it was obvious he never attended that school. He shamefacedly admitted that his only contact was taking a one-day seminar there.

One of my clients was about to hire a man who claimed to have a degree in accounting from a prestigious college. Only when I called to the client's attention that the school is a liberal arts college that doesn't give degrees in accounting did he realize the candidate was lying.

It's relatively easy to check colleges. Most schools will verify whether a student attended and graduated if you write to them. If you want a transcript, you must have written authorization from the applicant and may be charged a small fee.

Exaggerated or Misleading Claims of Expertise or Experience

Watch out for phrases like "supervised a department," "managed a team," "increased sales," or "created a program." They may be true but can be misleading unless they are related to and supported by specific accomplishments such as the size of the department or team, the percentage of improvement in sales, or the scope of the program. Be sure to question all such claims at the interview.

The Self-Employment Cover-Up

Many resumé fakers claim to be self-employed to cover up periods of unemployment or a job they don't want uncovered for a variety of reasons. It's very difficult for an employer to confirm self-employment. If it's legitimate, you can usually check the bank where the business had an account or through Dun and Bradstreet or other credit organizations. But this takes time and sometimes money, and many employers will not bother the check it out, particularly if it is for a relatively short period of time. Use your best judgment. Ask a lot of questions about the nature of the business, what customers or clients were served, and financial reports. Get the names of the accountants, attorneys, and bankers the company used.

Another ploy applicants use to hide periods of unemployment or jobs they'd rather not discuss is being a consultant. Often, this is literally true.

Employment Enigmas

Job applicants can buy fake college degrees, transcripts, and certifications on the Internet for a few hundred dollars. Make the sure college claimed is legitimate. The best schools are accredited by the regional accreditation association or are approved by the state in which they are located.

Many executives take on consulting assignments during periods of unemployment. It's a good way to make a few bucks while looking for a job. Don't just accept this at face value. Ask about clients and projects to verify the claim.

The "Out-of-Business" Excuse

It's not unusual for a resumé faker to claim employment with a company that is out of business. I've seen resumés that claim employment in well-known firms that have closed shop, and I've seen claims of employment in companies that never existed but are listed on the resumé as being out of business. It's sometimes not possible to check these claims. One way, of course, is to ask for paycheck stubs or W-2 forms issued by the company. This will at least prove that the individual worked there. If the person has no proof, be skeptical about the claim.

If, on the basis of the resumé, you decide to interview the applicant, make a list of questions to verify the facts and probe for details about the previous job. The following chapters will discuss how to do this and how to check the accuracy of the information.

The Least You Need to Know

➤ There is no such thing as a standard resumé. Many resumés fail to bring out qualities that are important to success on a job. Other resumés may exaggerate the candidate's experience and give an impression of competence that exceeds the reality.

➤ Set up a series of knockout factors based on your job specs. Unless the applicant has these qualifications for the job, there's no point in spending another second reading that resumé.

➤ Don't take what you read in the resumé at face value. Read between the lines. Applicants may have hidden negative factors or neglected to note assets that may be of value to your company.

➤ Chronological resumés present an applicant's background by listing jobs by dates of employment. Functional resumés present an applicant's background by listing duties, responsibilities, or accomplishments without regard to the job or company in which they were performed.

➤ Check colleges. Most schools will verify whether a student attended and graduated if you write to them. If you want a transcript, you must have written authorization from the applicant and may be charged a small fee.

➤ A candidate's resumé indicates experience in a desired area, but you can't tell from the description how deep the experience is. Make a note to probe for more details when you interview this candidate.

Chapter 14

The Application Form

In This Chapter

➤ Comparing applications and resumés

➤ Using the application form as a legal bulwark

➤ Designing meaningful application forms

➤ Using the application as a screening tool

➤ Using the application to prepare for the interview

If you've ever had to look for a job—and who hasn't—you've probably filled out dozens of application forms. Some probably were brief and simple and took a few minutes to complete. Others may have been multipage documents seeking to uncover hidden aspects of your background.

The application form is the basic first step in the selection process. This chapter looks at the various uses of these forms, how to design a form that will be useful in providing meaningful information, and some of the ramifications—legal and pragmatic—concerning these forms.

The Application Serves Many Purposes

The company application form serves several purposes. It's a rapid means of providing the interviewer with basic information about the applicant. It alleviates the need for the interviewer to ask for this routine information. It also provides legal protection and makes it easy to compare candidates.

All Applicants Must Fill Out the Form

Some candidates may be reluctant to complete an application. They may tell you that all the pertinent information is in the resumé. And sometimes it is. But as was pointed out in the preceding chapter, a resumé is designed to play up the strengths of the applicant—and sometimes to cover up negative factors. For this and for other reasons you'll learn as you read this chapter, completing the application is important and should be insisted on.

One of the common shortcuts applicants use is filling out their name and address on the application and then scrawling over the balance of the form "See resumé." This is not acceptable. Insist that every candidate fill out the form completely. If you mail an application form to a candidate, specify in your letter that the application must be completely executed. For applicants who come to the office, train receptionists or staff members who give out the forms to tell each applicant "Please complete the form in its entirety even if you have a resumé." Comment that the resumé can be a useful supplement but not a replacement for the company's form.

Employment Enigmas

"I don't have to fill out the application. I have a resumé." This is *not* a good argument. If an applicant doesn't want to take the time to complete your application form, he or she may be hiding something—or it may be an indication of laziness or unwillingness to follow instructions.

Hiring Hints

Never reprint your application form until your legal counsel reviews it to make sure it's in compliance with the latest laws and regulations.

It Protects You Legally

In this litigious age, a rash of suits have been filed against companies by applicants. Some have claimed discrimination when they didn't get the job, others have claimed a company jeopardized their current job by calling their employer for a reference, still others felt their privacy was invaded when a company investigated their background, and others filed for different reasons emanating from their applying for a job with a company.

In addition, if a company learns after a person is hired that the employee misrepresented his or her background on an application or resumé, the company should have the right to terminate that person.

Properly designed application forms may protect companies. For example, applicants will have a tough time proving you discriminated against them because of age if no questions on your application request age or related information. But it could work against you if the form contains illegal questions. As noted in Chapters 3, "What the Laws on Employment Cover," and 4, "Watch Your Language," make sure your form complies with the civil rights laws and does not ask questions that are prohibited.

It Provides Information You Need

It's convenient to have essential information in one easy-to-find place. The form provides an applicant's name, address, phone number, Social Security number, and educational background. Most useful is the work history with dates of employment, positions, companies, and a brief description of duties and responsibilities. Usually it includes salary, the reason for leaving, and the name of a person in the company who can provide information about the applicant.

It gives you enough basic information to determine whether the prospect is worthy of further consideration. Although most forms don't have enough space to give details about a person's activities, actions, and accomplishments, it provides, along with the applicant's resumé, adequate data to make preliminary judgments.

Many companies receive hundreds of resumés in response to help-wanted ads. From these, a group of viable candidates is culled; in many instances, before inviting them for interviews, they are sent application forms. The best applicants are then invited for interviews.

In some situations, particularly when filling the job rapidly is a factor, appointments are made for interviews before receiving the application form. In such cases, the applicant is usually asked to complete it and bring it to the interview or might be given the form to complete after arriving at the facility. In any case, the form should be filled out and read prior to interviewing the candidate.

The application and resumé serve as tools to assist the interviewer in preparing questions to ask. You'll learn more about this in Chapter 16, "Planning the Interview."

Recruiting Residuals

Instead of using paper job applications, Target stores and Home Depot substitute computer-based application forms. Kiosks have been placed in the stores so shoppers can apply for jobs by answering questions online. Then a formatted copy is sent electronically to the manager on duty who can set up an immediate interview.

It Makes It Easy to Compare Candidates

While resumés are written in a variety of styles, applications for jobs in a company are all formatted the same way. This makes it easy to compare applicants. By placing application forms side by side, you can immediately measure the education and experience of each candidate against the others. You can compare duration and types of experience and can note salary variations.

Impressive resumés may make a candidate stand out, but when the resumé and application are considered together, you may find that an applicant with a less imposing resumé actually has a better background.

Clauses to Protect You

In addition to being a selection tool, the application form is a contract. Of course, it's a one-sided contract in that it's written to protect the employer. Let's look at some of the important clauses that attorneys strongly recommend be included in this document.

Permission to Investigate Background

This covers two different types of investigation: checking references and using an investigative service to look into the applicant's background.

Reference checks: Because of their concerns about litigation, many companies refuse to give information about former or current employees. By getting a release from the applicant that authorizes the employer to provide information, you obviate this concern. Many companies have a clause to cover this in their application; some have this on a separate document.

Here is an example of such a clause: "In the event that (name of company) investigates my work and personal history and verifies the information provided on this application and related papers and in interviews, I authorize all individuals, schools, and firms (except my current employer if so noted) named herein to provide any information requested about me and hereby release them from all liability for damage in providing this information."

Hiring Hints

Some lawyers suggest that, even if a release clause is incorporated into the application form, a separate form should be signed for each school and employer to be contacted.

This may be followed by a box stating that "Permission is granted to contact my current employer" with a space for initials.

Investigative Reports

Under the Fair Credit Reporting Act, a federal law, if you consider using the services of an outside credit or investigative reporting agency, you must provide the applicant with a written notification stating that such a report may be ordered. The applicant must be advised that he or she has the right to request a copy of such a report from the agency that conducts the investigation and that the name of such agency will be provided upon request. If you plan to use this type of service on a regular basis, this clause should be included on the application form in print that is no smaller than the rest of the application. You also should include space for the signatures of the applicant and a witness. If you use investigative reports for only a few positions, instead of printing it on the application, develop a separate form to use when appropriate.

Employment at Will

Unless an employee is protected by an individual contract with the employer (a negotiated contract between the employer and a labor union or civil service employee), the individual falls under *employment-at-will* status. This means that the employer has the right to terminate the services of the employee at any time, for any reason, or for no reason at all, so long as it complies with applicable laws such as the civil rights laws. Most employees in American companies fall into this category. However, to ensure that new employees are aware of this, it should be indicated on the application form.

Words to Work By

Employment at will is a legal concept under which an employee is hired and can be fired at the will of the employer. Unless restricted by law or contract, the employer has the right to refuse to hire an applicant or to terminate an employee for any reason or no reason or all.

A typical clause may read: "I understand that this application is not a contract of employment. I understand that (name of company) follows an employment-at-will policy and that my employment may be terminated at any time for any reason consistent with applicable state and federal laws. This policy cannot be changed verbally or in writing unless authorized specifically by the chairman or president of this company."

Certification of Truth

After you hire a person, if you find out that he or she lied in his application or resumé about an important factor, you should have the option to take immediate action to terminate that person. The suggested clause reads: "I certify that the statements on this form and other information provided by me in applying for this position are true, and I understand that any falsification or willful omission shall be sufficient cause for dismissal or refusal of employment."

The prototype application form, which you'll find later in this chapter in the section "Sample Application Form," includes a variation of the preceding clauses. The wording may not be the same because each company's legal advisors word the clauses in their own way.

Different Forms for Different Jobs

Most companies use a standard application form for all jobs. This works well for obtaining basic information. However, application forms can be much more useful if questions are included that bring out specific information needed to screen applicants for the jobs for which they have applied. To do this, companies can design forms to fit the jobs involved.

Technical Jobs

Although some companies test applicants on their knowledge of the technical areas for which they apply, it is a separate process that is not part of the application. Applications for technical jobs should include questions that expand on any aspects of the applicant's education and experience that are related to the job.

Here are some questions I have seen on technical job forms:

➤ List any advanced courses taken in physics and math.

➤ List any courses or seminars taken in your field since receiving your degree.

➤ What honors were you awarded in school?

➤ To what professional societies do you belong?

➤ What technical or professional journals do you read regularly?

➤ List any patents that you hold.

➤ What projects have you worked on in (indicate field)?

➤ What certificates or licenses do you hold (for example, Professional Engineer or similar certification)?

➤ What do you consider your most significant accomplishment in your career?

Hiring Hints

In designing special forms for special job categories, test your questions on current technical employees and managers to ensure their relevance.

Sales Jobs

Another field for which special application forms are helpful is sales. Here are some questions used on forms for sales representatives:

➤ What products or services have you sold?

➤ What markets have you called on?

➤ List some of your customers or clients.

➤ If paid on an incentive basis, what percentage of last year's income was from base pay? What percentage was from the incentive plan?

➤ List your gross sales for each of the past five years (if all with the same company).

➤ What sales awards have you won?

➤ What percentage of time did you devote to servicing customers?

➤ Check all the fields in which you have had sales experience:

❑ Sales to food, drug, or other mass-market retailers

❑ Sales to department stores or discount stores

❑ Sales to industrial companies

❑ Sales to financial institutions

❑ Sales to hospitals, schools, or other institutions

❑ Sales to individual consumers

❑ Other (please specify): _____

Naturally, you should develop questions that will enable you to quickly identify whether the applicant has the type of sales experience that fits your needs.

Other Areas

There are specially designed applications for such diversified jobs as management executives, advertising and marketing staff members, accountants, and even clerical workers.

If a job requires good writing skills, the application form could include essay-type questions that require the candidate to demonstrate writing ability. Because such forms take much longer to read and evaluate, most companies prefer to test writing ability later in the screening process.

Evaluating the Application

Many things can be learned from the application form (and its accompanying resumé) that can help you eliminate candidates who are not worthy of the time and expense of additional screening. As you study the resumé, look for these factors: Does the candidate have the background to do the job? Has he or she shown a pattern of success in the past? Does he or she have a stable job history? Let's look at each of these.

Can the Individual Do the Job?

In reviewing the application form, determine whether the applicant has the basic requirements to do the job. Because application forms don't usually provide much space for details about experience, check to make sure at least the basic educational requirements are met and see if the jobs held are in line with the experience needed. If so, prepare to explore this at the interview.

It's reasonable to assume that an applicant who has worked in your field may have the background you are seeking. Some recruiters or team leaders are overzealous in their screening and eliminate well-qualified prospects because of lack of information. If it is not clearly stated on the application and resumé, don't automatically reject the candidate. Pick up the telephone and call him or her to clarify the situation. Don't make a rash decision to eliminate the applicant solely on the basis of inadequate information. On the other hand, applicants who don't meet the basic requirements should not be given further consideration.

The application should give the person reading it enough detail about the candidate's previous job duties to see how much can be transferred to the needs of the company. It can specify information such as experience using certain computer software, operating certain equipment, or possessing skills needed on the job. If the application form was designed for specific jobs (as described earlier in this chapter), the answers to special questions asked about background can be very helpful in making the decision as to whether the applicant should be brought in for further processing.

> ### Employment Enigmas
>
> Don't assume an applicant lacks experience on the basis of a job title or a one-line description of duties on an application form. Look for details on the resumé and prepare in-depth questions for the interview.

> ### Recruiting Residuals
>
> Some companies make it easy for tough-to-find applicants to apply for jobs. They conduct quickie interviews over the phone and invite applicants in for interviews—but only after there is mutual interest do they have them fill out the application form.

Progress

The applicant's progress and growth in jobs and career should be evaluated as well as specific experience. For routine jobs, this may not be significant; indeed, it may even be a negative. A person who has moved up rapidly will expect to continue to move up rapidly. If your company cannot offer opportunity for this continued progress, the employee will probably become unhappy and seek employment elsewhere in a short time. On the other hand, if a job offers opportunity but demands ambition and drive, the applicant should have manifested this by the progress made in previous jobs.

Progress can be measured by positions held and salaries earned. A person who has worked for the same firm for many years but has only received automatic annual salary increments has actually made no real progress even though earnings have gone up. Position and salary should be compared to those of other people in that field with similar education and experience.

If an applicant for the position of marketing administrator is a Harvard graduate, is 32 years old, and is earning well below what his classmates are earning, it may be indicative of some problem. It may indicate that the applicant has no drive and is content to work in a routine job with modest earnings and no real responsibility.

Caution: Again, never take anything of this sort at face value. There may be legitimate reasons for lack of progress. Some years ago, I almost rejected an applicant because she had worked for a company for several years and made no progress. When I probed, I learned that she had joined the company when it started with promises of big opportunity once it got off the ground. Unfortunately, the firm never could raise the capital needed to move ahead. It had nothing to do with her capability. When hired by my client, she became one of its most productive employees.

Hiring Hints

The earnings record should not be the only measure of progress. More important is determining whether the applicant shows a pattern of increasing responsibility in his or her career to date.

Recruiting Residuals

In today's hot market for technical personnel, qualified people are likely to move from company to company far more frequently than their nontech colleagues. Over the past few years, the typical tenure of techies on a job has fallen from five to three years.

The earnings record should not be the only measure of progress. More important is determining whether the applicant shows a pattern of increasing responsibility in his or her career to date. Have promotions been in line with the person's experience? Has he or she moved more rapidly than might be expected? If so, was this due to personal capability and accomplishments? Was it due to growth in the industry or the company rather than individual efforts? Was it based on nepotism?

Hiring Hints

Job-hopping is often an indication of an unstable personality but not always. Probe for reasons before making a no-go decision.

Comparing several applicants' progress in their careers will develop a pattern for growth in any occupation. One could find, for example, that advertising people move faster in both position and earnings than people in the banking field. Salespeople may make more money faster than in most jobs, but they don't move up to management positions as rapidly as their co-workers in administrative jobs. Comparison of progress rates must take all of these factors into consideration. One can't make arbitrary judgments and rate one occupation against another.

Stability

Another factor the application form indicates is job stability. Many employers will automatically reject an applicant who has changed jobs too often. Some companies have made this a knockout factor: If a person has had more than two jobs in five years (or some similar combination of years and jobs), he or she is knocked out.

There is much to be said in favor of this policy. Frequent job changes may indicate restlessness or boredom with a job. It's unlikely that the candidate's next job will be any different. Some people are "two-yearers"—the time it takes to master the intricacies of the job and then tire of it. Others may be marginal workers, employees who are not bad enough to discharge but are the first to be laid off when business slows down. In other cases, there may be personality problems. The employee may never have been able to get along with co-workers or bosses.

Employment Enigmas

People who have had a long period of employment with one company—but for some good reason leave that company—often have two or three short-duration jobs before they find a home again.

On the other hand, it may be just bad luck. The person may be on the job a short time when the company suffers a business reversal resulting in a mass downsizing or reorganization, which eliminates the job. Sometimes a person may start a job and rapidly realize it was a mistake. It's better to quit immediately than to stay around just to keep your work record from looking bad.

Young people, particularly, may make several job changes over a short period of time. They are feeling their way, and it may take a while to find the right career.

Before arbitrarily rejecting an applicant as a job-hopper, it's important to determine the reason for the apparent instability. There are often good reasons for changing jobs. Don't lose a potentially good employee because of some arbitrary policy on "instability."

What Else to Look For

The application form may give some insight into the applicant's personality. It also indicates whether the applicant can follow the simple directions required to complete it. In some employment offices, the length of time taken by an applicant to fill out the form is used as a measure of speed in performing clerical tasks. If the job calls for good handwriting, it can be observed on the application form.

In some companies, receptionists are trained to observe the manner in which applicants act when given the form. Do they get to work on it in a businesslike manner? Do they refer to notes? Do they ask questions about the form? If another person accompanies them, do they confer with that person before answering a question on the form?

Sample Application Form

The following application form is a prototype. This form can be used for any job. As noted earlier, it is often desirable to design special forms for special jobs, but the basic form should be similar to this.

Note that all the questions comply with EEO regulations.

Application for Employment

Date: _____

Name: _____ Social Security number:_____

Address: _____

City, State, ZIP: _____

Phone (1) _____ (2) _____

Fax _____ E-mail _____

Position sought: _____ Salary desired: _____

EDUCATION

Level: _____ School/Location: _____

Course: _____

Number of years: _____ Degree or diploma: _____

continues

---

continues

College: _____

Other: _____

EMPLOYMENT RECORD

1. Company/Address: _____

Dates: _____ Salary: _____ Supervisor: _____

Duties: _____

_____

_____

_____

Reason for leaving: _____

2. Company/Address: _____

Dates: _____ Salary: _____ Supervisor: _____

Duties: _____

_____

_____

_____

Reason for leaving: _____

3. Company/Address: _____

Dates: _____ Salary: _____ Supervisor: _____

Duties: _____

_____

_____

_____

Reason for leaving: _____

How were you referred to this company? _____

Are you 18 years of age or older? _____

If you're hired, can you provide written evidence that you are authorized to work in the United States? _____

Is there any other name under which you have worked that we would need in order to check your work record? (If so, please provide.) _____

APPLICANT'S STATEMENT:

I understand that the employer follows an "employment at will" policy, in that the employer may terminate my employment at any time or for any reason consistent with applicable federal and state laws. This employment-at-will policy cannot be changed verbally or in writing unless authorized specifically by the president or executive vice president of this company. I understand that this application is not a contract of employment. I understand that the federal government prohibits the employment of unauthorized aliens; all persons hired must provide satisfactory proof of employment authorization and identity. Failure to submit such proof will result in denial of employment.

I understand that the employer may investigate my work and personal history and verify all information given on this application, on related papers, and in interviews. I hereby authorize all individuals, schools, and firms named therein except for my current employer (unless indicated herein to provide any information requested about me and hereby release them from all liability for damage in providing this information.

[You may/may not contact my current employer]

I certify that all the statements in this form and other information provided by me in applying for this position are true and understand that any falsification or willful omission shall be sufficient cause for dismissal or refusal of employment.

Signed _____ Date _____

Example of a company application form.

In designing your own application form, add questions that are pertinent to the jobs you seek to fill, Check any questions against the "lawful and unlawful" questions listed in Chapter 4 to make sure that they don't violate any of the civil rights laws.

The Least You Need to Know

➤ The company application form is a rapid means of providing the interviewer with basic information about the applicant. It also provides legal protection and makes it easy to compare candidates.

➤ Make sure your form complies with the civil rights laws and does not ask questions that are prohibited.

➤ Application forms should indicate that the company is an employment-at-will employer. The company should be given permission to investigate the applicant's background and to check references, and the applicant should guarantee that information provided is true.

➤ It's a good idea to create special application forms for special jobs to provide specific information needed to screen applicants for these jobs.

➤ In evaluating application forms, determine whether the applicant has the basic background needed to fill the job. Prepare questions that ask the applicant to expand on what is in the application and resumé.

➤ Look for records of progress. Has the applicant advanced in position and salary commensurate with education and experience?

➤ Look for stable work histories, but understand reasons for job changes before making a decision on an applicant's stability.

Prescreening Applicants

It costs a bundle to interview an applicant. To fill many jobs, applicants have to be brought in from out of town for interviews. This is expensive, especially when you may have to interview several candidates before making a selection. Travel is only one part of interviewing expenses. Interviewing involves many more expenses, as you'll learn in this chapter.

Are there ways to reduce this cost? The answer: prescreening. This chapter explores several ways for a company to determine whether it's worthwhile to invite a prospect in for an interview.

Figuring the Cost

There is much more to computing the cost of bringing an applicant to your facility for an interview than just the actual expenses of the trip. Yes, those travel expenses can be formidable, but they represent only a fraction of the real cost.

Reducing Travel Expenses

Travel costs make up a large part of recruiting expenses. As you'll learn later in this chapter, effective prescreening keeps this cost down by eliminating unqualified people before incurring these costs. However, sometimes prescreening isn't appropriate. Personality often is more important than job experience and seeing the candidate is a top priority.

Barry G., sales manager of the Superior Institutional Supply Co., strongly believes in seeing all viable applicants. He finds telephone interviews frustrating.

Barry finds it less expensive to go out and see a prospect in his or her own town instead of bringing the prospect to Superior's office. Because his work requires extensive travel, there's a good chance he will be visiting a city near where the prospect is located. He arranges to see the candidate during the trip. If his itinerary doesn't bring him close to that vicinity, he asks a member of his sales staff who will be traveling there to see the applicant.

Claudia M., the human resources manager of a Texas-based computer company, makes periodic trips to California and Massachusetts, where several competitors are located, to interview applicants in those areas. By being able to see several people on each trip, she saves her company the expense of bringing individual applicants to the Texas office for interviews.

Hiring Hints

If you know that there may be several viable prospects in one area, concentrate your recruiting ads in that area. You can then arrange interviews with all of candidates in whom you have interest in one trip.

Words to Work By

The purpose of all screening is to eliminate unqualified applicants. The term **prescreening** is reserved for the aspect of the screening process that precedes inviting an applicant for an interview.

The High Cost of Interviewing

Even when no travel is involved, interviewing is expensive. Interviewing is time consuming, and time must be translated into money. If you can break the salaries of the people doing the interviewing into an hourly rate and then multiply the number of hours spent interviewing applicants by that rate, you begin to realize how much interviewing actually costs. This is compounded when several people interview a candidate.

In addition to this basic cost, there is the incalculable cost of lost productivity. If a manager is devoting part of the workday to interviewing applicants, other work suffers. Administrative work is not done, customers are not served, and employees are not supervised. All this is expensive.

Whenever possible, well-planned, thorough *prescreening* should be used so that only candidates who are likely to be qualified will be called in for interviews.

Using Special Application Forms

Some companies have designed application forms with built-in screening devices. Two of these are the graded application and the diagnostic application.

The Graded Application

Some application forms assign a rating of 1 to 10 for each of the qualifications a candidate possesses. Type of education and experience, depth of experience, and relevance of affiliations and activities determine the rating.

Recruiters and others who screen the applications are provided with guidelines specifying what standards the applicant must meet to rate a perfect 10. Here is an example:

Position: Training specialist

Education:

> Ph.D. or Ed.D.   10
>
> Master's degree   9
>
> Bachelor's degree in related field   8
>
> Other Bachelor's degree   7

Work Environment:

> Working in consulting dealing with a variety of companies   10
>
> Working in a technical company   9
>
> Working in a manufacturing company   8
>
> Working in an office environment   7
>
> Working in a trade school   6

Responsibility:

> Developing and delivering programs   10
>
> Developing but not delivering   8
>
> Delivering programs   7
>
> Assisting in developing programs   6
>
> Assisting in delivering programs   5

This continues for each of the other job requirements.

If the candidate meets a minimum total rating, depending on the job involved, he or she is invited in for an interview.

Hiring Hints

When rated applications are used, candidates can be compared easily by charting the scores on a spreadsheet.

In cases in which the information on the resumé isn't sufficient to make a rating, a telephone interview may be held to obtain what is needed.

The danger in using ratings is that they often are subjective. Despite guidelines, it may be difficult to rate depth of experience and true levels of responsibility from the application and resumé.

Another limitation is that the applicant may have omitted an area of importance to you in the desire to keep the resumé brief. Good candidates may be overlooked for the wrong reason.

Diagnostic Application Forms

One screening device that has been attempted from time to time is an application form designed to be predictive, known as a *diagnostic application form*.

Usually designed by psychologists, these forms include questions that aim to force the writer to disclose hidden drives, motivations, weaknesses, and strengths.

Some typical questions asked on these forms include …

What subjects did you like most (least) in school?

In what subjects did you get the best and poorest grades?

What aspect of your previous jobs did you like most (least)?

In what aspect of your jobs did you perform most effectively?

Words to Work By

Diagnostic application forms consist of a series of questions designed to uncover motivations, strengths, weaknesses, and other intangible characteristics of the applicant.

The purpose of these questions is to determine relationships between interest and performance. It also tells you the applicant's attitude toward important phases of the job. If the answer indicates that the applicant does not like or does poorly in a key aspect of the available job, it alerts you to potential problems if the person is hired.

"When you were in school, to whom did you go most frequently for advice?"

"When faced with a problem on your job(s), to whom did you go for assistance?"

The answer indicates relationships with family, friends, or teachers in school or supervisors, mentors, or peers at work.

"Where do you expect to be in five years?"

The answer to this may show whether the applicant has set realistic goals. A related question may be "How do you plan to reach these goals?"

The answer to the first question indicates ambition or lack of it. The answer to the second question determines whether, in answering the first question, the applicant just wrote something to impress you or really thought it out.

Although some psychologists find these applications useful, there is great danger in using them. Untrained persons may misinterpret answers or, more likely, use them incorrectly. The intent of the psychologist is to establish a complete picture of the applicant from the pattern of the answers. A common error in using the diagnostic application form is that laymen may overemphasize the answers to specific questions instead of taking them as part of the whole. Companies using diagnostic forms should require that only persons trained in their use should be allowed to interpret them.

Using Essay Questions

This is an excellent tool to use when screening for jobs in which communication skills are important. If the job calls for writing reports, composing marketing or advertising pieces, or answering correspondence, this is a good way to evaluate writing skills.

Essays measure more than just writing ability, however. They provide a good example of the thinking process the applicant follows. They show organization of ideas, clarity of thinking, mastery of technical nomenclature, and the ability to express oneself clearly, concisely, and comprehensively.

Some companies—like college admissions offices—include the essay questions in the application form. The form is then completed by the applicant and mailed to the office, where it is studied as part of the prescreening process. The essays are just one of the factors on which the decision to invite for an interview is made.

A few companies use essays as part of a preliminary screening given at the first meeting with a candidate. The applicant writes the essays at the employment office.

Skeptical recruiters want to ensure that the applicant—not a "ghost writer"—writes the essay. They want to read essays written under circumstances in which the applicant hasn't had time to prepare.

Employment Enigmas

The subjects chosen for the essay questions should be job related. Labor lawyers caution that, unless the answers to the questions can be related to ability to do the job, they may be deemed discriminatory.

The Telephone Screening Interview

Probably the most frequently used prescreening tool is the telephone call. In a relatively brief telephone interview, you can acquire a lot more information about a candidate than can be obtained from the application and/or resumé. Let's examine how to make a telephone interview most valuable.

Call the Applicant at Home

It's not a good idea to call the applicant at work to discuss your job opening. This not only is unethical, it puts the applicant in an awkward position because other people may be nearby who can hear the conversation. The call should be made to the person's home in the evening. This may mean you have to make these calls from your home or work late at the office. It's just one of the sacrifices that recruiters and managers have to make to get the people they want.

Some human resources managers notify an applicant by mail or e-mail to expect a call at a specific time so the applicant is prepared for the call and will be at home.

Plan the phone call as carefully as you would an in-person interview. Read the application and/or resumé carefully and note areas that require elaboration. Don't be afraid to ask hard questions such as reasons for desiring a job, accounting for periods of unemployment, relations with superiors, and specific details about work or educational background.

Ask Meaningful Questions

Study the job specifications carefully. It may appear from the resumé that the applicant meets the job specs, but often a person may meet some of the essential requirements but not others. Some candidates have superficial experience that is exaggerated in the resumé.

Probe to determine whether the applicant's experience and skills are close to what you are seeking. Prepare a series of job-related questions to test this. For example, if the candidate is applying for a job in a technical field, have the team leader of the group in which the vacancy exists provide you with several questions that will help determine the candidate's level of expertise in that field. Be sure to cover all the key points.

Hiring Hints

For technical jobs and other jobs in which specialized know-how is required, it's best to have a person who is well-grounded in that field conduct the telephone interview or participate in it via a conference call.

Take Notes

In a telephone interview, it's even more important than in a personal interview to note the answers to your questions. It's not a distraction to the interviewee as it might be in a face-to-face interview, so you have more freedom to be thorough in your note-taking. We tend to remember people and what they tell us more easily when we see them in person than when we just hear them over the phone.

Prepare a list of key questions on a sheet of paper and leave lots of room to write the responses. This is particularly important if you plan to discuss the interview with a team leader or a department head. In addition, when interviewing several candidates for the same job, referring to the answers each gives to the same or related questions will make it easier to compare them.

In Chapter 17, "Face to Face with the Applicant," you'll find a prototype interview note-taking form that you can use as a guide.

Be Flexible

The telephone interviewer who just reads a list of questions and jots down the answers without reacting is like the telemarketer who uses a canned sales presentation on the phone and becomes confused if the prospect doesn't answer as expected. The answer to one question may prompt you to ask questions not on the list. For example, when I was screening applicants for a client's opening for a budget director, a question concerning the applicant's relationship with the IT department brought a response that showed the candidate had so much depth of knowledge of information technology that the whole plan of the interview was changed to explore this attribute. It enabled the company to consider the applicant for a more responsible position than the one for which he originally was being considered.

What to Listen For

In addition to noting the applicant's substantive responses to your questions, the telephone interviewer should listen very carefully to the candidate's voice and method of responding. A voice often indicates the confidence or lack of confidence that an applicant has in his or her qualifications for the job. Hesitance, equivocation, and long pauses between thoughts often reflect weaknesses. Nervous laughter, frequent digressions, evasions, and nonresponsive replies are danger signals.

As in the face-to-face interview, some applicants may be nervous during a telephone interview, but after a few minutes of rapport-building, the tensions should be eased. If you feel the applicant is not giving you the information you want or seems to be hiding behind vague answers, let him or her talk for a while. Listen closely, giving nondirective responses such as "Yes," "Uh-huh," or just silence. If you still don't get the information you want, ask some specific questions about the work or request details of the applicant's activities in that area. Failure to obtain good information is a good reason to terminate the interview and reject the applicant.

Evaluating Personal Characteristics

Evaluating the applicant's personal traits is more difficult on the telephone than evaluating work experience. However, there are questions you can ask that are designed to determine such qualities as stability, resourcefulness, motivation, and other intangibles.

Here are some examples of these questions:

➤ **For stability**: Why did you leave each of your previous jobs?

➤ **For interpersonal relations**: Describe your relationship with your superiors, subordinates, and peers?

➤ **For resourcefulness**: What kind of problems did you face on the job? How did you handle them? When faced with a problem, at what point did you seek assistance? To whom did you go?

➤ **For motivation**: What do you seek in a new job that you're not getting in your present (or most recent) job?

Employment Enigmas

If there are any serious negative factors about the position or your company, give the prospect a chance to bring it up before extending an invitation for an interview. For example, "This job requires that you travel 75 percent of the time. Will this affect your thinking concerning this job?"

If the job calls for relocation, ask whether the applicant is familiar with the area in which the job is located. Get his or her reaction to living in a small town, a big city, a cold climate, or whatever situation applies to your company.

Discuss Salary

Many recruiters go through the entire telephone interview and then invite the applicant to the company without discussing salary. After the applicant has several interviews at the office, a serious discrepancy in what you are prepared to pay and what the applicant expects may occur. This embarrassment can be avoided if the salary situation is clarified during the telephone interview. You need not commit the company to a specific salary, but you should ask the prospect what salary is expected. If it's within the range, it's unlikely that a problem will arise. If you're far apart, it should be frankly stated.

Closing the Telephone Interview

Remember that the objective of the telephone interview is to determine whether to invite the applicant in for a face-to-face meeting. This should be made clear at the outset of the conversation. Job offers do not usually result from a phone call. The next step, if interest is shown on both sides, is an invitation for a personal interview.

In closing the interview, review your notes to make sure you have all the information you need. If you're sure you want to extend the invitation, do so. If you have some reservations or want to discuss your reaction with other people in your organization, tell the applicant you'll be in touch with him or her. Give a specific time when your next contact should be expected and be sure to keep your promise.

If you've decided that the applicant is not for your company, how you close the call will depend on the circumstances. If the reason is a lack of interest on the applicant's part, a polite "Thank you for your time" is enough. If the reason is a lack of technical qualifications and this became obvious during the interview, you should say so. "Our job calls for somebody with much more design experience. We'll keep you in mind if a spot develops that can use somebody with your background." If it's for any reason that cannot be easily communicated such as vagueness in responses, lack of self-confidence, or similar reasons, tell the applicant you will discuss the interview with others in the company and let him or her know. Be sure to write the applicant in a reasonably short time and inform him or her that another candidate met your needs more closely.

Enter the Chat Room

With the rapid increase in the use of the Internet as a communication device, some companies are prescreening applicants in chat rooms. Instead of telephoning for additional information, the recruiter e-mails the applicant and suggests that they set up a chat room date.

A two-way interchange of questions and answers gets the ball rolling. As the chat goes on, the interview metamorphoses into a conversation in which ideas and concepts can be discussed.

The advantage is that many young people today are very comfortable using chat rooms, and much information can be elicited that may have been missed because of the nervousness of the prospect in a telephone call.

The obvious limitation is that the telephone enables you to hear the voice, diagnose the tone, and listen for hesitance, evasions, and equivocations.

The Least You Need to Know

➤ Travel costs make up a large part of recruiting expenses. Effective prescreening keeps this cost down by eliminating unqualified people before incurring these costs.

➤ Interviewing is time consuming, and time must be translated into money.

➤ Some companies have designed application forms that contain built-in screening devices. Two of these are the graded application, in which job qualifications are rated, and the diagnostic application, which is designed to identify intangibles.

➤ Probably the most frequently used prescreening tool is the telephone call. In a relatively brief telephone interview, you can acquire a lot more information about a candidate than can be obtained from the application and/or resumé.

➤ Plan the phone call as carefully as you would an in-person interview. Read an application and/or resumé carefully and note areas that require elaboration.

➤ In addition to noting the applicant's substantive responses to questions, the telephone interviewer should listen very carefully to the candidate's voice and method of responding.

Part 5

Making the Interview More Meaningful

You've done the preparatory work. You've studied application forms and resumés. Now you're ready to see the applicant. Interviewing is both an art and a science. It's a science because it can be structured to bring out the information desired. It's an art because the interviewer must be able to tailor the questions and interpret the responses.

Interviewing can be tricky. Some applicants try to hide negatives and exaggerate positives. Some have hidden assets that you have to probe to uncover.

Some interviewers make mistakes that could result in hiring the wrong person or just as bad, failing to hire the right person.

Experienced interviewers know how to overcome these problems. After reading this part, so will you.

THE PLAN

NEW EMPLOYEE

Planning the Interview

Interviews are more than just pleasant conversations between you and the applicant. How the interview process is planned and followed can make the difference between hiring the best candidate and just selecting one by instinct. This process will be explored in detail in this and the following chapters.

The first step is to determine who will do the interviewing, what types of interviews will be conducted, and what other selection techniques will be used. Then questions must be framed to bring out the information needed to judge the qualifications of the candidates.

This chapter shows you how the process begins and discusses how to design and use a carefully structured interview.

Each applicant brings to the interview his or her own special qualifications and personal characteristics. Be prepared to tailor your interviewing plan to accommodate for this.

A basic part of any interview is proper preparation by the interviewer. The two essential sets of documents that must be reviewed are the application form and its accompanying resumé and the job description including the job specification.

Reread the Paperwork

Before an applicant enters the interview room, the application and resumé should be thoroughly studied. Any areas that require more information or that are indications of strengths or weaknesses should be noted so that questions may be asked about them.

Keep in mind the objectives of the interview: first, to determine whether the candidate has the technical qualifications needed for the position; second, to determine whether the applicant has the personality traits needed to be successful in the job.

Job skills are easy to identify and are clearly indicated in the job specification. Questions geared toward job skills should be prepared. They may take the form of test questions such as "What type of equipment would be most suited for this process?" Or they may be questions about experience such as "What software did you use to determine marketing trends?"

Personality qualifications are much more difficult to measure. Some of these intangibles may be listed in the job specs. For example, a person "must be able to work under pressure" or "should be able to present public speeches." It's not easy to reduce many personality factors to a simple statement. The interviewer's knowledge of the job, the people with whom the applicant will have to work, and the company culture must be taken into consideration.

Hiring Hints

Before an applicant enters the interview room, the application and resumé should be thoroughly studied. Be prepared to probe areas that require more information.

The First Interview

In most companies, the first interview is with a member of the human resources department. Because HR staffers are usually well-trained in interviewing, they generally do a credible job in determining whether the candidate is worthy of further consideration.

Many firms, however, particularly smaller organizations, don't have human resources departments. Even in larger companies, the HR department may be located at the home office while the job opening is in a distant facility. In these cases, some other manager or supervisor will conduct the first interview. Unfortunately, many of these people are not trained in interviewing.

The hiring decision is rarely made at the first interview, but it is a key phase of the process. Good applicants are lost because the interviewer didn't ask the right questions or misunderstood the answers. Good applicants also may be lost because they get a bad impression of the company at the interview and decide not to pursue the position. In addition, applicants who should have been rejected may be referred for subsequent interviews, wasting the time of higher-level managers.

Any person assigned to conduct these first interviews should be carefully trained in interviewing methods. If you are one of these people, study this and the following chapters for tips on becoming a better employment interviewer.

Subsequent Interviews: When and By Whom?

If, as a result of the first interview, the applicant appears to be viable, arrangements should be made for additional screening without delay. Particularly when jobs are plentiful and applicants scarce, qualified applicants are lost because of procrastination.

A candidate for all but the most basic jobs should be interviewed by at least one member of the HR department and by the team leader, supervisor, or manager for whom he or she will work. The HR staffer screens to determine whether the applicant meets broad job specifications and analyzes the applicant for personality, attitude, and general background. The team leader or supervisor is better suited to evaluate specific knowledge of the job and whether the prospect will fit in with the group.

In many companies, several managers may interview the candidate before a final decision is made. When teams are used, members of the team other than the team leader may also interview prospects for that team.

In most companies, the head of the department in which the employee will work makes the hiring decision. He or she is usually is the last interviewer. For example, a member of the HR department may first interview an applicant for a tax accountant position. If warranted, the leader of the tax accounting section will interview the applicant. If passed, the chief accountant or controller will conduct an interview and will make the hiring decision. In this process, the decision maker sees only the very top candidates.

This and other variations of the interviewing process will be discussed in detail in Chapter 19, "Special Types of Interviews."

Employment Enigmas

Even though applicants are rarely hired at the first interview, it's an extremely important part of the process. Poor interviewing can cost the loss of a good candidate and can waste the time of other managers to whom unqualified applicants are referred for further interviews.

Employment Enigmas

Line managers are busy and may procrastinate in arranging interviews with candidates you approve. The longer the manager stalls before seeing the candidate, the greater the chance he or she will be grabbed up by a competitor.

Planning the Questions to Ask

Some interviewers sit down with the applicant with only a general idea of the questions they plan to ask. They may start with a general statement such as "Tell me about yourself." From the response, they then pick aspects of the candidate's background to explore. This may be okay for an experienced interviewer who just uses this statement as an opening device and has thought out what added questions to ask. However, the danger here is that the applicant may tell you only what he or she wants you to hear, and you may never get around to asking about areas not mentioned.

Hiring Hints

To ensure attainment of all relevant information, prepare a list of key questions that must be asked during the interview before you sit down with the applicant.

Hiring Hints

It's important to prepare questions to ask an applicant at the interview, but don't limit yourself to asking just these questions. Be alert to responses and ask additional questions based on answers received.

Make a List of Key Questions

In planning for the interview, develop a list of the questions you plan to ask. An effective interview is well planned. The interviewer doesn't ad-lib questions.

Some interviewers write down the questions they plan to ask and refer to them during the interview. Others make notes on the applicant's application form to remind themselves about areas they wish to explore. Still other interviewers depend on their knowledge of the field to develop questions as they move along in the process.

General Questions About Work Factors

To evaluate the applicant's qualifications, questions should be developed to give you enough information to make a hiring decision. Some of these will be broad, general questions to get an overview of the candidate's education, experience, and personality. Once you are satisfied that he or she meets these requirements, you should be prepared to ask additional questions that will probe for very specific details. Let's first look at preparing general questions.

The following table provides a list of some of the areas the interviewer should explore.

Areas of an Applicant's Background to Explore

Education and Skills

Level of education (secondary school, college, grad school, and so on)

Majors or courses related to the job requirements

Scholastic achievements

Licenses and certifications

Other skills acquired (such as foreign languages, computer know-how, mechanical skills, and so on)

Experience

Jobs held

(Include in this category all full-time jobs, part-time jobs, volunteer work related to the job being filled, and military service.)

Titles

Companies

Descriptions of duties

Earnings

Progress

Achievements

Physical Qualifications (Where Relevant)

Energy

Strength

Health

Vision

Hearing

Appearance

Dexterity

The following traits can be observed at the interview, and questions can be framed to verify how these characteristics were manifested in previous jobs.

Character

Reliability

Honesty

Integrity

Conscientiousness

Values

Loyalty

Work ethic

Environment (where pertinent)

continues

Areas of an Applicant's Background to Explore   (continued)

Physical Qualifications (Where Relevant)

Ability to get to the place of work

Willingness to travel

Ability and willingness to be on the job during the hours required

Ability and willingness to work overtime when required

Willingness to work under the pay scale or pay system offered (such as a lower salary than previously earned or working on commissions or other incentives)

Level of intelligence

Mental ability

Judgment

Breadth of experience

Communication skills

Aptitudes

Personality factors

Reaction to pressure

Motivational factors

Drive

Initiative

Adaptability

Emotional stability

Self-confidence

Interpersonal relations

Cooperative nature

Framing questions to elicit the information needed is not easy. Here are some suggested questions about jobs. Note that most are open-ended questions:

➤ Describe your present responsibilities and duties.

➤ How do you spend an average day?

➤ How did you change the content of your job from when you assumed it until now?

➤ Discuss some of the challenges you encountered on the job. How did you deal with them?

➤ What do you consider to be your chief accomplishments in your present or previous jobs?

To determine qualifications other than work experience, ask the following questions:

➤ How do you view the job for which you are applying?

➤ What in your background particularly qualifies you to do this job?

➤ If you were hired for this job, in what areas could you contribute immediately?

➤ In what areas would you need additional training?

➤ In what ways have your education and training prepared you to do this job?

To probe for weaknesses, ask the following questions:

➤ What disappointments did you experience in your previous jobs?

➤ In what areas did you need help or guidance from your boss?

➤ For what actions or qualities have your supervisors complimented you? Criticized you?

➤ What do you like most about your current (or most recent) job? What do you like least?

Questions to Uncover Personality Traits

Work experience is important in determining applicants' qualifications, but there are other important factors. In order to select the best candidate, personality traits such as motivation, stability and resourcefulness must be considered.

To find out about motivation, ask the following questions:

➤ Why did you select this type of career?

➤ What do you seek in a job?

➤ What is your long-term career objective?

➤ How do you plan to reach this goal?

➤ What kind of a position do you see yourself in five years from now?

➤ What are you seeking in your next job that you are not getting now?

To find out about stability, ask the following questions:

➤ What were your reasons for leaving each of your jobs?

➤ Why are you seeking a job at this time?

➤ What were your original career goals?

➤ How have these goals changed over the years?

Words to Work By

Open-ended questions enable the respondent to answer in an unstructured manner, thereby giving more information and often answers that would not have been elicited from closed, specific questions. Instead of asking "Have you worked with Microsoft Excel?" say "Tell me about your experience with Microsoft Excel."

Hiring Hints

Read your job specs carefully. Discuss the job with the department head or team leader. Frame questions that will enable you to get the information needed to determine whether this applicant is best for the open position.

To find out about resourcefulness, ask the following questions:

➤ How did you change the scope of your previous jobs?

➤ What were some of the more difficult problems you faced on the job? How did you solve them?

➤ To whom did you go for counsel when you couldn't handle a problem on the job?

➤ What was the most radical idea you introduced to your company? How did you persuade management to accept this idea? How did you implement it?

To find out about a candidate's ability to work under direction or with others, ask the following questions:

➤ Describe your supervisor's supervisory methods.

➤ How would you evaluate these methods?

➤ On what task forces, committees, or teams have you served?

➤ What did you contribute to the work of this group?

➤ In previous jobs, how much of your work was done on your own? How much was done as part of a team?

➤ What aspect did you enjoy most? Why?

Preparing Specific Job-Related Questions

The responses to these general questions will give you enough information to determine whether the candidate is basically qualified for your job. However, in every job there are certain very specific areas of knowledge, experience, and expertise that the applicant must demonstrate to be capable of becoming productive rapidly. To determine this, you should also prepare a list of questions that will probe for these details.

Conducting the actual interview and interpreting the answers to these questions will be discussed in the next few chapters.

Because the questions differ from job to job—even jobs with the same or similar titles may require different specific factors—you must develop appropriate questions for each job.

To do this, you must study not just the job specification, which lists the qualifications required, but also the job description, which gives details of job functions.

Hiring Hints

In some cases, the interviewer does not see the application or resume until the time of the interview. Study the documents carefully before beginning the interview. Let the applicant wait in the reception area until you have had time to review them and prepare appropriate questions.

For example, if your opening is for a medical technician, you should prepare questions about the types of medical equipment the applicant has learned to operate in school, his or her experience in operating the equipment, and the venues in which the person worked (at a hospital? a clinic? a physician's office?). If you are not fully knowledgeable about the job, have the person to whom the job reports design these questions for you—and, of course, the answers.

Some HR staffers prefer to leave the asking of specific questions to the team leader or department head. However, if there are several applicants who appear to be qualified and the line managers are overloaded with work in their functional areas, it's advantageous for the first interviewer to use these questions as screening tools.

The Structured Interview

Most good interviews have structure, which is why they are known as *structured interviews*. If they don't, they often result in a chaotic exchange of questions and answers with little possibility of making reasonable decisions. However, some companies use specially prepared structured interview forms that interviewers must follow virtually line by line.

One reason for this is legal; another is psychological. Some labor lawyers advise that, by asking each applicant exactly the same questions in exactly the same order, you will have a defense against charges of discrimination. Some psychologists have designed structured interviews to uncover patterns of behavior by asking questions in the exact same order in the exact same way to all applicants.

> **Words to Work By**
>
> **Structured interviews** use a list of questions that must be asked in exactly the same way in exactly the same order. These are also called **patterned interviews, diagnostic interviews**, or **guided interviews.**

Advantages of Using a Structured Interview

Whether the reason is legal, psychological, or just pragmatic, there are some advantages to using some form of structured interview.

By asking questions printed on a form, you won't miss asking an important question. You have to ask it. The structured interview form provides space next to the questions to record answers. This helps the interviewer remember the responses. And, because all applicants are asked the same questions, it makes it easy to compare applicants when making the final decision.

> **Employment Enigmas**
>
> When using a structured interview form, don't fall into the trap of reading the question as if it's a questionnaire. Present the questions in a conversational tone and rephrase whenever necessary to put the question into the context of the conversation.

Consider the Downside

The negative side of a formal structured interview is that it stifles creativity and flexibility. In the formal structured interview, you are not allowed to deviate from the form. Both the forms developed for legal reasons and those with psychological implications require strict adherence to the structure.

As previously noted, flexibility is important in an interview. The answer to one question may require follow-up to obtain more or better information.

Using a Less Formalized Structure

One way to use the structured interview effectively is to use it as a guide. This cannot be done if the format you use is psychologically based because the exact words, where questions are placed in the interview, and the interrelationship of one question with another are designed to help the psychologist make the evaluation. However, most structured interviews are not of this nature, and variations and flexibility can be built into them.

The Personalized Personnel Profile in the following table is an example of a structured interview form. It is designed to serve as a guide and gives the interviewer freedom to be flexible. Feel free to adapt this for your own use. Follow the instructions at the beginning of the form.

Note that space is provided to take notes. Before using this form, read the discussion on taking notes during an interview in Chapter 17, "Face to Face with the Applicant."

The Personalized Personnel File

This is designed to ensure that each interview results in complete and significant information about the applicant.

Instructions

To use this profile effectively, it must be personalized for each specific job and each applicant. The printed questions should be used only as guidelines. They may or may not be asked of each applicant depending on pertinence.

MOST IMPORTANT: Specific questions relating to job requirements should be developed for each job based on the job description, the company's needs, and interviewer's follow-up to responses given by the applicant.

Write only brief phrases in the NOTES AND COMMENTS column—just enough to help you remember the applicant's responses.

NOTES AND COMMENTS

_____

_____

_____

_____

Name of applicant: _____

Address: _____

_____

Telephone: _____ Fax: _____ E-mail: _____

Position: _____

Department: _____

Interviewed by: _____

Date: _____

Education

Ask the questions in Part A of applicants who did not attend college. Use questions in Part B for college graduates and people who have taken some college courses. For applicants who have been out of college for five years or more, omit Parts A and B and ask only the questions in Part C.

Part A. Questions for applicants who did not attend college:

1. What is highest level of schooling you've completed?

2. Why did you decide not to continue your formal education?

3. How were your overall grades?

4. In what extracurricular activities did you participate?

5. Tell me about any class or club offices held.

6. If you worked, how many hours per week? Summers? What kind of jobs?

7. What steps have you taken to acquire additional education since leaving school?

8. What training have you had in high school or other schools that helped in your career?

9. What was the first significant job you held after leaving high school?

10. How did this lead to your present career?

continues

continued

Part B. Questions for college graduates and people who have taken some college courses:

1. I see that you attended college. Why did you select that school?

2. What was your major? Why did you choose it?

3. How were your overall college grades? How did they compare to your high school grades?

4. What courses did you start in college and later drop? Why?

5. In what types of extracurricular activities did you participate in college? What offices did you hold?

6. How did you finance your college education?

7. If you worked in high school or college, how many hours per week? Summers? What kind of jobs?

8. What were your vocational plans when you were in college?

9. If they are different now, when did you change your thinking? Why?

10. What additional education have you had since college?

11. How do you think college contributed to your career?

12. (If college was not completed) When did you leave college? Why? Do you plan to complete your degree? (If so, ask about plans.)

13. What was the first significant job you held after leaving (or graduating from) college?

14. How did this lead to your current career?

Part C. Questions for people out of school five years or longer:

1. How has your educational background contributed to success in your career?

2. What courses or seminars have you taken recently? If job related, how did you apply them to your job?

3. What are you doing now to keep up with recent achievements in your field?

4. What are your plans at present to continue your education?

5. Other than job-related programs, what else are you doing for self-development?

6. What magazines do you read regularly?

7. What books have you read recently?

Work Experience

Make copies of this section so you have one set of questions for each job held.

1. On your application, you indicated you worked for _____.
   Are you still there? (Or: When were you there?)

2. Describe your duties and responsibilities in each of your assignments with this company?

3. What did you particularly enjoy about that job?

4. What did you least enjoy in that position?

5. What do you consider to be your major accomplishment in that assignment?

6. Tell me about some of your disappointments or setbacks in that job.

7. Tell me about the progress you made in that company.

8. If progress was significant, ask: To what do you attribute this fine progress? If not, ask: Were you satisfied with this progress? If not satisfied, ask: How did you attempt to overcome this?

9. What was the most valuable experience you obtained in that position?

10. Why did you leave that company? (Or: Why do you want to leave?)

Specific Questions

Write here a list of specific questions to be asked based on the job description. Use additional pages if needed. _____

_____

_____

_____

_____

_____

_____

Intangible Factors

To obtain a complete picture of the individual, not just as an applicant, but as a person, ask these questions:

1. What are you seeking in this job that you are not getting in your present job?

2. Tell me about your long-term career goals? Short term?

continues

continued

3. In what way could a job with our company meet your career objectives?

4. What goals have you set in previous jobs or at school? What have you done to accomplish them? With what results?

5. What are your criteria for your own success?

6. What factors have contributed most to your own growth?

7. What factors have handicapped you from moving ahead more rapidly?

8. If you had to do it over again, what changes would you make in your life and your career?

9. What aspects of a job are the most important to you?

10. Think of a supervisor you particularly respected. Describe his or her management style. Describe your least effective supervisor.

11. For what have supervisors complimented you? For what have they criticized you?

12. Tell me about some of the significant problems encountered in any of your jobs. How did you solve them?

13. If hired for this position, what can you bring to it that will rapidly make you productive?

14. In what areas could we help you become even more productive?

The Curtain Is About to Go Up

Once you've prepared the questions you're going to ask, you are ready for the actual interview. Whether the interview will be loosely structured or you will follow a guided pattern such as the Personalized Personnel Profile, most of the questions you've prepared will be the same for all applicants for the same job.

Keep in mind, however, that each applicant brings to the interview his or her own special qualifications and personal characteristics. Be prepared to tailor your interviewing plan to accommodate for this. Study the applicant's application form and resumé. Frame additional questions based on what is reported in these documents. This may call for rephrasing some questions, adding new questions, and placing emphasis on aspects of the job you hadn't originally planned to emphasize.

When you are confident that you're well-prepared to conduct a meaningful interview, go out to meet the applicant and bring him or her in for the interview. What you do then will be discussed in the next chapter.

The Least You Need to Know

➤ A basic part of any interview is proper preparation by the interviewer. Review the application form and its accompanying resumé and the job description including the job specification.

➤ Any person assigned to conduct first interviews should be carefully trained in interviewing methods.

➤ To ensure attainment of all relevant information, prepare a list of key questions that must be asked during the interview before you sit down with the applicant.

➤ Most good interviews have structure. If not, they often result in a chaotic exchange of questions and answers with little possibility of making reasonable decisions.

➤ One of the limitations of a structured interview is the tendency to stick to just the questions on the list. Flexibility is important. The answer to one question may require follow-up to obtain more or better information.

➤ Basing the interview on the job specs is only part of the picture. Because each applicant brings to the interview his or her own special qualifications and personal characteristics, tailor your interviewing plan to accommodate for this.

Chapter 17

Face to Face with the Applicant

In This Chapter

➤ Determining what the interview seeks to accomplish

➤ Breaking the ice

➤ Getting down to business

➤ Encouraging the applicant to open up

➤ Probing for personal characteristics

➤ Giving the applicant information about the job

The interview serves several purposes in the selection process. It's obvious first purpose is to obtain enough information from the applicant to determine whether he or she is qualified for the job. It is not just an interrogation, however. It also enables the interviewer to observe the candidate, interpret and evaluate the answers to questions, and compare the candidates. In addition, an important function of the interview is to give the applicant information about the company and the job.

In this chapter, you'll learn to implement the preparations discussed in the preceding chapter. The planning is over. You're ready to meet the applicant. It's show time!

Getting Started

To obtain the best results from an interview, the interviewer must put the applicant at ease. Tense applicants are ill at ease and don't respond fully to your questions. Establishing rapport with the applicant takes a little time, but even in a brief interview it's well worth it.

An important objective of the interview is to create a favorable image of the company in the eyes of the applicant. The reputation of the firm can be improved or harmed by the manner in which applicants are treated. You want an applicant to accept a job offer, and even rejected applicants may be potential customers.

Establish Rapport

To make the applicant feel at ease, the interviewer must be at ease and feel comfortable about the interview process. An ideal setting for an interview is a private room, comfortably furnished with a minimum of distracting papers on the desk. To avoid telephone interruptions, turn on your voice mail or have somebody else answer your phone.

Go out and greet the applicant. It's much better to personally go to the reception area than to send a secretary to fetch the applicant. So get up from your chair and get out there. Introduce yourself and escort the applicant to the interviewing room.

When greeting the applicant, use his or her full name. "David Livingstone, I'm Henry Stanley." This makes the applicant feel that you identify him or her as an individual, not just as another candidate. Dale Carnegie said, "Remember, a person's name is to that person the sweetest and most important sound in any language."

By using both the first and last name in addressing the applicant and introducing yourself, you are putting both of you on equal footing. If you call yourself "Mr." or "Ms." and call the applicant "Dave," it sounds condescending.

Start the interview by making minor observations and asking noncontroversial questions. It's not necessary to talk about the weather or last night's game or television special.

The opening should be related to the interview but should not make the applicant defensive or upset. Don't start with such questions as "What makes you think you could handle this job?" or "Why were you fired from your last job?"

A better approach is to select an innocuous area from the application and comment on it. It may be based on something in the applicant's background to which you relate. For example, "I see you went to Lincoln High School. Did you know Mr. Salkin, the drama teacher?" or "I see you live in Chelsea. That neighborhood is growing rapidly."

Employment Enigmas

The use of first names has become a common practice in America, but there are many older people and people from other cultures who consider it disrespectful.

Nervous Applicants

At this point, the ice is generally broken, and you can move into the body of the interview. However, occasionally you run into an applicant who is overly tense and limits responses to nervous nods and monosyllabic mumbles. Here are some suggestions to calm this person down:

➤ Identify and sympathize with him or her. You might say to a young person, "When I was interviewed for my first job, I was terribly uneasy." Making the applicant realize that being nervousness is not unusual often helps.

➤ Comment on his or her accomplishments. For example, "I see your grades were well above average," or "I was impressed by your being chosen for the Math Olympics."

> **Words to Work By**
>
> The word **interview** is derived from *inter* meaning "between" and *view* meaning "a look." An interview is not a one-way interrogation. It's a look at a situation (in this case, a look at a job) between the interviewer and the candidate.

➤ Some mature people, when returning to the job market after years of employment in the same company, are very tense. They may be self-conscious, embarrassed, worried, and overly cautious. To draw them out, start the interview with a few comments about their past successes so they can talk about something of which they are proud.

Asking Questions

Now is the time to ask the questions you prepared when planning for the interview. If you use a structured interview system, begin now to follow the structure. If you follow a less formal procedure, ask the questions you prepared as well as others that will help gather the information needed.

Guidelines

To get the most out of the interview, here are some guidelines to follow when asking questions:

➤ DON'T ask questions that can be answered "Yes" or "No." This stifles information. Instead of asking, "Have you any experience in budgeting?" say "Tell me about your experience in budgeting."

➤ DON'T put words in the applicant's mouth. Instead of asking, "You've called on discount stores, haven't you?" ask "What discount stores have you called on?"

Employment Enigmas

Glib applicants may come up with high-sounding solutions to situations, but they may not really be practical. Follow through by asking what problems might be encountered if the idea was implemented.

Hiring Hints

Elicit information from applicants about what they have done in previous jobs that they are particularly proud of. Past successes are good indicators of future achievements.

➤ DON'T ask questions that are unrelated to your objectives. It might be interesting to follow up on certain tidbits of gossip that the applicant volunteers, but it rarely leads to pertinent information.

➤ DO ask questions that develop information as to the applicant's ...

Experience: "What were your responsibilities regarding the purchasing of equipment?"

Knowledge: "How did you (or how would you) cope with this problem?"

Attitudes: "How do you feel about heavy travel?" "Why do you wish to change jobs now?"

An effective way to probe for full information is to use the "W" questions: What, When, Where, Who, and Why. With the addition of How, you can draw out most of the information needed. Here are some examples:

➤ What computer software was used?

➤ When did you design that program?

➤ Where was the program installed?

➤ Who was responsible for supervising that project?

➤ Why did you make that decision?

➤ How did you implement the new system?

Ask Situational Questions

Give the applicant a hypothetical situation and ask how he or she would handle it. The situations should be reasonably close to actual problems found on the job. Judge the response by the knowledge of the subject, approach to the solution, value of the suggestions, and clarity in communicating the answer.

A variation of the situational question is to ask the applicant to describe difficult situations faced on previous jobs and how they were resolved.

Summary Questions

When you have completed questioning the applicant about a phase of his or her background, ask a question that will summarize what has been presented. For example, "You certainly have extensive background in quality control. Briefly summarize what you can contribute to make our company more effective in that area."

This gives the applicant a chance to bring together the highlights of his or her experience in that area, and it enables you to review the highlights of the person's background.

At the end of the interview, a good summary question is "Now that you've learned a bit about our job and have had to chance to tell me about yourself, please tell me briefly what you bring to this job that will ensure your success."

Hiring Hints

Try this: After the applicant responds to your question, count to five slowly (to yourself, of course) before asking the next question. By waiting five seconds, you'll be surprised how often an applicant adds something—positive or negative—to the response to the previous question.

Using Nondirective Techniques

It's not always possible to obtain necessary information by direct questioning. *Nondirective* approaches may help in these cases. Nondirective questioning uses open-ended questions such as "Tell me about ...." The applicant then tells whatever he or she feels is important. Instead of commenting on the response, you nod your head say "Uh-huh," "Yes," or "I see." This encourages the applicant to keep talking without you giving any hint as to what you are seeking.

In this way, the applicant may talk about problems, personality factors, attitudes, or weaknesses that might not have been uncovered directly. On the other hand, it may bring out some positive factors and strengths that were missed by direct questioning.

Words to Work By

In **nondirective interviewing,** instead of making a substantive remark after an applicant's response, the interviewer makes a noncommittal comment such as "Uh-huh" or just nods or remains silent. This encourages the applicant to continue talking and brings out information not directly asked about.

Another way of using the nondirective approach is to be silent. Most people can't tolerate silence. If you don't respond instantly, the applicant is likely to keep talking.

Ferreting Out the Intangibles

It's relatively easy to frame questions to get information about experience and accomplishments. It's equally important, however, for the interviewer to learn as much as possible about the personal characteristics that often make the difference between hiring a mediocre employee and a standout.

In the Personal Personnel Profile—the structured interview guide described in the preceding chapter—there is an entire section of questions to ask about intangible factors. Even if you interview on a less formal basis, you can pick up some good questions from the form to use in your interview.

Resourcefulness

In the old days when jobs were primarily routine, companies did not want employees to be resourceful. The worker's job was to follow orders and stick to the system. Innovators were looked upon as troublemakers. As more and more jobs today fall into the category of "knowledge work," resourcefulness is an important factor.

Here are some questions to ask about resourcefulness:

➤ Give me an example of how you dealt with a situation in your job that you had never encountered previously.

➤ How did you change the scope of your job from the time you started it until now (or when your left it)?

➤ What was the most radical idea you contributed to your company? How did you persuade your boss to accept it? How did you implement it? What was the result?

➤ You are under extreme pressure to complete a job by a deadline. Two days before the deadline, you discover a major error in your calculations. How would you deal with this?

➤ You're a sales rep. You just learned that another company has acquired your biggest customer, and the acquiring company will do all purchasing. How will you handle this?

In evaluating the responses, look for the degree of resourcefulness used, the applicant's determination to overcome the problem, and the applicant's capability to handle unforeseen circumstances and bounce back from the shock.

Taking Criticism

Nobody likes to be criticized. Some people are very sensitive and become upset and resentful. Here are some questions to ask about this topic:

➤ In your last performance review, what did your boss tell you that you felt was accurate. In what areas did you feel the boss was unfair in the assessment? In evaluating the response, consider the importance of the "unfair" areas and the applicant's attitude when he or she discussed it. Did he or she sound upset or resentful? Did he or she dwell on it? Did he or she pass over it rapidly?

➤ Your boss blasts you for making a decision with which she disagrees. You feel you were right. What will you do?

➤ One of your employees files a complaint against you with the union, claiming you treat him unfairly by assigning him all the "dirty work." Your argument: "That's all he's capable of doing." During the period that this is being adjudicated, how will you deal with the complainant? The other employees in the department? Your boss? In evaluating the responses, look for the emotional reaction. Did the applicant keep cool? Did he or she deal with the situations adequately?

Working Under Direction and with Others

Interpersonal relations are essential to almost every job. The employee must relate well to the supervisor or team leader, subordinates, and of course, peers. Here are some questions regarding this area:

➤ Describe your supervisor's supervisory methods? If you were the supervisor, what would you do anything differently?

➤ Give me an example of an order or an instruction you received from your boss with which you disagreed. What did you do?

➤ You are a member of a team. When the team is assigned a project, all team members participate in planning the work. You disagree with the majority. What will you do?

➤ In your previous jobs, how much of your work was done as an individual? As part of a team? Which did you enjoy more? Why?

➤ How would you describe your relationships with your co-workers on your present (or past) jobs?

Employment Enigmas

Companies seek employees who have drive and motivation and are success oriented. However, many jobs don't offer the opportunity to obtain the rewards these people seek. For these "dead-end" jobs, it's better to hire less ambitious people.

From the responses, determine whether the candidate is a team player, an easy-going conformist, an individualist, and so on. You should base your judgment on the culture of your company.

Potential and Self-Concept

How a person views his or her life to date is an indicator of that person's future. People who look upon themselves as being successful are likely to continue to be successful. People who are dissatisfied with their lives will likely become dissatisfied employees. On the other hand, people who are complacent with their progress may not have the motivation to push ahead. These questions will bring out the applicant's self-concept:

➤ How would you evaluate the progress you have made so far in your career?

➤ What do you think has contributed most to the successes you have made?

➤ What have you done in the last five years that has given you the greatest personal satisfaction?

➤ What has been your biggest disappointment in your career? How has it affected your life?

➤ Why do you think you can be successful in this job?

➤ In what way can we help you become successful in this job?

➤ How does this job fit into your career plans?

➤ Do you have a plan for self-improvement? What have you accomplished in this plan thus far? What do you plan to accomplish this year?

Hiring Hints

Elicit information from applicants about what they have done in previous jobs (or other areas of their lives) that they're particularly proud of. Past successes are good indicators of future achievement.

From the answers to these questions, determine the applicant's level of self-confidence and success orientation and whether the applicant can realize his or her goals in this job.

There are many other intangibles that might be measured. Questions can be framed to bring out the ones specifically needed for your job opening. Use the preceding sample questions as a guide to developing your own questions.

Giving Information to the Applicant

An important part of the interview is giving the applicant information about the company and the job. All the work and expense undertaken to get good employees is lost if the applicants you want don't accept your offer. By giving them a positive picture of the job at the interview, you're more likely to have a higher rate of acceptances.

When and What to Tell About the Job

Some interviewers start the interview by describing the job duties. Some give the applicant a copy of the job description in advance of the interview. *This is a serious error.* If an applicant knows too much about a job too soon, he or she is likely to tailor the answers to all of your questions to fit the job.

For example, you tell a prospect that the job calls for selling to department-store chains. Even if the applicant has only limited experience in this area, when you ask, "What types of markets did you call on?"—guess which one will be emphasized.

The best way to give information about duties and responsibilities is to feed it to the applicant throughout the interview—after you have ascertained the background of the applicant in that phase of the work. Here's an example:

> **Interviewer:** What types of markets did you call on?

> **Applicant:** Drug-store chains, discount stores, department stores, and mail-order houses.

The interviewer then should ask specific questions about the applicant's experience in each of these markets. If the department-store background is satisfactory, the interviewer might then say, "I'm glad you have such a fine background in dealing with department-store chains since they represent about 40 percent of our customer list. If you should be hired, you'd be working closely with those chains."

If the background in this area was weak, the interviewer might say, "Because a great deal of our business is with department-store chains, if you should be hired, we would have to give you added training in this area.

Employment Enigmas

Don't give applicants copies of the job description before an interview. Their responses to your questions will be influenced by what they read.

At the end of the first interview, the interviewer should have a fairly complete knowledge of the applicant's background, and the applicant should have a good idea of the nature of the job. At subsequent interviews, the emphasis will be on obtaining more specific details about the applicant and giving the applicant more specific data about the job.

Answering Applicants' Questions

Most interviewers give the applicant an opportunity to ask questions about the job and the company at some point (usually at the end of the interview). The questions asked can give some insight into the applicant's personality and can help you in your evaluation.

Are the questions primarily of a personal nature (such as vacations, time off, raises, and so on) or are they about the job? People who are only concerned about personal aspects are less likely to be as highly motivated as job-oriented applicants. Their questions can also provide clues about their real interest in the job. If you feel from the questions that a prospective candidate might not be too enthusiastic about the job, it gives you another chance to sell the prospect on the advantages of joining your company.

You are always "selling" when you interview. It's important that you present your company and the job in a positive and enthusiastic manner. This doesn't mean, however, that you should exaggerate or mislead the applicant.

Tell the applicant the negatives at the interview, but show how the positive aspects outweigh them. For example, "Our company does require its engineers to put in a great deal of overtime because we're working on very urgent matters. However, even though, as an exempt employee, we are not obligated to pay for your overtime, we do give extra pay for the extra time. Moreover, the work is exciting and rewarding. I'm sure you'll get as much satisfaction as all our engineers do from the challenges of the job."

Closing the Interview

Once the interviewer has all the necessary information and the applicant has been told about the job and has had the opportunity to ask questions, the interview can be brought to a close.

End on a Positive Note

All interviews should end on a positive note. The applicant should be told what the next step would be. In most cases, if there is an interest in the candidate, additional interviews—sometimes with the same interviewer, more often with another person—will be arranged. This should be done as soon as feasible. If possible, make the appointment for that interview before the applicant leaves the office. If testing, a psychological appraisal, or other steps are part of the process, tell the candidate what to expect and set dates for them.

In many cases, the first interviewer will see several applicants before deciding which ones to send for subsequent interviews. Unless you have already decided that this applicant is not to be considered further, tell him or her that, once you have interviewed the other candidates, you will select the ones who will be invited for further discussions. Tell the applicants that you will contact them as soon as this decision is made.

Telling the Decision to the Applicant

If, on the basis of the first interview, you have decided that the applicant is not to be considered, it's only fair to tell him or her. In most cases, the reason may be obvious. During the interview, it probably became clear to both of you that the applicant was not qualified. Just say, "Joe, since you don't have experience in areas X and Y, which are essential to being able to do this job, we cannot consider you for it."

If the reason is not directly job related (such as lacking personal characteristics or your reaction to the applicant), rather than rejecting him or her outright say, "We have several more applicants to interview. Once we've seen them all, we'll make a decision."

Remembering the Applicant

You've seen a dozen applicants for the open position. Unless you take notes, it's unlikely that you'll remember what each one has told you and your reaction to them. It's essential that some method be devised to record the highlights of the interview and, in due course, the decisions made. It's not possible or even desirable to take stenographic transcriptions or tapes of every interview. Enough information should be noted, however, so that you're able to remember who each applicant is, what makes one different from another, and how each applicant measures up to the job specifications.

Hiring Hints

Don't keep applicants on a string waiting to hear from you. If you are not interested in a candidate, write or phone him or her no later than a week after the interview. If the applicant is still being considered but the decision is delayed, keep the applicant advised of the status.

Good Notes Keep You Out of Trouble

When you evaluate several candidates for the same job, if you've kept good records of the interviews, it's easier to compare them. By rereading your notes rather than depending on your memory, you are more likely to make sounder judgments. When several people interview the same candidate, a consistent system of recording information will facilitate an in-depth analysis of the applicant's qualifications.

Good records also help if you face legal problems. In the case of an investigation by government agencies such as the EEOC or state civil rights divisions, good records of the interview can be your most important defense. When no records or inadequate records have been kept, the opinion of the hearing officer is dependent on the company's word against the applicant's. Good, consistent records provide solid evidence.

231

Taking Notes

Taking notes often has a negative effect on applicants. Some get very nervous when they see you write down everything they say. They may be inhibited from talking freely and may hold back on important matters.

Taking notes also may have a negative effect on you, the interviewer. You might be so busy writing what the applicant just said that you don't listen to what is currently being said.

Some companies have designed special forms for interview record keeping. Others suggest that you make notes on the application form or on a paper attached to the form after the interview. In any case, a summary form should be completed *immediately* after the close of the interview.

The following figure is a good example of a form that's useful in summarizing interview results. Note that it provides space to list the job factors as indicated in the job specification, and there's space in the next column to record highlights of the applicant's background in that factor.

On the reverse side of the form (see the next section) is a place to record personal factors and the interviewer's overall comments.

Recommendations of Interviewers

Each person who has interviewed the applicant should make comments on the same type of form. After going over the comments, a recommendation should be made:

_____ Recommend hiring

_____ Recommend considering as a possible hire

_____ Don't hire

Reasons for recommendations should be given. Compelling the interviewer to succinctly state a reason can help overcome intuitive decisions based on some vague like or dislike. Interviewers must remember that the reason may be challenged by EEOC or other agencies.

Chapter 22, "Making the Decision," discusses in detail the factors to consider in making the hiring decision.

INTERVIEW SUMMARY SHEET

Applicant _____   Date _____

Position applied for _____   Interviewer _____

JOB FACTORS[1]   **Applicant's
                                                    Background[2]**

Duties: _____

_____

_____

_____

Responsibilities: _____

_____

_____

_____

Skills Required: _____

_____

_____

_____

Education Required:[3] (level) _____

    Specific types: _____

_____

    Educ. achievement: _____

_____

Other Job Factors: _____

_____

_____

_____

[1] Job factors should be listed from job specifications for position applicant applies for.

[2] Interviewer should note aspects of applicant's background that apply to each factor in this column.

[3] Level of education – how much schooling completed; type represents subjects related to job taken; achievement represents grades or standing.

An interview summary sheet.

INTERVIEW SUMMARY SHEET *(CONTINUED)*

PERSONAL FACTORS	Comments
Growth in Career	
Accomplishments	
Intangibles:	
Appearance	
Motivation	
Resourcefulness	
Stability	
Leadership	
Creativity	
Mental alertness	
Energy level	
Communication skill	
Self confidence	

Applicant's strengths: _____

Applicant's limitations: _____

☐ Applicant should be hired: _____

　　Recommendations for additional training: _____

☐ Applicant should not be hired: _____

　　Reasons: _____

Additional comments: _____

An interview summary sheet (reverse side).

The Least You Need to Know

➤ To obtain the best results from an interview, the interviewer must put the applicant at ease. Tense applicants are ill at ease and don't respond fully to your questions.

➤ An effective way to probe for full information is to use the "W" questions: What, When, Where, Who, and Why. With the addition of How, you can draw out most of the information needed.

➤ Use nondirective interviewing. Instead of making a substantive remark after an applicant's response, make a noncommittal comment such as "Uh-huh" or just nod or remain silent. This encourages the applicant to continue talking and brings out information not directly asked about.

➤ Frame questions that will tell you about the applicant's work experience and that will enable you to determine his or her resourcefulness, ability to follow instructions, ability to work with others, and other intangible factors.

➤ If you tell the applicant too much about the job in the beginning of the interview, his or her answers will be tailored to what the job requires. The best way to give information is to feed it to the applicant throughout the interview—after you have ascertained the background of the applicant in that phase of the work.

➤ Taking notes is important, but it may stifle applicants, and it may keep you from fully listening. Write brief notes during the interview. Immediately after the interview, review them and write a summary while the interview is still fresh in your mind.

Chapter 18

Barriers to Good Interviewing

In This Chapter

➤ Interviewing bloopers and how to avoid them

➤ Improving communication between interviewer and interviewee

➤ Becoming a better listener

➤ Surviving applicants who drive you crazy

Interviewing can be tricky. You think you're asking the right questions, but the answers don't give you the information you expected. Maybe you're doing it wrong. Maybe the applicant is maneuvering around the questions. Maybe you lost control of the interview.

Applicants judge you and your company by the way you conduct the interview. Be friendly but businesslike. Be organized but flexible. Keep in mind your objective: to get enough information to make a sound hiring decision.

This chapter looks at some of the barriers that prevent interviewers from getting the most out of interviews.

Ten Common Mistakes Interviewers Make

By being aware of some of the traps interviewers fall into, you can catch yourself and keep the interview moving along productively.

The Haphazard Interview

In the preceding chapter, you learned that by establishing a systematic approach to the interview, you'll get the information you need. Although using a formal

Hiring Hints

By planning the questions you'll ask in a systematic manner, you'll cover all the bases. Be flexible within the structure, though, so you don't fail to probe areas of interest that may develop as you go along.

structured interview has advantages, many people are not comfortable working within its limitations. It was suggested that an informal structured format be used.

Unfortunately, in their attempts to be flexible, some interviewers go to the other extreme; they ask questions in a haphazard manner and, as a result, get little information.

Bill W., who had been interviewed for a job in the accounting department of the Goody Gumdrop Candy Co., left the interview with the feeling that the chief accountant, who conducted the interview, had obtained little information about his qualifications. Bill reported that the interviewer had jumped from one subject to another—talking for a moment about education, shifting to some phases of work experience, back to schooling, over to attitudes, to job objectives, and then back to work background.

Not only did the interviewer fail to get a comprehensive view of Bill's fitness for the job, he also turned Bill off. Bill realized he didn't want to work for a person who was so disorganized.

Interviewing for the Wrong Job

Some interviewers don't pay adequate attention to the job specifications. This is likely to happen when you are interviewing for a variety of jobs in the same department. Barbara P. applied for a job analyst's position. The interviewer asked all kinds of questions about every aspect of human resources administration, but very few were about job analysis. Barbara commented that the questions were very good for somebody applying for a more general job in the department, but they didn't bring out information about her background for the open job.

Always reread the specs before the interview. It will help you set your mind on what you really seek in the applicant's background and will enable you to frame appropriate questions.

Letting the Applicant Dominate the Interview

A savvy applicant can so dominate the situation that he or she only tells you what is most favorable and manages to de-emphasize negative facets. A good interviewer must maintain control. When you have an applicant who doesn't let you get one word in, who twists your questions to fit his or her desires, who keeps adding information that is not relevant but is designed to boost the applicant's assets, *cut it off.*

One polite way of doing this is to say, "That's most interesting; however, would you mind giving me specific details on ...." The best way to counteract an applicant's attempt at domination is to insist the he or she answer your questions to your satisfaction.

Playing God

One of the major complaints applicants have about interviewers is that they condescend to them. They act so superior that the applicant feels uncomfortable. Because the interviewer has the power to hire or at least to refer the applicant on for further consideration, there is a tendency to "play God" and smugly savor the power.

Cool it. Keep your objectives in mind. You don't want to turn off the candidate. A little humility will pay off in better rapport, more and more meaningful information, and if an offer is extended, a better chance of the candidate accepting it. It will also win friends for you and your company.

Employment Enigmas

Don't let the applicant dominate the interview. If he or she spins answers that are not responsive to the question asked, repeat the question and demand specific information, not just broad generalities. Keep probing until you get a satisfactory response.

Telegraphing the Right Response

Some interviewers are so anxious to fill a job that they help the applicant respond correctly to their questions. They "feed" the applicant the expected answer. "This job calls for experience in handling customer complaints. You've done this, haven't you?" Nobody ever says "No."

Talking Too Much

Some interviewers talk too much. They start the interview by telling the applicant all about the company. Then they spend more time talking about the job. Sometimes they'll tell you about their own job. Finally, they get around to asking a few questions. But before the applicant has a chance to complete the answer, they often interrupt to make a comment or, worse, to tell you about something in their history that your answer reminded them of.

There's an old saying that you can't learn anything when your mouth is open. The interview is a two-way process. If you do all the talking, you'll stifle the applicant and will get little information. Let the applicant do most of the talking, but keep him or her on track by asking good questions.

Playing the District Attorney

Some interviewers get a kick out of catching the applicant in inconsistencies. They repeat questions in several forms to ascertain that the answers are the same. If they find an "error," they pounce on the victim.

Such people should not be interviewing applicants. They belong in the police department or the CIA. Most of the so-called inconsistencies found by this type of interrogation are insignificant and have little or no bearing on a candidate's ability to do the job.

It not only is a waste of time, it also may cause the company to lose highly qualified prospects who are rejected by these "DAs" for the wrong reasons.

Playing Psychologist

Just because you took Psych 101 in college, it doesn't qualify you to be a psychologist. Some interviewers assume far more psychological knowledge than they have. They look for hidden meanings in everything the applicant says. They ascribe Freudian motives to work experience, family relations, attitudes, and even casual comments made by the applicant. The fact that they are not really qualified to make these judgments doesn't bother them one bit. They are so absorbed in their "psychological" evaluations that they fail to determine whether the applicants can or cannot do the job for which they are being interviewed.

Falling in Love (or Hate) with the Applicant

Sometimes an interviewer is so impressed by one aspect of an applicant's background that it dominates the evaluation. As noted in Chapter 1, "20 Mistakes Companies Make in Hiring People," this is called the halo effect. It may be a person's appearance or charisma. It might be the possession of a specific skill that is needed by the company. Although the trait may be impressive, there may be other important facts in the applicant's background that negate it.

Here's a good example: The interviewer was so impressed by Lara's high score on the word processing test that he hired her. Only after she was employed did he discover that she didn't have sufficient background in some of the other functions the job called for.

The opposite of the halo effect is the pitchfork effect. The applicant displays one characteristic that turns you off. You ignore his or her other excellent qualifications.

A good interviewer will recognize that this charm or skill is an asset and that one negative factor is *only* one aspect of the total person. These characteristics should be put in proper perspective.

Failure to Probe for Details

You can't accept every answer at face value. Some applicants may lie outright; more often, applicants play up their strengths by exaggerating their qualifications. You may ask about experience in a certain area. Even if the experience is very light, the applicant is likely to make it sound more impressive that it really is.

To overcome this, probe for details. Study the job specs. If you are not fully familiar with the job for which you are interviewing, ask the person to whom the job will report to suggest questions to ask.

An applicant says he designed a training program for computer operators. Don't stop there. Ask specific questions about the content of the program, the problems faced in implementing it, the results of the training, and other pertinent questions.

Get examples of what was actually done. Another applicant, a customer service representative, states that she has dealt with irate customers. Ask for some examples of how she handled a customer. Probe for details. Don't move on to another question until you feel you have adequate information.

Employment Enigmas

A glib applicant can often make up examples to back up claims of accomplishments. If the example *is* too vague or you suspect the applicant is fabricating, ask for another example and then yet another. Even glib people can't come up with realistic stories that rapidly.

Check Your Interviewing Techniques

After interviewing an applicant, review your own performance. Use the following checklist to guide your self-evaluation:

1. Introduction
   - ❑ Did the interviewer use the application form in planning the interview?
   - ❑ Did the interviewer establish rapport?
   - ❑ Did the interviewer move smoothly into the body of the interview?
2. Getting Information
   - ❑ Did the interviewer ask questions that elicited information?
   - ❑ Did the interviewer follow answers through?
   - ❑ Did the interviewer look beyond the obvious?
   - ❑ Did the interviewer avoid telegraphing desired responses?
   - ❑ Did the interviewer control the interview?

❏ Did the interviewer encourage the applicant to speak freely?

❏ Did the interviewer really listen?

❏ Did the interviewer obtain adequate job factor information?

❏ Did the interviewer obtain adequate intangible factor information?

3. Giving Information

❏ Did the interviewer describe the job adequately?

❏ Did the interviewer give the applicant some background information about the company?

❏ Did the interviewer "sell" the job to the applicant?

❏ Did the interviewer encourage the applicant to ask questions?

4. Closing the Interview

❏ Did the interviewer control when the interview closed?

❏ (if the applicant was to be rejected)
Did the interviewer handle the rejection diplomatically?

❏ (if the applicant was to be considered further)
Did the interviewer inform the applicant of the next step of the procedure?

❏ Did the interviewer leave the applicant with a good impression of the firm?

❏ Did the interviewer make appropriate notes after the applicant left?

By reviewing the answers to these questions, you can evaluate how well the interview was conducted and learn in what ways you can improve your interviewing techniques.

Poor Communication

Good interviewing is not interrogating—asking questions and getting responses. To be effective, it must be a two-way communication with feedback flowing from one party to the other on a continuous basis. The response to your question may not provide the information you desired. Why might this be?

You May Not Be Speaking the Same Language

You may not be speaking the same language. I don't mean you were speaking Latin and the applicant was speaking Greek. You may be using *jargon*—words or terms unique to your company that are not likely to be understood by an outsider. You may be using technical terminology that would be appropriate when interviewing a person experienced in that field but meaningless to an applicant for a trainee position. If you see a puzzled look on the applicant's face when you ask a question, rephrase it immediately. There is an exception: If knowing the terminology is essential to job performance, this may indicate that the applicant lacks the qualifications for the job.

Psychological Barriers

The following list details some of your attitudes that influence the way you interpret what you say and what you hear:

➤ **Assumptions.** You're a person whose highest priority in life is work. You've always worked 12-hour days, and you assume that all ambitious people are willing to put in the hours you do. You're likely to be wrong. Probe to learn how an applicant really feels about this and the other conditions incumbent to this job.

➤ **Preconceptions.** People tend to hear what they expect to hear. The responses to your questions are distorted by any information you have already known about the subject. If what the applicant says is different from what you expected, you might reject it as being incorrect. What does this mean to you? Keep your mind open. When an applicant tells you something, make an extra effort to listen and to evaluate the new information objectively instead of blocking it out because it differs from your preconceptions.

➤ **Prejudices.** Your biases for or against a person influence the way you receive what he or she says. If you have a good first impression of the applicant, more than likely you'll be inclined to accept whatever he or she says. If you took an instant dislike to the applicant, you'll most likely discount anything that's said.

Words to Work By

Jargon consists of the special initials, acronyms, words, or phrases used in your field or company and nowhere else. A statement like "We booked a perp on a 602A" won't mean anything to somebody who is not in law enforcement in your city.

Are You Really Listening?

The applicant starts answering a detailed question. You begin listening attentively. But before you know it, your mind begins to wander. Instead of listening to the problem, your thoughts are moving on to other things: the pile of work on your desk, the meeting you have scheduled with the company vice president, the problems one of your children is having at school. You hear the applicant's words, but you're not really listening.

Employment Enigmas

As soon as you realize you haven't been fully listening to the applicant—when you start hearing a droning sound instead of words, when you hear only words but not ideas, or when you're anticipating what you *think* will be said—stop! Then start listening!

Does this happen to you? Of course, it does. It happens to all of us. Why? Our minds can process ideas 10 times faster than we can talk. While the applicant is talking, your mind may race ahead. You complete the applicant's sentence in your mind—often incorrectly—long before the applicant does. You "hear" what your mind dictates, not what's actually said.

This is human nature. You must anticipate that it will happen, and you must be alert and take steps to overcome it. Read on to learn how to become a better listener.

"Sorry, I Wasn't Listening"

Suppose your mind was wandering and you didn't hear what the applicant said. It's embarrassing to admit you weren't listening, so you fake it. You pick up on the last few words you heard and comment on them. That's good. If it makes sense, you're lucky, but you may have missed the real gist of the response.

When you're not sure what really was said, you don't have to admit, "I'm sorry, I was daydreaming." One way to get back on track is to ask a question or make a comment about the last item you did hear: "Can we go back a minute to such-and-such?"

Another method is to comment: "To make sure I understand your view on this, please elaborate."

Overcoming Psychological Barriers to Clear Communication

You *can* become a better listener. You can stop some of the main causes of ineffective listening before they begin. All you have to do is make a few changes in your work environment and in your approach to listening—a small effort with a big return.

Hiring Hints

If you use a structured interview form like the Personal Personalized Profile (see Chapter 16), space is provided on the form to take notes. If you interview on a more informal basis, make your notes on a separate sheet of paper or use a form (see Chapter 17, "Face to Face with the Applicant").

➤ **Eliminate distractions.** The greatest distraction is probably the telephone. You want to give the applicant your full attention—and then the phone rings. Answering the call not only interrupts your discussion, it also disrupts the flow of your thoughts. Even after you've hung up, your mind may still be thinking about the call. Before the applicant comes in, arrange for someone else to handle your calls or set your voice mail to pick up all calls right away. If this isn't possible, get away from the telephone. Go to a conference room. Of course, there's probably a phone in the conference room, but no one knows you're there, so it probably won't ring.

➤ **Get rid of excess paper to reduce distractions.** If your desk is strewn with paper, you'll probably sit there skimming them until you realize too late that you're reading a letter or a memo instead of listening. Put those papers away in a drawer. If you go to a conference room, take only papers related to the interview.

➤ **Don't get too comfortable.** Some years ago, I was interviewing an applicant for a management position. As was my custom, I sat in my comfortable executive chair with my hands behind my head. Maybe I rocked a little. I was suddenly shaken from my lethargy when the applicant said, "Dr. Pell, you're not listening to me." I hemmed and hawed and awkwardly continued the interview, but I learned a lesson. Ever since then, rather than taking a relaxing position when interviewing, I've made a point of sitting on the edge of my chair and leaning forward rather than backward. This position not only brings me physically closer to the applicant, it also enables me to be more attentive and helps me maintain eye contact. It also shows the applicant that I'm truly interested in getting the full story being related and that I take seriously what is being said. And because I'm not quite so comfortable, I have less of a tendency to daydream.

➤ **Be an active listener.** An *active listener* doesn't just sit with open ears. An active listener asks questions about what's being said. You can paraphrase ("So the way I understand it is that …"), or you can ask specific questions about specific points. This technique not only enables you to clarify points that may be unclear, it also keeps you alert and paying full attention.

➤ **Be an empathetic listener.** Listen with your heart as well as your head. Empathetic listeners not only listen to what other people say, they also try to feel what other people are feeling when they speak. In other words, you put yourself in the applicant's shoes.

➤ **Take notes.** It's impossible to remember everything that's said in a lengthy interview. Take notes but, as pointed out in the preceding chapter, don't take stenographic transcriptions. If you're concentrating on what you're writing, you can't pay full attention to what the applicant is saying.

Words to Work By

An **active listener** not only pays close attention to what the other party says, he or she asks questions, makes comments, and reacts verbally and nonverbally to what is said.

More Listening Tips

Become an active listener. There's more to listening than just hearing what the applicant is saying. Here are some pointers:

➤ Look at the applicant. Eye contact is one way to show interest, but don't overdo it. Look at the whole person; don't just stare into his or her eyes.

245

➤ Show interest by your facial expression. Smile or show concern when appropriate.

➤ Indicate that you are following what is being said with nods or gestures.

➤ Ask questions about what the applicant says. You can paraphrase by saying, "So the way I understand it is …," or you can ask specific questions to clarify points that may be unclear.

➤ Don't interrupt. A pause should not be a signal for you to start talking. Wait.

➤ Don't argue. The interview is not a forum to discuss your opinions. If you disagree with the applicant's response, note it, but this is not the time or place to rebut it.

Watch the Body Language

Body language is a lot more important than people think. Interviewers should take a hint from top salespeople. They make a practice of carefully studying the body language of a prospect from the first few minutes of the interview. They note how the prospect's expressions often emphasize what is really important to him or her. They especially note the prospect's body language in reaction to their sales presentation, and they adapt their pitches accordingly. All of us can benefit from following this practice. It will enable us to become better interviewers.

Dealing with Problem Applicants

When you invite people in for interviews, you're sure to get some applicants who may present special problems. As previously noted, some may be too timid or too nervous to give adequate information. Some may be so verbose that you can't get a word in edgewise. Others may try to control the interview. Let's look at some of these special issues.

The Digresser

This applicant answers every question with long explanations and examples—most of which provide little meaningful information. Here's an example:

> **Interviewer:** "What experience have you had calling on food chains?"

> **Applicant:** "I've called on every major chain in the East. You know Joe McGrath at A & P? He and I are old friends. Last year, I took him to the Dodgers-Mets game. You remember that one when the Mets got only one hit, etc., etc., etc."

Every question will elicit a similar response. If the interview is to be brought to a successful conclusion before nightfall, the interviewer must assume control.

This can be done by frequent interruption with key questions. When the applicant digresses, wait for him or her to pause for breath and then quickly ask a very specific question, preferably a closed question that can be answered in a few words.

The "Shopper"

These people are literally trying to "shop" the job market. They want to see if there are any jobs for which they qualify that will pay better than what they're getting in their present position. They have no real desire to change and may use a job offer only as a means of getting a raise at their current jobs. Some people do this periodically to determine whether they are still marketable. Job offers are rarely accepted, but it satisfies their egos.

The Belligerent Applicant

Some people are naturally confrontational. They try to put the interviewer on the defensive. They may accuse the company of discriminatory practices or of bias against creative people. They often argue with the interviewer about specific qualifications.

If faced with this, remain calm at all times. Keep the initiative. Bring the interview to a close as quickly and diplomatically as possible. Never get maneuvered into an argument. Let the applicant feel that you are interested in the comments and that you appreciate him or her bringing them to your attention. Conclude by saying, "This was a most interesting interview, Mr. Jones. You certainly have a fine background. Let me discuss this with the department manager and see how it fits our current needs." A few days later, send a polite rejection letter.

The Know-It-All

Have you interviewed applicants who are so well-prepared for the interview that they know the answer to all your questions before they're asked? They are so articulate that they may even lecture you about the specs.

Deal with these people by asking specific, probing questions. Glib people are great on generalities but are unable to provide details. Some only know the language of the job, not the job itself. Good interviewing will bring out discrepancies and superficialities, enabling you to determine whether the applicant is a doer not just a talker.

Employment Enigmas

No matter how provocative an applicant may be, never lose your cool. If an applicant becomes belligerent, bring the interview to a close rapidly and diplomatically.

The Pseudo-Psychologist

Just as some interviewers play psychologist, you may run into applicants who weigh every question to figure out what your "real" intent is. Even the most obvious questions are interpreted as a hidden attempt to disclose a personality aberration. The answers are often meaningless and unrelated to the question. Here's an example:

Interviewer: "What experience have you had with spreadsheets?"

Applicant: (thought) "Ah-ha. He wants to find out if I'm computer oriented or people oriented."

247

(statement) "Although computers contribute to better productivity, it's the people in the organization who make or break it."

Such an applicant is usually not employable. The best solution is to dismiss him or her with a statement like this: "Your emotional setup and the climate in which this position functions will create an ambivalence not conducive to an optimum behavior pattern." While the applicant is trying to understand this, escort him or her to the door.

The "Interviewer"

Sometimes the applicant tries to turn the situation around and interview you instead of you interviewing him or her. Here's an example:

Interviewer: "Can you give me some details about your current duties?"

Applicant: "I'll be glad to, but first tell me about your job opening."

Interviewer: "I'll be glad to, but first tell me about your experience."

This obviously will lead nowhere. Here's a better response:

Interviewer: "I appreciate your interest in our position, but first I would like to know more about you. If you come close to our needs, we can discuss the job."

Fortunately, most applicants don't fall into these categories and provide a good two-way interface. However, running into one of these problem people may waste your time and even give you some headaches. Identify the problem early in the interview. If you can't bring it under control rapidly, curtail the interview and get the applicant out of the office as tactfully as possible.

The Least You Need to Know

➤ Applicants judge you and your company by the way you conduct the interview. Be friendly but businesslike. Be organized but flexible. Keep in mind your objective: to get enough information to make a sound hiring decision.

➤ Always reread the specs before the interview. It will help you set your mind on what you really seek in the applicant's background and will enable you to frame appropriate questions.

➤ Good interviewing is not interrogating—asking questions and getting responses. To be effective, it must be a two-way communication with feedback flowing from one party to the other on a continuous basis.

➤ You *can* become a better listener. All you have to do is make a few changes in your work environment and in your approach to listening.

➤ Don't let the applicant control the interview. Bring digressers back on track with specific questions. Get rid of eccentrics rapidly but diplomatically.

Chapter 19

Special Types of Interviews

In This Chapter

➤ Getting others into the act

➤ Utilizing assessment centers

➤ Using simulations, games, and puzzles

➤ Calling in a "shrink"

No matter how good your interviewing skills may be, it's a good idea to get the opinion of others before you make a hiring decision. You may have missed some important points in your interview that might be noted by another interviewer.

Your judgment of the applicant may be influenced by a personal bias, and the views of other managers or team members may help you make a more objective decision.

In addition, companies have developed a variety of multiple-interview approaches. In this chapter, you'll learn about these techniques and how to integrate them into your organization's interviewing process.

Interviews by Several People

Most companies require applicants to be interviewed by several people. Each interviewer looks at the candidate from his or her own viewpoint and seeks different things. The first interviewer, usually a member of the HR department, is most concerned with overall qualifications. Does the applicant meet the specs? Will the applicant work well in the organizational culture? Is the applicant better than or at least as good as other candidate being considered? Applicants who don't pass muster are eliminated; the others are sent for additional interviews.

Going Up the Ranks—Survival of the Fittest

In most companies, the interviewing process is hierarchical. If the applicant passes the first interview, he or she is sent for a second interview—sometimes with a higher-level HR staffer but more likely with the department head or team leader of the group where the job exists. Survivors of this interview may then be sent to a higher-ranking manager, often the department head's boss, who makes the final decision. For complex jobs or jobs at higher levels, several managers may see the survivors. The decision will be made by the highest executive involved in the process.

Among the interviewers will be technical specialists who can determine the depth of the candidate's expertise and experience for the open job and managers to evaluate the candidate's overall background and personality.

Collaborative Interviews by Several Managers

A more formal version of multiple interviews is the *serialized interview.* Several people, not all of whom are from the department for which the prospect is being considered, will conduct interviews. Each interviewer will rate the candidate on a standard evaluation form. The ratings are compared, and opinions from all the interviewers are elicited before the hiring decision is made.

Words to Work By

Unlike the hierarchical interviewing system in which only applicants approved at early interviews continue through the process, in **serialized interviews**, all applicants who are not eliminated at the first screening are seen and rated by several interviewers. The decision is made after reviewing all the ratings.

Because there is a great deal of subjectivity in a hiring decision, ratings from several interviewers minimize biases. However, the decision is not made by a vote. It is not an election. It is a collaborative effort.

After all the candidates have been interviewed, the interviewers meet to discuss them. Ratings are compared, and comments are made. The relative merits of each of the prospects are discussed. The final decision may be made by consensus of the participants. However, since the responsibility of training, supervising, and coordinating the work of the new employee rests with the immediate supervisor, the final decision may be delegated to that person.

Interviews by Team Members

Teams are a collaborative group. The key to team success is the cohesiveness of the team members. When a new member is being considered for a team, it's a good idea for other team members to interview him or her.

Ideally, every member of the team should interview prospects. This takes time, however, and when team members are interviewing prospects, their other work suffers.

To save time, give each team member a chance to meet and get an impression of the prospect. It's not necessary for each person to conduct a full interview. Each team member should concentrate on the part of the applicant's background in which he or she has the greatest knowledge. All team members will have the opportunity to size up an applicant and to share their evaluations with the rest of the team.

Panel Interviews

One-on-one interviews are very valuable, but as previously noted, they are very time consuming. One way to save time and still get reactions from several people regarding an applicant is the *panel interview*.

In this setup, several people interview the prospect at the same time. If the job is for a new team member, the panel may be made up of members of the team. For some jobs, the panel may consist of an HR staff member, a technical expert, the department manager, and perhaps other managers.

Typically, they sit around in a circle. The prospect is asked a question by one of the panelists. Any other panelist can follow through with a question to augment the response or to obtain additional information.

Some candidates may feel intimidated by being "ganged up on" by several people. To avoid this, prepare the applicant by explaining the process before the meeting. Keep the discussion noncontroversial. The objective is to get a good deal of information from the applicant and, more important, to see how the applicant interacts with the group.

Employment Enigmas

Because supervisors or team leaders have the responsibility of making the new employee successful, their input in making the decision is important. They must be confident that the applicant chosen has the right stuff.

Hiring Hints

If the job calls for working closely with another team, arrange for an interview with the leader of that team.

Words to Work By

In **panel interviews,** a group of interviewers sit down with the applicant and collectively conduct the interview.

251

After the session, the panel members discuss what has been learned and their reactions to the prospect.

The Assessment Center

Although companies usually use assessment centers as a means of evaluating current employees to determine their advancement potential, this approach can be adapted for screening applicants.

Here's how it works. After interviews with the human resources staff and the team leader or supervisor, if there is a serious interest in the candidate, he or she may be invited to participate in the assessment process.

Recruiting Residuals

Assessment centers are an excellent way to test the mettle of employees or applicants by giving them problems or exercises to complete in a brief time frame. Major corporations such as IBM, Hewlett-Packard, AT&T, and Motorola have used assessment centers as part of their career-development programs.

The Assessment Team

Members of the assessment group usually are drawn from team members, members of other teams, representatives of higher-level management, and others who are knowledgeable about the job for which the applicant is being considered. In some companies, a psychologist participates in the assessment. A human resources manager or a consultant facilitates the meeting.

How large should the group be? This varies with the type and complexity of the job. A typical panel has five to eight members. In some setups, the participants sit in the center of the room, and the panel is dispersed around the sides with the chairperson up front. In other setups, the participants see only the chairperson; the others are in an adjacent room separated by a one-way window.

Assessment centers work best when several applicants participate. This gives assessors the opportunity to observe not only how the prospects approach and solve the problems presented, but also how they interact with each other. The assessors note which people take leadership roles, which come up with the most creative ideas, and which cooperate with the others.

Sometimes assessment participants are rivals for the same job; sometimes candidates are for different jobs; sometimes current employees being considered for promotion (not necessarily for the same jobs) are included.

The Process

Assessment centers are not just a variation of a panel interview. Candidates may be questioned by members of the panel on various aspects of their background or their thinking, but this is just the beginning. Most assessment centers go much deeper.

There are many variations of this process. Some include a series of situational exercises in which candidates must respond to real-life problems likely to be faced on the job. They may be asked to prepare and make a presentation of a new product, to study a situation, or to make recommendations and then defend their position.

The situations presented often are drawn from actual problems the company has faced in the past or even at the present time. Some companies find that using games, puzzles, and non-job-related exercises is more effective in uncovering personality and character traits.

Games and Exercises

In one company, applicants for jobs as consultants and computer programmers are asked to solve mathematical equations, brainteasers, or riddles and to participate in group games and exercises that test their ability to collaborate and think under pressure.

Some of the typical areas explored in assessment centers are leadership, decision-making ability, oral and written communication, energy, forcefulness, dependence on others, and willingness to collaborate.

One typical appraisal method is the leaderless group discussion. In this method, each participant may be given a point of view or certain information in advance. He or she must attempt to sell that point of view to the group but still help the group arrive at the best decision regarding a problem it has been asked to resolve.

Paper and pencil tests are often part of the procedure as are written assignments in problem analysis, appraisal simulations, and fact-finding exercises. Each task is designed to evaluate one or more of the dimensions shown by the company's analysis of what is important to succeed in the job.

Some companies use unconventional approaches. At an Internet-solutions firm in Boston, an applicant was asked "to build something" with a box of Lego blocks. He was told, "You have five minutes to build whatever you want, then we'll talk about it."

Employment Enigmas

Any exercises or games used in assessing candidates should meet EEOC standards. They must be relevant to job success and should not have an adverse effect on minorities or women.

The applicant didn't waste time. He constructed an aerated cognac snifter and then explained its functional and aesthetic qualities. His ingenuity paid off. He got the job.

In another company, the participants were given one hour to plan the construction of a shopping mall. They were given a budget, a copy of the city building code, the union contract, and several other pertinent factors. The objective was to see how they approached a complex problem with many impediments to easy solution.

Games, exercises, and other techniques should not be developed haphazardly. They should be designed by experts in this field to measure specific traits or qualities that are indicative of success on the job. Assessors should be given criteria on which to base their assessments.

Digging Deeper

Many companies have members of the human resources department conduct in-depth interviews or send applicants for evaluation by industrial psychologists.

Psychologically Oriented Interviews

Ascertaining competence to perform the job is important in making the hiring decision, but it's not the only factor. Equally important are the intangibles: the ability to work with others, stability, intelligence, adaptability, and many others.

A variety of psychologically based interviewing techniques are used to probe these areas. Although often conducted by outside professional psychologists, human relations staffers who have been given the necessary training in these techniques sometimes use them.

The key to any psychological interview is the free flow of ideas. Unlike the structured interview discussed in the preceding chapters, the candidate and the interviewer have an ostensibly casual conversation guided only loosely by the interviewer. The real purpose is not to get information but to find out what motivates the applicant and what personality factors are dominant.

The interviewer uses a nondirective approach to get the applicant to express his or her thoughts. Rather than commenting on the answers or asking questions about what has been said, the applicant is encouraged to expand thoughts using a nondirective technique.

254

As pointed out in Chapter 17, "Face to Face with the Applicant," silence is an effective means of doing this. For example, the applicant might say, "My last boss was an autocrat." Instead of asking a specific question that might influence the applicant's comments, the interviewer remains silent and looks expectantly while the applicant adds the reasons for making the statement. This discussion may be quite different from what might have been elicited if the interviewer had asked a question.

An interview of this sort takes a great deal of time. It may be several hours in duration. Some interviewers conduct part of the interview over lunch or dinner. It should be completely informal. The applicant should be made to feel that he or she can talk freely.

The Stress Interview

The objective of this approach is to determine how an applicant will react to stress on the job. Since many positions do put the incumbent under pressure, it's useful to determine if similar stress affects an applicant's ability to function effectively.

In a typical interview of this sort, the applicant is made to feel uncomfortable by being put on the defensive. The interviewer probes for weaknesses in the candidate's background and plays against them much as a tennis player hits the ball to his opponent's weak spots.

For example, a sales rep might mention that he doesn't like to write reports (a common complaint of sales people). In an ordinary interview, this would be ignored. In the stress interview, the sale rep is asked why he doesn't like to write reports. He may be accused of not wanting his boss to know what he is doing with his time or of being afraid to be compared to other sales reps. If he becomes upset about this and loses control, it could indicate inability to take stress.

Critics of the stress interview argue that the interviewing situation is artificial and has little relationship to the real pressures of a job. They believe it doesn't measure true stress. Most psychologists agree that there are more effective psychological tools to measure the ability to take pressure.

Recruiting Residuals

Some interviewers have gotten into trouble by using stress interviews. When an interviewer focused on an applicant's several short-term marriages as a stress point, she slapped him in the face and walked out.

Using Professional Psychologists

Many companies retain outside psychological consultants to evaluate applicants for certain jobs—particularly for senior-level positions but often for sales or other jobs in which personal factors may be a major aspect of the work.

Psychologists differ in how they approach these interviews. Some rely extensively on batteries of tests. Others prefer in-depth interviews. Most use a combination of both.

The chief concern of the psychologist is the behavior pattern of the applicant. By probing into the manner in which the applicant has dealt with ups and downs faced over the years, a comprehensive picture of the individual can be developed.

Questions will be asked about joys and sorrows, successes and failures, likes and dislikes—not only on the job but in all aspects of life.

By eliciting detailed information about the applicant's actions and reactions in a variety of situations, the psychologist can develop a behavioral profile. This can be compared with the personality pattern needed for the job.

Employment Enigmas

There are many "consultants" who claim to offer psychological evaluations of applicants. Check the credentials. A qualified professional psychologist has a Ph.D. in psychology, is licensed by the state, and is a member of the American Psychological Association.

The psychologist's report will indicate the applicant's strengths and weaknesses and will recommend to hire or not to hire. If positive, it may add suggestions for working effectively with the individual.

Typical concluding comments may read like this:

➤ **Negative:** Mr. S's track record is not overly spectacular and is basically limited in scope. If he were to join your company, we do not think he would attain the kind of results required. Intelligent as he may be, we believe his personality and temperament would prevent him from functioning as anticipated, either as assistant to the president or as a potential line or operating manager.

➤ **Positive:** Although Ms. N. is not an outstanding candidate, she can work well under moderately close supervision. However, she does not show much imagination or innovation. Inasmuch as your job as office supervisor involves relatively structured and routine work, there is no doubt that she can perform this work satisfactorily. However, it is unlikely she will ever advance above this level. My final recommendation, in the absence of a superior candidate, is to employ her.

The use of psychological consultants is not recommended unless the company has a definite interest in the applicant. It's too expensive and time consuming to be undertaken otherwise.

Fitting the Evaluation into the Total Picture

You hire a total person—not just his or her job skills. More people fail in jobs because of personality problems than because of inability to perform the work. It is important to evaluate these factors.

The big danger in using psychological evaluations is that many managers do not really understand the results. They may misunderstand a comment or overemphasize a factor and reject a well-qualified applicant—or worse, hire someone for the wrong reason who most likely will fail.

For example, the trait that Rachel L. looked at first was initiative. She wanted people for her department who could work on projects, make decisions, and move ahead without having to be prodded. But the position for which she was hiring was highly structured and didn't require much initiative.

Another type problem may arise when the decision maker interprets the psychologist's report in a self-serving manner. For example, the report read: "The applicant has high leadership potential and a strong desire to move ahead in her career." The department supervisor thinks, "She'll be after my job. I don't want her."

Some reports use technical terminology that could be easily misunderstood by laymen. For example, a report refers to some arcane neurosis, which may be innocuous, but the supervisor worries that he'd be hiring a "nut case."

Hiring Hints

Decisions based on psychological reports should be restricted to human resources staffers who have the background to understand and interpret the report. If the applicant is hired, the psychological report should be kept in a confidential file, not with his or her personnel records.

The Least You Need to Know

➤ In a serialized interview process, each interviewer will rate the candidate on a standard evaluation form. The ratings are compared, and opinions from all the interviewers are elicited before the hiring decision is made.

➤ When a new member is being considered for a team, it's a good idea for other team members to interview him or her.

➤ Assessment centers are an excellent way to test the mettle of employees or applicants by giving them problems or exercises to complete in a brief time frame.

➤ Some of the typical areas explored in assessment centers are leadership, decision-making ability, oral and written communication, energy, forcefulness, dependence on others, and willingness to collaborate.

➤ Ascertaining competence to perform the job is important in making the hiring decision, but it's not the only factor. Equally important are the intangibles: the ability to work with others, stability, intelligence, adaptability, and many others.

➤ For certain jobs—particularly for senior-level positions but often for sales or other jobs in which personal factors may be a major aspect of the work—consider using a professional psychologist to evaluate candidates.

Part 6

Making the Hiring Decision

You've interviewed the applicants and have made some preliminary judgments. Were they good judgments? To give you more information about the candidate, additional steps could be taken.

A great many companies will test applicants. They may give them paper-and-pencil tests or performance tests at the facility, or they may send them to outside professionals for evaluation. In Chapter 20, you'll learn about testing and when and how it can be used effectively.

In addition, it's important to get as much information about a person you plan to hire before making that critical decision. How to get complete and honest information from former employers and others will be discussed in this part.

Once all the information is in place, you have to make up your mind. If you were fortunate enough to have several candidates, which one should you pick? If there is only one in the hopper, should you hire or pass and keep looking? We'll give you some guidelines.

And finally, you'll learn how to make an offer and persuade the person you want to accept it. You'll also pick up some tips on how to keep them once they're hired.

Chapter 20

Using Tests

In This Chapter

➤ To test or not to test

➤ Learning about the types of tests

➤ Determining who's qualified to administer tests

➤ Testing for honesty

➤ Giving the preemployment physical exam

In the effort to minimize subjectivity in making the hiring decision, for many years companies have used a variety of tests to help appraise applicants. These tests vary from gimmicky quizzes that are purported to predict success or failure on a job to well-designed, carefully validated instruments.

How and when can you use these tests in the employment process will be discussed in this chapter. In addition, we'll look at some nontraditional appraisal tools.

How Good Are Employment Tests?

Do tests help in choosing employees? Some companies swear by tests; others swear at them. In companies in which tests are used extensively as part of the screening process, the HR department or an independent testing organization does the testing. Except for performance tests (discussed later in this chapter), if you are not in the human resources department, it's unlikely that you will have to administer tests.

If testing is used in your company, however, it's important for you to be familiar with the types of tests used and to understand exactly what the test is designed to show.

Let's look at the most frequently used preemployment tests.

Intelligence Tests

Like the IQ tests used in schools, these tests measure the ability to learn. They vary from brief, simple exercises (such as the Wonderlic tests) that can be administered by people with little training to highly sophisticated tests that must be administered by someone who has a Ph.D. in psychology.

Recruiting Residuals

The first extensive use of testing to measure intelligence and aptitude was during World War I, when some two and a half million men were given the Army Alpha test before being assigned for military training. In World War II, more than 13 million servicemen and –women were tested as part of the military assignment process.

You've taken intelligence tests in school, if you served in the military, when you applied for college, and probably when you were being considered for past or present jobs. They are designed to measure mental capacity such as general intelligence, verbal fluency, numerical ability, and reasoning ability.

The best-known are the Binet-Stanford Test (the IQ test still used by many schools), the Scholastic Aptitude Test (SAT), the American College Test (ACT) the Graduate Management Aptitude Test (GMAT), and similar tests for law school, medical school, and other graduate programs.

These tests all measure cognitive ability such as reading comprehension, spatial relations, and other specific areas that make up general intelligence. Measures of general intelligence are known to be a good predictor of performance for many jobs.

The major flaw in using general intelligence tests is that two individuals who receive the same score can earn this score in very different ways. One may be high in reasoning, low in numerical skills, and average in verbal skills. The other may be high in numerical skills, low in reasoning, and average in verbal skills. They display entirely different intelligence profiles. Judging them by total score can be misleading. To get a true picture, the test has to be evaluated by the scores of its components.

Many companies stopped using intelligence tests after the Supreme Court case of *Griggs vs. Duke Power Co.* The court ruled that, for a test to be used in employment screening, it must be *validated* to be free from *cultural bias,* and the score on the test must be directly related to the ability to do the job. Since that time, testing has made a comeback. Tests have been rewritten to eliminate cultural bias, and companies have taken steps to validate the tests to prove that they do have relevance to job success. For example, "intelligence tests" contained questions about classical literature or Greek mythology—subjects biased against minorities who come from a culture where these subjects are less likely to be studied, and which are not relevant to ability to learn the job.

Words to Work By

When a test includes questions related to matters more likely to be familiar to people coming from a white, majority culture than to people from minority cultures, the test is considered to be **culturally biased.**

Aptitude Tests

These tests are designed to determine the potential of candidates in specific areas such as mechanical ability, clerical skills, and sales potential. Such tests are helpful in screening inexperienced people to determine whether they have aptitude in the type of work for which you plan to train them. Most aptitude tests can be administered and scored by following a simple instruction sheet.

Aptitude tests are very helpful in screening trainees. Because many applicants will have no work experience, these tests will give you a good concept of whether they are trainable. If a person is being considered for a job that calls for manual dexterity, there are tests that measure how fast and accurately the person can put pegs into holes, pick up parts with tweezers, or assemble minute parts using a magnifying glass.

Words to Work By

Tests must be proven to be **valid.** That is, they must actually measure what they are designed to measure. They must also be **reliable.** People must earn the same relative scores each time they are measured.

Clerical aptitude tests measure the ability to alphabetize names, remember series of numbers, or find and identify icons on a computer rapidly.

Performance Tests

These tests measure how well applicants can do the job for which they apply. Examples include operating a lathe, entering data into a computer, writing advertising copy, and proofreading manuscripts. When job performance cannot be tested directly, written or oral tests on job knowledge may be used.

It makes sense to ask an applicant to demonstrate his or her skill in performing the job. This is easy to do when the job is manual or routine. You can dictate a letter to a stenographer, have a word-processing operator set up a mass mailing, or watch an automobile mechanic fix a carburetor.

If the job calls for heavy physical activity such as climbing ladders, lifting heavy loads, or other strenuous activity, tests can be given to determine whether the applicant has the strength to perform them. Caution: Don't automatically reject a man or woman for these jobs because they "look weak." You must test all applicants being considered.

It's not so easy, however, when the job is more complex. There are no performance tests for managerial ability or most advanced jobs.

Some companies, as part of the screening process, have asked applicants for to develop programs or projects for them. This makes sense. Asking an applicant for a marketing position to develop a marketing program for a new product can provide insight into his or her methods of operation, creativity, and practicality. However, such tests can be carried too far.

One company asked an applicant for a training director's position to create a leadership-training program for team leaders. He worked on it for several days, submitted it, but didn't get the job. Some months later, he learned that the company was using his plan to train their team leaders. He billed the company for providing consulting services. When the company ignored his bill, he sued and won the case.

Interest Inventories

Vocational interest tests are primarily used by guidance counselors to help people choose careers. In these tests, The person taking the test is asked a series of questions to determine in what areas they have shown real interest. For example, he or she may indicate a long term interest in collecting coins or stamps, participating in competitive sports, playing a musical instrument and so on. Companies or guidance counselors then compare the pattern of interests shown in the test to the patterns of interest of people who have been successful in the type of work applied for. They compare the testee's answers against the profiles of people who have been successful in various fields. The basic philosophy behind the use of interest tests is that a person is more likely to do well and remain on a job that he or she enjoys. For example, successful salespeople may have a profile showing interests in sports, debating, and participating in social activities. Candidates for sales jobs who have similar profiles are more likely to be successful in sales.

Personality Tests

Personality tests are designed to identify personality characteristics. They vary from quickie questionnaires to highly sophisticated psychological evaluations. A great deal of controversy exists over the value of these types of tests. Supervisors and team leaders are cautioned not to make decisions based on the results of personality tests unless experts make the full implications clear to them.

A large number of organizations offer personality tests. You can obtain information about approved tests from the American Psychological Association, 750 First St., Washington, DC, 20002. Phone: 202-336-5500.

Selecting tests and similar assessment tools must be done very carefully. In buying a published test, ascertain the legitimacy of the publisher and the test by checking with the American Psychological Association and by contacting current and, if possible, past users of the test for their opinions.

Eric Samuelson, president of Management Development Institute of Alexandria, Virginia, poses five questions to ask when choosing an assessment tool:

➤ What traits does it measure and are they related to the job?

➤ Is it validated? What studies have been done to prove it works?

➤ Does it detect faking? How does it let you know about the accuracy and objectivity of the results?

➤ Does it compare applicants against a standard for the job?

➤ What can I do with the information after I hire someone? For instance, can I use the results to coach and supervise the applicant?

Employment Enigmas

Sometimes you just can't win. If you hire someone with a low test score and that person fails, management may blame you for not considering the test results. If the person succeeds, management often credits the test instead of complimenting you for using good judgment.

Human resources managers should always remember that the administration of one or more personality tests is not the same thing as a comprehensive personality assessment provided by an organizational psychologist. A comprehensive preemployment assessment by an industrial psychologist should include ability and personality measures plus an extensive interview. These assessments typically cost in the neighborhood of $500–$1,000 per candidate and should be based on an hourly rate charged by the psychologist. The professional psychologists association in your region will usually have a published recommended rate schedule for their members, and this may be used to verify that quoted charges for candidate assessments are within reason. Keep in mind that psychologists with training in industrial/organizational work should be entitled to charge slightly more than the minimum recommended rates due to the demand for their specialization.

Who Uses Employment Tests?

In 1998, the American Management Association (AMA) conducted a survey about workplace testing. Approximately 1,100 human resources managers participated. Because AMA corporate members are mostly mid-size and large companies, the data does not reflect the policies and practices of the U.S. economy as a whole, where small firms predominate.

In that survey, 48 percent of American employers reported that they use some form of psychological testing to assess abilities and behaviors for applicants. Tests measured cognitive ability, interests, managerial abilities, and personality. This was a significant increase from 1997, when only about 39 percent surveyed used some form of psychological testing.

Hiring Hints

Don't give up if at first the test doesn't seem to be predictive. It takes about two years to fine-tune a test that will best suit a company's needs.

In particular, the use of personality tests is on the rise. Such tests are used by 28 percent of respondents this year compared to 19 percent in 1997. Researchers said the high cost of recruiting—coupled with the high cost for making the wrong choice when hiring or promoting—has helped spur the increase.

As is true with all forms of testing, smaller organizations are less likely to conduct psychological tests than larger firms (39 percent of firms grossing less than $10 million compared to 54 percent of billion-dollar companies).

Nearly 65 percent of employers test applicants' job skills. This includes such tests such as typing, computing, or specific professional proficiencies (such as accounting, engineering, or marketing).

Administering Tests

As pointed out, some tests should only be administered by professional psychologists. However, many tests are designed for easy administration and evaluation. Company employees can be trained for this relatively easily.

If you choose to administer tests, they must be standardized to ensure accurate and consistent results. The test administrator should be thoroughly familiar with the test and should have answers ready for possible questions. Good test manuals provide these. Practice exercises and illustrations are helpful. Everything should be done to make the applicant feel at ease.

A satisfactory testing room should be available. It should be quiet, well-lit, and free from distractions, and it should have adequate desk space, computers, and other required equipment. Because many tests are timed, a stopwatch (or even better, an electronic timer) should be in place. Scoring of the tests should be prompt and accurate.

Manual tests usually are marked by comparing answers to a scoring stencil. To assure accuracy in grading, it's highly desirable to have more than one person mark the test. Today, many tests are administered and marked on a computer. Tests can be scored immediately.

For companies that don't have their own testing facilities, a Web-based centralized testing service is available. Test-and-train.com provides and scores tests covering computer programming, languages, arithmetic reasoning, word knowledge, and other skills. It also can customize tests for your special needs. Details can be found on the Web site or at 1-800-376-1118.

Nontraditional Approaches

For decades, companies have been seeking easy ways to identify applicants' personality traits and potential for success. Some study an applicant's horoscope to predict his or her potential. Others have retained consultants who promise amazing results by using a variety of "magic formulas." Do these methods work? Perhaps yes, perhaps no. Because objective studies are rarely made on these approaches, we must depend on the reports of the users. As you might expect, they are mixed. Companies usually start out enthusiastic about such tests, pointing out the early successes. But the majority of such companies tire quickly of these gimmicks, drop them, and go on to another gimmick that some sharp sales rep pitches to them.

Face Reading

Recently, a television magazine program discussed a new and controversial approach to evaluating personality characteristics—face reading. Originally developed by Mac Fulfer, a Texas attorney, as a tool for jury selection, its use has been expanded to personnel selection.

Fuller conducts seminars and has been retained by several large companies to train their HR staffs in this technique. With much anecdotal evidence as proof, Fulfer claims that the structure of a person's face reveals his or her thinking style. It can also identify problem-solving preferences, stress level, degree of openness, intimacy requirements, and even the basic truthfulness of the person.

Most psychologists pooh-pooh this approach as quackery and point out there have been no scientific, objective studies made of its effectiveness.

Hiring Hints

Over the years, hundreds of "short-cut" programs for effective hiring have been available ranging from lists of knockout factors to computerized personnel profiles. Consider them with skepticism. Some may have some value, but most disappear after a few years.

However, Fulfer presents much anecdotal evidence of its accuracy. Is it a gimmick or a useful tool? You can judge for yourself.

For more information, read Mac Fulfer's book, *Amazing Face Reading* (Creative Alternatives, 1997).

Handwriting Analysis

Not all, nontraditional screening techniques fit into the "gimmick" category. Some, like handwriting analysis, have been around for years. Although determining personality characteristics by analyzing handwriting has been used for decades in Europe, it has not been used extensively in the United States.

By studying a sample of the applicant's handwriting, the handwriting analyst (graphologist) can pinpoint strengths and weaknesses of the candidate. Handwriting can also measure specific factors such as attention to detail, persistence, self-esteem, stubbornness, energy, creativity, honesty, and ability to relate to others.

For more information about graphology, see the Web site of the American Society of Professional Graphologists (web.singnet.com.sg/~tjlow/graphology/grapho.htm).

Organizations using handwriting analysis say they prefer it to a typical personality test because it only requires job candidates to take a few minutes to jot down a short essay. By contrast, a battery of personality tests and interviews with psychologists can take several hours and can cost several thousand dollars.

HR executives in companies that use handwriting analysis report that they are relatively good predictors of personality as compared to other personality tests, but their predictability for job performance is questionable. It's a helpful tool, but it cannot replace well-conducted interviews and performance tests.

Words to Work By

Polygraph tests are purported to determine whether a person is telling the truth by measuring changes in heartbeat, blood pressure, and respiration when responding to a series of questions.

Other Tests

Companies test for other things in addition to personality, intelligence, performance, and aptitude. Two areas that are of particular concern are honesty and drug use.

Polygraph Tests

To ensure that applicants are responding to their questions honestly, some companies request that applicants submit to *polygraph tests*, also known as lie-detector tests. Polygraphs have been used for years in criminal investigations. By applying this to job seekers and sometimes current employees, misrepresentations can be uncovered.

As pointed out in Chapter 4, "Watch Your Language," the Employee Protection Act of 1988 has prohibited the use of polygraphs except in certain special cases.

Honesty Inventories

To replace the polygraph, some employers instituted the use of paper-and-pencil honesty and integrity tests. Questions are asked about attitudes and opinions on such things as the frequency of theft in our society, white lies, punishment for theft, and related matters.

These tests tend to be quite expensive (in the range of $30 to more than $100 per examinee). Test developers have justified the price of these tests based on development costs and potential savings arising from not hiring employees who steal, who are unreliable, or who are likely to take stress leave or abuse the company benefits plan.

There is no solid evidence that these tests are valid, but many companies who have used them feel they do provide information about the applicant's attitudes that can predict possible lack of integrity.

Hiring Hints

There are no official licensing requirements for people practicing handwriting analysis. To ensure that the person you are dealing with is qualified, verify their certification by the American Society of Professional Graphologists, the organization that maintains professionalism in this field.

Testing for Drug Use

Drug testing has become more commonplace in recent years. Many companies require applicants to be tested for drug use as part of their preemployment physical exam or as a separate test.

By far, the most frequently used test is urine sampling. In some cases, people who test positively are given blood tests to verify the original results.

It is not illegal to give drug tests, but there are limitations imposed on government contractors. The Federal Drug-Free Workplace Act requires that all federal contractors with contracts of more than $25,000 do the following:

➤ Publish a statement notifying employees that manufacturing, distributing, and using controlled substances is prohibited in the workplace.

Employment Enigmas

Drug test results may be wrong. Retest applicants who test positively. In addition, a urine analysis may incorrectly indicate signs of drug use. Some medications cause the same reaction that drugs do. Before rejecting the applicant, have this possibility investigated by medical experts.

➤ Establish a drug-free awareness program to inform employees of (1) the danger of drug abuse in the workplace, (2) the employer's policy of maintaining a drug-free workplace, (3) any available drug counseling, rehabilitation, and employee assistance programs, and (4) the penalties for drug-abuse violations.

➤ Employees must be given a copy of the policy statement and agree to abide by it.

➤ Violators will be punished or will be required to undertake rehabilitation.

To enforce this regulation, most government contractors require applicants to take a drug test and may require employees to take such tests periodically.

Companies who are engaged in interstate transportation are required to follow even stricter rules.

Medical Exams

Companies give preemployment medical exams to applicants for several reasons. One reason is that they want to make sure the health of the applicant is adequate to meet the job requirements. Some applicants may have medical conditions that would be aggravated by the work involved. For example, people with back problems should not be hired for jobs calling for heavy labor. Another reason is that the preemployment medical exam serves as a baseline against which subsequent medical exams can be compared. This is important in determining work-caused disabilities in workers' compensation matters.

The Health Questionnaire

Part of many preemployment medical exams is the health questionnaire. Applicants are asked a series of questions about their health and often that of their families. They may be asked to indicate any diseases or medical conditions they have suffered at any time in their lives.

The purpose of this is to aid the physician in making a through evaluation of the applicant's medical condition. It may be a great help to the doctor, but in the past, it often led to rejection by the company without the benefit of a medical expert. When the interviewer noted an "undesirable" condition, the applicant was dropped.

Carol L. checked off the box that asked if she had ever had cancer. Although her mastectomy occurred 10 years ago and she has been cancer-free since her operation, she was rejected and was not even sent for a physical exam. Allan D. checked the box that inquired about hypertension. Although his medication keeps his blood pressure under control, he too was rejected without a medical exam. In both cases, it's likely the physicians would have considered the applicants suitable for most jobs.

Under the Americans with Disabilities Act, no questions may be asked about health until after the decision is made to send the applicant for a medical exam. Health questionnaires may be given to the applicant only by the medical department. The completed forms are not seen by HR or line managers. If the person is hired, they should be placed in the employee's personnel file and should be kept in a separate file with other medical records.

Who Gives the Exam—and When?

Most large companies have their own medical department. Smaller companies either retain a physician or, more likely, contract a medical group in the community to do the testing.

Because it's costly to give a thorough medical examination, most companies will only send applicants in whom they have serious interest for these procedures.

The American with Disabilities Act (ADA) requires that a medical exam be given only after the decision to hire is made. The exam cannot be used as a reason for rejection unless a person's physical condition is a job-related issue and the company cannot make accommodation for it.

Can Medical Exams Be Knockout Factors?

The Americans with Disabilities Act has made it almost impossible to reject an applicant on medical grounds. As pointed out in Chapter 3, "What the Laws on Employment Cover," the company is obligated to find ways to accommodate the disability.

If it can be proven to the satisfaction of the authorities, however, that there is a legitimate medical reason for requiring certain physical standards for a job and that accommodation is not feasible, the qualification can be required.

For example, a job calls for continuous heavy physical exertion that would strain the heart; being free from any heart problems would be a legitimate requirement. Determination of these factors, however, must be made by physicians and not by line managers, human resources staffers, or just a long-established custom.

Medical exams have a place in the hiring process, but consideration must be given to the job relatedness of the medical requirements, the confidentiality of the information, and the company's compliance with the Americans with Disabilities Act.

The Least You Need to Know

➤ Intelligence tests are designed to measure mental capacity such as general intelligence, verbal fluency, numerical ability, and reasoning ability.

➤ Aptitude tests are designed to determine the potential of candidates in specific areas such as mechanical ability, clerical skills, and sales potential. Such tests are helpful in determining whether applicants have the aptitude to perform the type of work for which you plan to train them.

➤ In performance tests, applicants are asked to demonstrate how they'd perform an actual part of the job for which they are being considered. For these tests to be valid, you must give the same test in the same manner to all applicants.

➤ Personality tests are designed to identify personality characteristics. They vary from quickie questionnaires to highly sophisticated psychological evaluations.

➤ Medical exams have a place in the hiring process, but consideration must be given to the job relatedness of the medical requirements, the confidentiality of the information, and the company's compliance with the Americans with Disabilities Act.

HELLO,
STATE
PEN

Checking References

Applicants can tell you anything they want about their experiences—but how do you know they're telling the truth? A reference check is one of the oldest approaches to verifying a background, but is it reliable? Former employers unfortunately don't always tell the whole truth about candidates. They may be reluctant to make negative statements, either because they don't want to prevent the person from working—as long it's not for them—or because they fear they might be sued. Still, a reference check is virtually your only source of verification.

Conducting the Reference Check

The purpose of the reference check is to verify the information obtained in the interview and to learn as much as possible about the applicant from people who are knowledgeable about his or her experience and background. A thorough reference check will also give you an idea of what you can expect in the future based on what has been done in the past. Check references after you believe an applicant has a reasonable chance of being hired. If you have more than one finalist, check each one before making a final decision.

Recruiting Residuals

According to a study conducted by the Society for Human Resources Management, 55 percent of applicants lied about the length of previous employment, 52 percent about past salaries, 44 percent about criminal records, and 28 percent about degrees attained.

Letters of Reference

One of the oldest and best-known types of reference is the letter of reference given to an employee when he or she leaves a company. This is not as common today in the United States as it was years ago, but it is still used extensively in other countries. Such a letter may state the following:

To whom it may concern:

Mr. William Crane was in our employ as a transportation clerk from September 1994 to March 2000. He is diligent, honest, and reliable. His performance reviews have always been at the highest levels.

Hiring Hints

Shakespeare said, "What is past is prologue." A comprehensive investigation of an applicant's past may be the best predictor of his or her potential for the open position.

Unfortunately, due to a company downsizing, the transportation department has been discontinued.

We highly recommend Mr. Crane to you.

This same letter with various wordings has been written an infinite number of times. What does it convey to the reader? Very little. It has as little meaning as the usual answer to "How are you?"

Some executives, when asked for a letter of reference, tell the employee to write it himself for the executive's signature. No employer writes a bad letter of reference. No applicant in his or her right mind would show such a letter to a prospective employer.

Writing to Former Employers

Many companies send routine form letters to former employers. All they ask are simple verification questions: job title, dates of employment, reason for leaving, and perhaps a few comments on the quality of work.

Some employers write individual letters to former employers asking for an opinion of the applicant's work. Often these letters are vague and, of course, result in vague responses.

Other letters are more detailed, asking specific questions about performance, personality, and other pertinent data. These letters, if answered frankly, can give far better information than a general letter or brief form. The questions must be worded carefully and should cover the key areas important to your job requirements.

The downside is that many people are reluctant to put anything of an adverse nature in writing. If a former employer writes anything derogatory in a letter and it gets into the wrong hands, the writer and the company may be sued for defamation. Even if what has been written is perfectly true, the writer must go through the trouble and expense of a defense. And if the information is subjective, such as "Ms. K. was lazy" or "Mr. L. was stubborn," it may be hard to prove.

The Telephone Check

Most reference checks are made by telephone. To make the best of a difficult situation, you must carefully plan the reference check and use diplomacy in conducting it.

The following list provides some tips for making a telephone reference check:

> ➤ **Call an applicant's immediate supervisor.** Try to avoid speaking to the company's HR staff members. The only information they usually have is what's on file. An immediate supervisor can give you details about exactly how that person worked in addition to his or her personality factors and other significant traits.

> ➤ **Begin your conversation with a friendly greeting.** Then ask whether the employer can verify some information about the applicant.

Most people don't mind verifying data. Ask a few verification questions about date of employment, job title, and other items from the application.

Hiring Hints

Unless company policy requires that the human resources department make reference checks, the team leader or supervisor should do it. That person has more insight into the job and can react to responses with follow-up questions to determine whether the applicant's background fits the needs.

➤ **Diplomatically shift to a question that requires a substantive answer.** This question should not call for an opinion, however. Respond with a comment about the answer, as in this example:

You: Tell me about her duties in dealing with customers.

Supervisor: [Gives details of the applicant's work.]

You: That's very important in the job she is seeking because she'll be on the phone with customers much of the time.

By commenting about what you have learned, you make the interchange a conversation—not an interrogation. You're making telephone friends with the former supervisor. You're building a relationship that will make him or her more likely to give opinions about an applicant's work performance, attitudes, and other valuable information.

➤ **Move into evaluative questions.** Continue in this manner for next five or six questions. By this time, you and the former supervisor are telephone friends, and he or she is more likely to give opinions about the applicant's work, personality, strengths, and weaknesses.

➤ **"Listen" for reluctance and uncertainty.** Once the conversation is moving along, you can sense when the former supervisor is holding something back. You can tell you're not getting the full story by the voice, the hesitation in responding, or the vagueness of the answers. In the section "All I Can Tell You Is That She Worked Here" later in this chapter, you'll learn how to deal with this.

Employment Enigmas

Follow the same guidelines in asking questions of the reference as in interviewing applicants. You can't ask an applicant whether she has young children, and you can't attempt to get this type of information from the reference.

To ensure that you cover all bases, it's a good idea to prepare a telephone reference worksheet.

Complete the top section before you pick up the phone. Note that, after the introduction, the first three questions are "verification" questions. Then some questions are asked to probe duties and responsibilities, and finally, questions ask for an opinion of the applicant. Item #6, specific questions related to the job, is very important. Here you can probe for such things as technical knowledge, leadership responsibilities, creativity, and matters that are indicators of ability to do the job involved.

Use it as a model to develop your own form to meet the special needs of your company.

Telephone Reference Worksheet

Name of applicant _____

Position applied for: _____ Dept. _____

Company contacted: _____

Person spoken to: _____ Title: _____

Suggested introduction: Hello, I'm _____ of (company) _____ . We are considering one of your former employees, (name of applicant), for a position as (job title) _____ . I'd appreciate a few minutes of your time to verify some facts about his/her background.

1. (State applicant's name) said that he/she was employed as (job title) _____ _____ from _____ (date) _____ to _____ (date) _____ .

Is this correct? _____ (If not, insert correct dates: _____ .)

2. He/she stated that her salary was $ _____ per _____. Is this correct? (If not, indicate correct figure: _____ .)

3. He/she stated that his/her work included (list a few major activities from resumé, application form, and interview notes):

Activity	Comments
_____	_____
_____	_____
_____	_____
_____	_____
_____	_____

Is this correct? _____

4. Can you tell me some of the other activities in which he/she was engaged?

_____
_____
_____

5. In which of these activities did he/she perform most effectively?

_____
_____
_____

continues

continued

6. List here additional specific questions related to your job specs or other facets of background you wish to explore.

_____

_____

_____

_____

_____

_____

_____

_____

_____

_____

7. In which of these activities did you have to give him/her added support?

_____

_____

_____

_____

8. What were some of his/her greatest accomplishments in this job?

_____

_____

_____

_____

9. During the time spent in your company, what progress did he/she make in terms of being given added responsibilities, promotions, and salary increases other than routine cost-of-living raises?

_____

_____

_____

_____

10. How did (applicant's name) get along with co-workers?

_____

_____

11. Can you comment on:

Attendance _____

_____

Dependability _____

_____

Ability to take on responsibility _____

_____

_____

Potential for advancement _____

_____

_____

Degree of supervision needed _____

_____

_____

Overall attitude_____

_____

_____

12. Why did he/she leave the company? _____

_____

_____

13. If there were an opening in your company for a person with (applicant's name)'s background, would you consider him/her for that position? _____

(If not, why?) _____

_____

_____

14. Is there anything else we should know about (applicant's name) before we make our hiring decision?

_____

_____

_____

Notes and comments: _____

_____

_____

_____

Reference check conducted by _____ Date _____

Personal Visits

When checking the references of future key personnel, a personal visit to the former employer can be extremely effective. It has all the advantages of the telephone conversation plus the personal touch that only a face-to-face meeting can establish.

Much valuable information and a clear analysis of the prospective employee can be obtained. The time spent is usually well worth it.

Before making the visit, carefully decide what information you are most interested in obtaining. There's no point in just verifying routine background information. Concentrate your time on the soft skills. Learn as much as you can about the applicant's ability to work with others, to be a leader, to innovate, to communicate idea to people at all levels, and if pertinent, to represent the company in dealing with customers, banks, vendors, the government, and stockholders.

Don't be afraid to ask hard questions. You may not get all the answers you'd like, but you may pick up information that could make the difference between hiring an average person who could do the job just okay and a superior person who would be a significant contributor to the company's bottom line.

Hiring Hints

When checking with a former boss in person, watch the face and body language of that executive. Look for hints that there's more below the surface than is being conveyed. If so, probe for the respondent's attitudes and deep feelings about the candidate. Explore all areas of doubt.

What About Personal References?

Companies often ask applicants to give them some personal references—people who know them and can vouch for their character. These often are clergy, the family physician, or personal friends.

This is usually a waste of time. Applicants are unlikely to name somebody as a reference who might say something unfavorable. The time and effort spent checking personal references would be better spent with someone who has had business contacts with the candidate. For young people with little or no work experience, teachers or school administrators are your best bet.

Schools and Colleges

One area that is frequently misrepresented is education. Applicants claim degrees they don't have, years of schooling in excess of the actual number, majors in subjects in which they took only one course, and extracurricular activities in which they never were involved.

Surprisingly, many companies never check education. Most schools will, at a minimum, verify whether a person is a graduate of that institution. But this is not enough. Schools will send you transcripts of the student's grades and other activities. Most schools and colleges require written permission from the former student and often charge a small fee. If you have serious interest in the applicant, it's worth the time it takes and the money spent.

Contacting teachers or guidance counselors may be helpful. Letters given to the students by teachers should be considered in the same way as other letters of reference handed to you. The only way to get meaningful information is to telephone the teacher and ask specific questions, just as you would when phoning a former supervisor.

How to Avoid Getting Meaningless Information

Reference checks can be a valuable tool or a waste of time and effort. It all depends on whom you talk to and what you ask. To complicate matters, many companies are reluctant to give any information at all. Let's look at how to cope with these matters.

Who to Talk To

As noted earlier in this chapter, try to avoid speaking only to somebody in the human resources department. The best source is usually the applicant's immediate supervisor. Either on the application form or at the interview, get this person's name, title, and telephone number or extension.

Before making the call, check with the company to make sure the person named is (or was) actually the applicant's supervisor. Debbie was sure that her ex-boss, Arlene, would give her a mediocre reference, so she listed Amy, a co-worker, as her supervisor. In checking the reference, the HR staffer who made the check routinely asked the telephone operator for the name of the department supervisor. When she was told, "Arlene," she commented, "Isn't that Amy's department?" "Amy works there," was the response, "but Arlene's the manager."

One of my clients was taken in by this scam. When Harold was fired from his job, he knew he'd get a bad reference. On his application form, he noted that his work was under the supervision of an outside consultant. He listed the name of a consultant-friend who had no connection at all to the company. When my client called, he received a glowing reference. A few months after the man was hired, my client attended a business luncheon and was seated next to an executive from Harold's former company. He casually commented that he had hired one of his former people. He could tell from that executive's facial expression that he seemed surprised. My client commented that he was disappointed in his performance and couldn't understand how he could have done so well in the old job and so poorly in the new. That's when he learned that Harold had been fired and that the man from the old company had never heard of the "consultant" given as a reference.

Seven Questions You Must Get Answers To

In the telephone reference checklist (see the section "The Telephone Check" earlier in this chapter), you'll find several good questions to ask. As pointed out, it's important to ask specific questions about job activities and performance. Whether or not you use this checklist, here are seven key questions that will provide significant information to help you make a good hiring decision:

1. What is your opinion of the applicant's work in relation to other people assigned to similar work?

2. What do you consider to be his or her strengths?

3. In what areas does he or she need to improve?

4. Why did he or she leave your company?

5. If the applicant were to reapply for a position with your company or another company where you had the power to hire or reject, would you hire him or her? If not, why not?

6. Is there anything else of significance we should know about (applicant's name) that will help us make him or her more effective if we should hire him or her?

    Thank the reference for taking the time to talk to you and for the frankness and sincerity with which he or she responded to the questions. Then, as almost an afterthought, ask:

7. Do you have any further comments you'd like to make about (applicant's name)?

Because you've developed a good rapport with this person, and because you seemingly have concluded the questioning by your thanks, his or her guard has been lowered and additional information—good or bad—may be added.

All I Can Tell You Is That She Worked Here

In today's litigious climate, companies have been advised by their attorneys to be extremely careful about what they say in response to a call for a reference. There have been lawsuits for defamation of character against firms that gave negative information. As a result, many employers will only verify that the former employee worked at the company and give dates of employment, little else.

Sometimes you can still obtain needed information using diplomacy and persuasion. It's worth a try.

If the former employer refuses outright to answer a question, don't push. Point out that you understand his/her reluctance. Then ask another question (but don't repeat the same one). After the responses begin coming more freely, you can return to the original question, preferably using different words.

What happens if you believe the person you're speaking to is holding something back? What if you sense from the person's voice that he or she is hesitating to provide answers? What if you detect a vagueness that says you're not getting the full story? Here's one way to handle this situation:

> "Mr. Controller, I appreciate you taking the time to talk to me about Alice Accountant. The job we have is very important to our firm, and we cannot afford to make a mistake. Are there any special problems we might face if we hire Alice?"

Here's another approach: "Ivan will need some special training for this job. Can you point out any areas to which we should give particular attention?" From the answer you receive, you may pick up some information about Ivan's weaknesses.

Dealing with Poor References

Suppose everything about Carlos seems fine, and in your judgment he's just right for the job. When you call his previous employer, however, you get a bad reference. What do you do?

If you have received good reports from Carlos's other references, it's likely that the poor reference is based on a personality conflict or some other factor unrelated to his work. Contact other people in the company who are familiar with his work and get their input.

Anna's previous boss tells you she was a sloppy worker. Check it out some more. Anna's ex-boss may be a perfectionist who isn't satisfied with anyone.

Employment Enigmas

In answer to the question "Would you rehire?" don't accept the response, "It's against company policy to rehire people who have left." Rephrase the question as "If you were in my position, would your hire (applicant's name)?"

Hiring Hints

Don't automatically reject an applicant if you get a poor reference. Arrange for another interview. Don't mention the poor reference but ask questions that may uncover the reason for it. Hold your judgment until you know the entire story.

When you contact Pierre's former supervisor, you hear a diatribe about how awful he was. But you notice that he held that job for eight years. If he had been so bad, how come he worked there for such a long time? Maybe his ex-boss resents his leaving and is taking revenge.

Lucy's ex-boss comments that her work was unsatisfactory. References from her other jobs are excellent. Don't take this one at face value. Interview Lucy again. You may find that she had a personality conflict with this last boss. Elicit the names of others in the company who could give you an unbiased report.

Words to Work By

If you check an applicant through a **credit bureau,** you'll get information about his or her financial stability, lawsuits, bankruptcies, and related matters. If you check through an **investigative agency,** you'll learn about an applicant's reputation in the community, criminal records, and verification of employment history.

Using Outside Investigators

Sometimes there's information you'd like to know about an applicant that cannot be obtained from a standard reference check. For example, for jobs with fiduciary responsibility, it's important to learn about the financial stability of an applicant. You don't want embezzlers, people with money problems, or people with unstable backgrounds.

Types of Investigative Services

There are two basic types of investigative services:

➤ National credit-checking companies
➤ National investigative agencies

National credit-checking companies are the most frequently used investigative service. These companies have ongoing dossiers on almost everybody in the country. Every time you take out a bank loan, finance a car or furniture, or sign up for a credit card, information about you is reported to these organizations. They often claim to know more about people than they know about themselves.

Subscribers to one or more of these firms can get credit reports on any applicant—and often do. Whether this information is pertinent to the job is disputable. Some employers feel it gives them a more complete picture of a prospect than just his or her job record.

The three major credit-checking organizations are Equifax, www.equifax.com, 1-888-532-0179; Experian, www.experian.com, 888-EXPERIAN; and Trans Union, www.transunion.com (no toll-free line, check local listings for an office near you).

National investigative agencies have trained investigators, often former FBI or police agents, who are skilled in checking people out. The major services in this area have their own staffs or correspondents in every major city and can uncover information about the applicant's personal life as well as job factors.

An employer using these services gives the nearest branch office of the investigative firm the basic facts about an applicant. These are transmitted to the various agents in cities where the applicant has worked and lived. The agents make personal visits to former employers, neighbors, and others who may know the applicant. They check his or her work history, attitudes, sobriety, personal habits, and reputation.

The advantage of using outside agencies to verify the applicant's work background is that they are professionals and know where to go and how to get information. Their national facilities make it possible for personal checks to be made wherever the applicant may have worked. Their reports are objective and concise.

The major problem in using these services is that the investigators rarely understand the specific job and the personality factors needed to succeed in it. Only people close to a job know these factors, and these intangibles are often difficult to communicate to others. Only company personnel or consultants working closely with the company can uncover these factors.

Employment Enigmas

Never tell an applicant that he or she is hired "subject to a reference check." If the references are good but you choose another candidate, an applicant will assume you received a poor reference. Also, never tell a person that the reason for rejection is a poor reference. Reference information should be treated as confidential.

The Law

The Fair Credit Reporting Act requires that, if you use an outside credit or investigating service, you must provide the applicant with written notification that you might obtain a report on his or her background from an outside agency and that, if such an investigation is conducted, he or she can request a copy of that report from the investigative agency.

If the applicant requests such a report, you are only obligated to refer him or her to the agency that made the report. It's the agency's responsibility to provide it within a reasonable period of time.

Many companies incorporate the request for permission to order the report into their application forms. Because the law requires that applicants be given written notification that such a report may be requested, some companies prefer to print the notification on a separate form with a copy for the applicant.

Some states have stricter laws that require a company to obtain written permission from the applicant before an investigative report can be ordered. Check your state laws for what is applicable to your company.

The Least You Need to Know

➤ The purpose of a reference check is to verify the information obtained in the interview and to learn as much as possible about the applicant from people who are knowledgeable about his or her experience and background.

➤ If a former employer writes anything derogatory in a letter and it gets into the wrong hands, the writer and the company may be sued for defamation. Even if what has been written is perfectly true, the writer must go through the trouble and expense of a defense.

➤ When making a telephone reference check, avoid speaking to the company's HR staff members. An immediate supervisor can give you details about exactly how that person worked in addition to his or her personality factors and other significant traits.

➤ Don't automatically reject an applicant if you get a poor reference. Arrange for another interview. Don't mention the poor reference but ask questions that may uncover the reason for it. Hold your judgment until you know the entire story.

➤ The Fair Credit Reporting Act requires that, if you use an outside credit or investigating service, you must provide the applicant with written notification that you might obtain a report on his or her background from an outside agency and that, if such an investigation is conducted, he or she may request a copy of that report from the investigative agency.

Making the Decision

The interviews are over. References have been checked. You now have to decide which candidate to hire. This can be one of the most important decisions you are required to make as a manager.

This has become even more significant today. In his book *Effective Leadership Programs* (ASTD, 1999), Dr. Franklin C. Ashby points out that the old hierarchical structure in which top management made all the decisions has been replaced with a more collaborative, team-based, cross-functional organization in which important decisions are made at all levels. This means that, no matter what level the job is at, choosing the right person is key to the success of your organization.

You have all the information about the applicants that is needed to make your choice. In this chapter, you'll find out what to do and what not to do at this critical juncture.

Don't Kid Yourself

Some people boast about their ability to judge people. Yet when asked upon what basis they make this judgment, the reason is often superficial:

"He had a firm handshake."

"She looked me straight in the eye."

"He went to the same college I did."

"She comes from a fine family."

When hiring a person, the decision must be made on much more substantial bases. Let's look at some of the common fallacies that result in hiring the wrong person.

Employment Enigmas

Finding the perfect employee is virtually impossible. In today's market, you'll be lucky if you can find a person who is 80 percent ready for the job. In making the choice, keep in mind that whoever you hire will require training, coaching, and support.

Overemphasis on Appearance

In most contacts with people, our immediate reaction is to their appearance. A person whose physical characteristics, dress, and presence are pleasant, neat, and attractive starts off on the right foot in most interpersonal relationships. This does not mean that you should judge the book solely by its cover or that you should give preference to handsome men and beautiful women. Neatness, a pleasant countenance, and good taste in dress and grooming are important.

This doesn't mean that certain aspects of appearance shouldn't be considered. For example, if the applicant's mode of dress or other aspects of his or her appearance are unconventional, it may turn you off. "How can I hire a man with a handlebar mustache?" "Why does she wear such an odd outfit?" For jobs calling for dealing with customers, these may be negative factors. But for other jobs, they shouldn't influence your decision. Some psychologists point out that such idiosyncrasies provide insight into the applicant's personality. Probing questions and, perhaps, interviews by psychologists might bring out what the applicant is consciously or subconsciously projecting.

We Favor People Like Ourselves

Tom's staff members were all alumni of his university. Even though Beth worked in Chicago, her assistant and secretary were both from Iowa, her home state. When Tom and Beth were questioned on why they selected these people, their responses included comments on job qualifications, personality traits, and intelligence. Neither manager considered the similarity of their backgrounds to be a factor.

One tends to subconsciously favor people whose backgrounds are close to one's own. There is a comfortable feeling when dealing with people who have shared a similar environment or experience. This can be an asset in that working relationships can be developed more rapidly and more easily. However, it may lead to choosing a less qualified candidate. When all the people in a work group have analogous backgrounds, there's an inclination for them to think alike and be less open to new ideas.

Hiring Hints

Be aware of your own biases—pro and con. If you know you are influenced positively or negatively by certain aspects of an applicant's background, neutralize it when you make the hiring decision.

Can the Applicant Do the Job?

Your basic tools to determine job qualifications are the job description and the job specifications. As pointed out earlier in this book, some job specs are absolutely essential. Applicants who don't meet these specs be eliminated early in the process. All applicants under consideration at this stage of the process should be qualified to do the job. Your responsibility is to select the best one.

Although all the surviving applicants meet the basic specs, they all offer different degrees of expertise in key areas as well as additional qualifications. For example, Betty and Sue both have been operating room nurses. Betty's experience has been in a hospital in a small community, and she hasn't worked with the sophisticated equipment that Sue, who worked in a large hospital, has. Your hospital doesn't have this equipment at this time but is planning to install it. Your decision between Betty and Sue would depend on their total backgrounds. Sue's experience is an asset, but perhaps Betty is a better overall candidate with the potential to learn to use the new equipment when it is installed.

Do They Have Those Critical Intangibles?

Meeting the job specs is just part of the decision-making process. Equally important is having the intangible factors that make the difference between just doing a job and doing it well. Let's look at some of these factors and how to evaluate them when interviewing the candidates.

Self-Confidence

When Jeremy was interviewed, he exuded self-confidence. He was not afraid to talk about his failures and was unlike people who try to impress interviewers by bragging about their accomplishments. Jeremy was matter-of-fact about his successes. He projected an image of being totally secure in his feelings about his capabilities. It is likely that Jeremy will manifest this self-confidence on the job, enabling him to adapt readily to the new situation.

Fluency of Expression

Laura was able to discuss her background easily and fluently. She did not hesitate or grasp for words. When the interviewer probed for details, she was ready with statistics, examples, and specific applications. This indicates not only her expertise but her ability to communicate—an essential ingredient in many jobs.

There are some glib people, however, who can talk a great job but have only cursory experience or knowledge of it. They learn and use the jargon of the field. To determine if an applicant is a talker but not a doer, ask in-depth questions and probe for specific examples of his or her work. Glib phonies cannot come up with meaningful answers.

Alertness

Diane sparkled at the interview. She reacted to your questions and comments with her facial expressions and gestures. You could see she was on her toes. Alert, sparkling applicants are usually dynamic and exciting people who give their all to their jobs.

Maturity

Maturity cannot be measured by the chronological age of a person. Young people can be very mature, and older people may still manifest childlike emotions. Mature applicants are not hostile or defensive. They do not interpret questions as barbs from a "prosecutor out to catch them." They do not show self-pity or have excuses for all their past failures or inadequacies. They can discuss their weaknesses as readily as their strengths.

Sense of Humor

Evan was a sourpuss. At no time during the interview did he smile or relax. Even when you tried to lighten up the interview with a humorous comment, he barely reacted. This may be due to nervousness, but it's more likely that Evan is one of those very serious people who never look at the lighter side of things. They are difficult to supervise and are impossible to work with in a team. It is easier and much more fun to work with a person who has a sense of humor. On the other hand, applicants who are too frivolous, tell inappropriate jokes, laugh raucously, or act inconsistently with the situation may be immature.

Intelligence

Although some aspects of intelligence can be measured by tests, we can pick up a great deal about the type of intelligence a person has at an interview. If the job calls for rapid reactions to situations as they develop (for example, a job in sales), a person who responds to questions rapidly and sensibly has the kind of intelligence needed for the job. However, if the person is applying for a job in which it is important to ponder a question before coming up with an answer (for example, a job as a research engineer), a slow but well-thought-out response may be indicative of the type of intelligence required.

Warmth

This very important intangible asset is difficult to describe but you know when it is there. A warm person reacts to you, is empathetic, and shows real concern about the matters discussed. This person will talk freely about interpersonal relations. He or she is comfortable at the interview and makes you feel comfortable. An individual with this type of personality is at ease in any environment and will fit into the department rapidly and naturally. They are likable people and are easy to live and work with.

Sensitivity to Feedback

Applicants who understand what you are projecting—not only in your questions and in your comments but also with your body language—will probably do the same on the job. This is an asset that is invaluable in the workplace. Such people are easy to train. They readily accept and implement instruction and criticism, and they work well with their peers.

Naturalness

A person who is natural and relaxed probably is a well-integrated person. However, do not automatically negate a nervous applicant. Reaching such a person and determining what latent characteristics may exist beneath his or her uneasiness calls for skill, patience, and determination. The person's nervousness may be masking his or her real self.

Growth Potential

The job for which you are hiring can lead to rapid advancement into more responsible positions. In making your decision, keep in mind the potential of the candidate. Does he or she have what it takes to move up the ladder? Potential for growth is an important factor in choosing the best candidate for this opening.

Leonora L., an African American woman, couldn't understand why she was rejected for a position as a data-entry clerk. She had three years of excellent experience and had been told she did very well in the performance tests. She noted that the job had been filled with a white woman, and she felt her race had been a factor.

In response to the complaint, the company stated that Leonora was rejected because she didn't have any background in working with spreadsheets. When the EEOC investigator noted that the job description didn't mention working with spreadsheets, she was told that, to be promoted from the data-entry job, it was necessary to know that area. The EEOC ruled in favor of Leonora. They pointed out that an applicant cannot be rejected for an open job on the grounds that he or she is not qualified for a possible future job. If knowledge of spreadsheets is needed in the future, she could be trained in that work while employed in the lower-level position. The company must hire Leonora or work out a financial settlement.

It used to be that top management made all the decisions and filtered them down through a series of layers to the rank-and-file workers. We have seen and continue to see this being replaced by a more collaborative organization in which people at all levels are expected to contribute to every aspect of their organization's activities.

Getting things done is now assumed by groups of people usually headed by a team leader. Together as a team, they plan, implement, and control the work.

The essence of a *team* is common commitment. Without it, the members of the group perform as individuals; with it, they become a powerful unit of collective performance.

Words to Work By

A **team** is a group of people who collaborate and interact to reach a common goal. The team is made up of a team leader who coordinates the work of team members, often referred to as associates.

In the ideal team, each associate performs his or her function in such a way that it dovetails with other team members to enable the team to achieve its goals. Using this collaboration, the whole becomes greater than the sum of its parts.

An excellent example of this is a surgical team. Every member of the team—the surgeons, the anesthesiologist, the nurses, and the other technicians—carries out his or her individual functions expertly. When they work as a team, interactions flow seamlessly among them. All are committed to one goal—the well-being of the patient.

There are examples of successful teams in every endeavor: championship sports teams, disease-curing research teams, fire-fighting rescue teams, and teams in every aspect of business.

In selecting members for a team, it is extremely important for you to pick people who will fit in with the team. This does not mean that all members should come from the same race, ethnic group, sex, or social backgrounds. But they should have certain personal characteristics, attitudes, and philosophies of work in common.

If a team consists of men and women who are dynamic and fast thinking, an applicant who is a plodder, who ponders ideas before expressing them, won't fit in no matter how competent or intelligent he or she may be.

It's a good idea to have all team members interview applicants who are being seriously considered. The team leader should elicit the opinions of all team members before the hiring decision is made. On teams in which decisions are made by consensus, all members must agree on the candidate.

The danger here, of course, is that the biases of individuals may influence their judgment. Careful training must be given to all members to alert them to these problems so they can work to overcome them.

Choosing Among Several Top-Level Applicants

In a tight job market, you may have only one viable candidate. Your choice now is easy. Hire or don't hire. In most cases, however, you'll have several good people from which to make your final selection.

Decision-Making Blunders

Comparing candidates must be done systematically. Watch out for these common blunders:

➤ **The rule of recency.** You've interviewed a dozen applicants over several weeks. When the time comes to make a decision, you have forgotten much about the first few candidates, but the ones you interviewed most recently are fresh in your mind. You're more likely to hire one of them. To overcome this, keep good records of each interview. Discuss all candidates who have been passed on for subsequent interviews with all the people who have interviewed them. If your notes indicate that an early applicant appeared to be a good prospect, but after seeing several others you have only a vague memory of his personality, it's worthwhile to arrange a refresher interview before making the final decision.

➤ **Overemphasis on one factor.** You were very impressed with Jonathon because he has an excellent background in designing Web pages. This is one of the first tasks the new employee will be assigned. However, the job will involve other areas in which Jonathon is not as well qualified as other candidates. Put all the applicants' backgrounds in perspective. Keep in mind the entire job—not just one part of it.

➤ **The applicant's interest in the job.** When an applicant shows interest in the job and follows up with phone calls, e-mail, or letters, it's an indication of interest in the job. This is good, but it also can influence you more than it should. Yes, you want the person you hire to be excited about the job and really want to be accepted. This is a factor that should be taken into consideration, but it does not mean he or she is the best candidate for the job.

➤ **Pressure from another source.** Stacey L. has gone through the process and is one of four candidates to reach the final stage. You get a call from a customer, a good friend, or maybe your boss, pressing you to hire Stacey. She's obviously qualified or she wouldn't have reached this stage, but it's your decision to make. Is she the best of the four? If you select another candidate, you'll have to explain why you didn't hire Stacey to that customer or friend—or most difficult, to your boss. The easy way out is to hire Stacey, but if, in your judgment, one of the others is better suited, don't let others influence you.

The Final Selection Spreadsheet

To systematize making the decision, compare applicants by placing their backgrounds side by side. One way of doing this is to use a worksheet such as the one shown in the following table.

Final Selection Spreadsheet

Job Specification	Applicant #1 Name:	Applicant #2 Name:	Applicant #3 Name:	Applicant #4 Name:
Education:				
Experience:				
Intangibles:				
Other:				

In the first column, list the specs as shown in the job specification sheet made at the start of the search. In the column for each applicant, list the individual's qualifications that are related to that spec.

Final Selection Spreadsheet

Job Specification	Applicant #1 Name:	Applicant #2 Name:	Applicant #3 Name:	Applicant #4 Name:
Education:				
BA or BBA:	BBA Mgmt	BA Econ	BA Mgmt	BS Engrg
Major:	Mgmt	Cum laude	MBA Mgmt	MBA
Experience:				
Intangibles:				
Other:				

Follow the same system for each of the other job specs. This way, you have the key aspects of each applicant's background side by side with the specs and can make an objective comparison.

From this, you can choose the applicant closest to the job requirements.

Intuition or Gut Feelings

Candidates often are very close in their qualifications for the job. You have to make a choice between relatively equally competent people. Now it is a matter of your judgment. Choosing a candidate purely on gut feeling without systematically analyzing each prospect's background in relation to the job specs is a mistake. But when the decision is choosing the best among equals, you have to trust your gut feelings on which one to pick.

As we said, hiring is both a science and an art. When you've exhausted the "science" (the systematic comparison of candidates) the "art" (your *gut feelings*) takes over.

Words to Work By

Gut feelings are not purely emotional. They have developed during your years of experience in interacting with other people on and off the job. You have built up a treasury of reactions to people, and your gut feelings have been formed by these experiences.

The Least You Need to Know

➤ Don't hire or reject an applicant because of superficial aspects of his or her background. Look at the whole person in relation to the job for which he or she is being considered.

➤ Be aware of your own biases—pro and con. If you know you are influenced positively or negatively by certain aspects of an applicant's background, neutralize it when you make the hiring decision.

➤ Meeting the job specs is just part of the decision-making process. Equally important is having the intangible factors that make the difference between just doing a job and doing it well.

➤ In selecting members for a team, it is extremely important for you to pick people who will fit in with the team. This does not mean that all members should come from the same race, ethnic group, sex, or social backgrounds. But they should have certain personal characteristics, attitudes, and philosophies of work in common.

➤ To systematize making the decision, compare applicants by placing their backgrounds side by side. Use a candidate-comparison spreadsheet to make this comparison easier.

HEY! GUESS WHAT!

Chapter 23

Making the Job Offer

In This Chapter

➤ Making the offer

➤ Resolving doubts and concerns about the job

➤ Clarifying job duties and responsibilities

➤ Selling the job to the applicant

➤ Negotiating the compensation package

➤ Making the formal offer

➤ Rejecting the runners–up

Once you've made your decision as to the person you want to hire, you are now ready to make a job offer. All through the interviewing process, you have been getting feedback from the applicants regarding their interest in the job. Any applicant who has not expressed serious interest in the job should not have reached this point, but this does not necessarily mean he or she will automatically accept your offer. Before making the formal offer, there should be a clear understanding between the applicant and the company as to what the job entails, what the company expects from the applicant, and what the applicant expects from the company.

This chapter discusses the final stages of the process as well as the negotiations preceding the formal offer and, we hope, acceptance of it.

Before Making the Offer

Don't take anything for granted. During the entire process, the candidate has been enthusiastic about the job, has expressed sincere interest, and seems anxious to start work. Before making the offer, it's important to review the job and make sure both you and the applicant are on the same track.

Clarifying the Job Duties

Go over the job description point by point. Although the candidate may have read it already, most job descriptions are not comprehensive, and many facets are not specified. Discuss each aspect of the job to make sure it is what the applicant has understood.

During the interviewing process, Ken L. was so excited about the job that the team leader was sure he would accept the offer. But when the team leader went over the details, Ken was not so sure it was the job he wanted. He had misunderstood some of the major duties and had assumed the job was at a higher level. He said, "I've done all of these things for years. What I'm looking for is more advanced work, not just a repeat of what I have now." Unless the team leader can convince Ken that the opportunity to do the type of work he desires will develop in a relatively short time, the offer should be withdrawn.

Hiring Hints

Before making a formal job offer, make sure you and the candidate know exactly what the job entails. The applicant not only should be qualified for it, it should fits his or her career goals.

What the Company Expects

In addition to the job duties expected of a staff member, most companies have policies and practices that should be made clear to an applicant before making a job offer. If the job requires travel, overtime, work on weekends, or unusual working conditions, this should be made clear to the applicant before making a formal offer. Indeed, this should have been brought up early in the process so that, if there is a problem in complying, the applicant could withdraw before reaching this point.

What appears to the company to be minor matters may be important to an applicant. Raul's resumé mentioned that he taught two nights a week at a local university. Nothing was said about this during his interviews. After he accepted the job and started work, he was told it was company policy not to permit employees to hold any other job, and he would have to give up his teaching position. Had Raul known this, he wouldn't have accepted the job. The result is a discontented employee who will probably be looking for another job.

What the Employee Can Expect from the Company

In today's competitive market, the applicant often has to be sold on accepting your job offer. Salary and the entire compensation package are important, and this will be discussed in the next section. But it often isn't money that will make the difference between acceptance and rejection of a job offer by the person you really want.

For years, companies have provided "fringe benefits" such as company cars, memberships in country clubs, and the usual insurance packages. Recent innovations include such things as child-care facilities, fitness programs, flexible hours, and casual-dress days. Let's look at some unusual "fringes" that companies have instituted to attract and keep good workers.

Motorola's Semiconductor Products Sector has launched an employee program called "etc." that offers activity or fitness centers, nearby child-care services, and an errand-running service.

Three activity centers, operated by Club One of San Francisco, offer fitness classes ranging from kickboxing aerobics to yoga and tai chi; softball, basketball, and volleyball leagues; social outings such as skiing and rafting trips; and other outdoor adventures.

Bright Horizons Family Solutions will operate a 15,000-square-foot childcare center for 234 children of Motorola workers at the Arizona State Research Park near the company's Tempe facility.

Recruiting Residuals

Here's a benefit busy people will appreciate: Motorola also has arranged for errand-runners for workers. Workers pay $5 per hour to send someone to shop, run to the dry cleaners, or walk a dog.

A utility company in the Southwest offers long-term medical insurance for employees, their parents, and in-laws and provides consultation and referral service to help workers choose elder care or child care.

In addition, other perks cropping up in the workplace include casual dress codes, in-office therapeutic massages, and pizza parties.

Employment Enigmas

Don't let your anxiety over losing a desirable candidate tempt you to make an informal offer—promising a higher salary or other conditions of employment that haven't been approved—with the hope that you can persuade management to agree to it. Failure to get this agreement not only will cause the applicant to reject the offer, it can also lead to legal action against your company.

Employment Enigmas

Because women usually have been paid less than men, basing the salary you offer on current earnings isn't always equitable. If the job had been offered to a man and you would have paid a higher rate based on his salary history, you should offer a woman the same rate even though her earnings record has been lower.

Do these perks sell the job to applicants? There are no studies to prove it, but it probably helps when an applicant compares two or more job offers.

The Compensation Package

In most companies, the final offer, including salary, is handled by the HR department. Usually the HR representative discusses directly with the applicant the starting salary, benefits, and other facets of employment. If you're responsible for making the offer in your company, however, it's a good idea to check all the arrangements with your boss and the HR department to avoid misunderstandings.

Most companies set starting salaries for a job category, although you may have a narrow range of flexibility depending on an applicant's background. When jobs are difficult to fill, however, and for many higher-level positions, starting salaries are negotiable.

In these types of jobs, several people usually interview an applicant, and you may have several interviews with finalists before making a decision. You should obtain a general idea of each person's salary demands early in this process so you don't waste time even considering people whose salary requirements are way out of line.

Companies traditionally have used an applicant's salary history as the basis for their offer. Ten or fifteen percent higher than a person's current salary is considered a reasonable offer.

In negotiating salary, keep in mind what you pay currently employed people for doing similar work. Offering a new person considerably more than that amount can cause serious morale problems.

There are exceptions to this rule, of course. Some applicants have capabilities that you believe would be of great value to your company, and to attract these people, you may have to pay considerably more than your current top rate. Some companies create special job categories to accommodate this situation. Others pay only what they must and hope it won't lead to lower morale.

Some companies believe they can avoid these types of problems by prohibiting their employees from discussing salary. This "code of silence" is virtually impossible to enforce. People talk—and discussion of who makes how much is fodder for great gossip. One of my clients gave an employee a significant raise to keep him from leaving. He and the others in the company who were aware of the raise were sworn to secrecy. His boss told me, "That very afternoon our manager in Los Angeles called to ask whether the rumor about this raise was true. Asked where he picked up this information, he said it was on his e-mail when he got back from lunch." The grapevine in action again!

Salary alone isn't a total compensation package. It also includes vacations, benefits, frequency of salary reviews, and incentive programs. All these items should be clearly explained.

Hiring Hints

Even when the salary you offer is less than an applicant wants, you might persuade that person to take your offer by pointing out how the job will enable him or her to use creativity, engage in work of special interest, and help reach career goal.

Hiring Bonuses

When applicants are scarce, companies resort to whatever they can to fill positions. One rapidly growing approach is the hiring bonus. According to the American Management Association's 1998 survey of 334 HR managers, 44 percent of them said their companies offer bonuses, up from 30 percent the previous year.

Bonuses are no longer reserved for senior executives. Companies are using signing bonuses to secure all kinds of employees including technicians, IT staff, skilled factory workers, and specialists in most areas.

One advantage of the hiring bonus is that it saves money down the road because base salary and benefits are not affected. It also is less likely to cause tension between old and new employees because it doesn't upset the compensation program.

The amount of the bonus may range from $50 for rank-and-file positions all the way to $25,000 for executives. The average bonus is about $5,000. Most companies pay the bonus in one lump sum with the new employee's first paycheck. Some companies stretch it out over the first six months or year. Some companies require the new employee to sign an agreement to remain on the job for a specified period of time, but such agreements are difficult to enforce.

Overcoming Obstacles

What do you do if, at the time you make the offer, the applicant brings up new objections? Just as a salesperson must be prepared to overcome last-minute reservations to buy a product, you must be ready to face and overcome these objections. Let's look at some common problems.

The Salary Is Too Low

Your first choice is Hillary. Early in the interview process, you explored her salary requirements, and your offer is in line. At least that's what you thought. Now Hillary demurs. "If I stay where I am, I'll get a raise in a few months that will bring me above that salary. You'll have to do better."

Having received approval of the hire at the salary offered, you have to either reject it, persuade her to take the job by selling her on other advantages, or go back to your boss for approval of the higher rate. What you do depends on many factors. Do you have other viable candidates for the job? If not, how urgent is it to fill the job?

Employment Enigmas

Salary should not be a reason for rejection. This should be agreed upon before the offer is made. Any discrepancies should have been worked out early on.

Determine whether you can legitimately offer other benefits such as a salary review in six months, opportunity for special training in an area in which she is particularly interested, or other perks. Think over the situation carefully and discuss it with your manager. Caution: Don't make commitments you don't have the authority to honor.

If you and your boss agree that Hillary should still be considered for the position, determine how much above your original offer you're willing to pay and what else you can offer. The meeting with Hillary should take place as soon as possible after you and your manager have determined the maximum deal you can offer. With this in mind, you can negotiate with her and try to reach an acceptable arrangement. Usually, if this new negotiation doesn't lead to agreement, discontinue the discussion and seek another candidate. Continuing to haggle over terms of employment is not advisable.

Words to Work By

At some companies, instead of all employees working the same hours (8 to 4 or 9 to 5), the hours are staggered so that some employees come in and leave early and others come in and leave later in the day. This is called **flextime** or **flexible hours.**

I Need Flexible Hours

This should have come up early in the process. However, some people feel that, if they mention a special need, they may be rejected. After they get the offer, they bring it up.

Some companies have an established policy on *flextime.* If the job for which the candidate is being considered falls into this policy, there's no problem. All that has to be worked out are the hours. If there is no policy, however, whether to grant this request depends on a variety of circumstances. If you give a new employee flexible hours, will the current staff also want their hours changed? There are some jobs in which flexible hours are more appropriate than in others. Is filling this job so difficult that it pays to bend the rules?

Doubts and Skepticism

Some applicants are skeptics. Perhaps they've been misled by other employers and doubt that all the great benefits you offer are for real. Some may actually challenge you; others may just look or act doubtful. Be alert for these doubts and be prepared to rebut them.

Dorothy is frank with you. She says that one of the reasons she left her last job was that they promised her she would be trained in advanced computer techniques. After she started work, she received no advanced training. When she asked when to expect the promised training, the company kept putting it off. "What guarantee do I have that you won't do the same?"

One way is to show her your schedule of training in the areas discussed. Point out that all employees at her level are sent through a structured program to upgrade their skills. Tell her that the main reason for hiring her not only is her current expertise but also her potential for advanced work.

You may refer her to current employees who have gone through the training so she can get first-hand reports on what it did for them.

If a training class is in session at this time, you may invite her to sit in for a short period of time to see it for herself.

What Are My Opportunities for Advancement?

Of course, you can't promise automatic advancement in most jobs. Employees have to earn promotions. You should point out that the company conducts periodic performance reviews and that advancement is based on these reviews. To show the applicant the possibilities within the organization, display an organizational chart indicating the starting position and showing the various higher-level positions to which it can lead. If the company has a career pathing program, take this opportunity to describe how it works.

Hiring Hints

Even if your company's policy is to review all new employees after six months and usually give a salary increase, don't state this as a guarantee. Circumstances may change; the applicant may not have made expected progress.

I'm Considering Other Offers

It's not unusual for a good applicant to be looking at several possibilities. All through the interviewing process, you should be feeling the applicant out to determine what he or she is really seeking in the new job. Keep a record of this. Does he seek rapid advancement? Does she want special training? Has he commented on a particular type of job interest? Has she expressed concern about health benefits? Here is where you can use that information to persuade the candidate you want to accept your offer.

One way to counteract this is to ask the prospect to write down all the advantages of joining the other company or staying on the present job. Then you list all the advantages of joining your team. Be prepared to show how your job—which may even pay less or have fewer benefits than other offers—is still the best bet. Use all the information gleaned at the interviews as to what the candidate desires, and show how your job will help the prospect meet the goals he or she has set for the future. If this prospect is the one you really feel will be the best for your team, it's well worth it to make this effort.

Countering the Counteroffer

You've knocked yourself out reading resumés, interviewing applicants, and comparing candidates. You make the decision that you'll hire Valerie, and she accepts your offer. A week later, she calls to tell you she has changed her mind. When she told her boss she was leaving, her boss made a counteroffer.

Frustrating? You bet. To minimize the possibility of a counteroffer, assume that any currently employed candidate will get one. At the time you make your offer, bring it up and make these points:

➤ You know she has done a great job in her present company. You also realize that, when she notifies her company that she's planning to leave, it will undoubtedly make a counteroffer. Why? Because they need her now.

➤ If the company truly appreciated her work, it wouldn't have waited until she got another job offer to give her a raise. It would have given it to her long ago.

➤ Many people who have accepted counteroffers from a current employer find out that, after the pressure is off the company, it will train or hire someone else and let her go.

➤ From now on, she will always be looked at as a disloyal person who threatened to leave just to get more money.

➤ When the time for a raise comes around again, guess whose salary has already been "adjusted"?

When these arguments are used, the number of people who accept counteroffers decreases significantly.

Formalizing the Offer

Although most companies make a job offer orally (no letter and no written agreement), an oral offer is just as binding as a written one. Some companies supplement an oral offer with a letter of confirmation so there are no misunderstandings about the terms.

The Job-Offer Letter

If you make a job offer in writing or as a confirmation of an oral offer, it should contain the following elements:

➤ The title of the job (a copy of the job description should be attached)

➤ The starting date

➤ The salary (including an explanation of incentive programs)

➤ The benefits (may be in the form of a brochure given to all new employees)

➤ The working hours, location of the job, and other working conditions

➤ If pertinent, a deadline for acceptance of the offer

Employment Enigmas

When you make a job offer, the salary should be stated by pay period—not on an annual basis. Rather than specifying $36,000 per year, specify $1,500 per half-month. Why? Some courts have ruled that, if you quote a salary on an annual basis, you're guaranteeing the job for one year.

Employment Contracts—Yes or No?

In some situations, the employer and employee sign a formal contract. These contracts are often used with senior management people and key professional, sales, or technical personnel. Although it's rare, some organizations require all salaried employees to sign a contract, which often is little more than a formalized letter of agreement concerning conditions of employment. In many cases, they're designed for the benefit of the company. The employee has little room for negotiation.

One of the most controversial areas covered in many contracts is the so-called "restrictive covenant," which prohibits employees who leave the company from working for a competitor for a specified period of time. Although these types of contracts have been challenged, they're usually enforceable if they're limited in scope. Prohibiting a person from working for a competitor for a limited period of time, for example, is more likely to be upheld than prohibiting that type of employment forever.

Senior managers and other employees who hold critical positions in a company and applicants who have skills that are in great demand have the clout to negotiate personal contracts with the company. Any contract, whether it's generic or a negotiated special agreement, should be drawn up by a qualified attorney, not by HR or other managers.

Recruiting Residuals

Employment contracts supersede any employment-at-will policy. If an employee is covered by a contract, you may not terminate that employee except as specified in the contract.

Rejecting the Unsuccessful Candidates

It's not necessary to write or call every person who sent you a resumé to notify them that they didn't get the job. It is a good policy, however, to notify every person who has gone through the interviewing process.

Immediate Rejections

If at the interview it became apparent that the applicant didn't qualify, tell him or her right there. "Mr. J., the job calls for much more experience in CAD than you have, so I cannot consider you for it."

However, if the reason for rejection is intangible, it may not be a good idea to bring it out at the time of the interview. Instead, a few days after the interview, write a thank-you note to the candidate for coming in to interview. Note that since other candidates were closer to your requirements, he or she is no longer being considered.

Notifying the Runners-Up

Some companies just assume that, if applicants don't get an offer, they'll realize they were rejected. This is not only discourteous, it gives your firm a poor image. It's good business practice to notify the men and women you have interviewed that the job has been filled. You want to make them leave with a favorable feeling about the company. Who knows, you may want to hire them at some time in the future. Also, they may be potential customers, vendors, or others with whom you may do business.

You don't have to tell applicants why they didn't get the job. Explanations can lead to misunderstandings and even litigation. The most diplomatic approach is just to state that the background of another candidate was closer to your needs.

Five Things You Never Tell Unsuccessful Candidates

Candidates who are rejected often want to know why you didn't select them. It's not a good idea to go into detail. It can lead to problems. In particular, avoid using these common reasons companies frequently tell an unsuccessful candidate:

➤ "Your references didn't check out." References are confidential. You are morally bound to maintain that confidence. In addition, there are legal ramifications. If information provided by you leads to a defamation suit, you will be dragged into the court as a witness and may be sued yourself.

➤ "You're overqualified." Too often the term "overqualified" is a euphemism for being too old. Even if you feel the applicant will be bored by the job or would be taking a backward step by working on it, don't use that phrase.

➤ "We decided not to fill the job." This is okay if it's true, but some companies use it as an excuse rather than inviting an argument over the applicant's qualifications.

➤ "You wouldn't fit in with our team." Careful! This could be construed as discrimination against a person because of race, religion, national origin, gender, age, or disability.

➤ "In order to meet our affirmative action goals, we had to hire a minority." You might be sued for reverse discrimination.

Again, your standard rejection statement should be: "We hired another candidate who was closer to our job specifications."

If the applicant asks: "In what way was he closer?" you don't have to explain. Don't get into a comparison of qualifications. Just say, "I cannot discuss another applicant's background with you. It would be a violation of his (or her) privacy."

The Least You Need to Know

➤ Before making a final offer, the company and the applicant should have a clear understanding of the job's duties and responsibilities.

➤ The compensation package should include salary, benefits, and any extras such as bonuses, stock options, or incentive pay.

➤ Hiring bonuses are not reserved for senior executives. They are now common practice to attract applicants for hard-to-fill jobs.

➤ Be prepared to help an applicant choose your job over other offers. Learn what he or she really seeks in a new job and point out how, by taking your job offer, this can be achieved.

➤ To minimize the possibility of a counteroffer, assume that any currently employed candidate will get one. At the time you make your offer, prepare the applicant to reject any counteroffer.

➤ You don't have to tell applicants why they didn't get the job. Explanations can lead to misunderstandings and even litigation. The most diplomatic approach is just to state that the background of another candidate was closer to your needs.

Chapter 24

Once You Have Found Them, Never Let Them Go

In This Chapter

➤ Understanding the cost of employee turnover

➤ Conducting the separation interview

➤ Determining causes of turnover

➤ What some companies are doing to retain good people

➤ Why recently promoted people quit

It's rare today for a person to join a company after graduating from high school or college and remain there until retirement. Most people have several jobs during their work life. Sometimes the reason for changing jobs is involuntary—the worker is fired, or due to downsizing or reorganization, a job is eliminated. But quite often the employee leaves voluntarily. For some reason, the individual is not getting from the job what he or she had hoped for.

Every time a person leaves a job, whether it's voluntary or involuntary, the company suffers. Productivity is curtailed until a replacement can be found and trained. As noted earlier in this book, it is expensive to recruit and select a new employee.

This chapter looks at some of the reasons people quit and what we can do to minimize this expensive turnover.

The Cost of Turnover

The Bureau of National Affairs reported that, in the first quarter of 1999, companies were losing 1.1 percent of their work force every month. This is a 13-year high.

We know turnover is costly, but how costly? Most managers haven't an inkling. Kepner-Tregoe, a management-consulting firm in Princeton, New Jersey, asked 1,290 managers what the cost of losing an employee is. Two-thirds couldn't answer the question.

Calculating the Cost

The cost, of course, varies with the type of job and the location of the organization. For example, the cost of replacing a human resources manager in the automobile industry was calculated to be over $130,000; the loss of a machinist, $100,000; replacing a store manager in a fast food chain, $20,000.

Select a department or job function that has a high turnover rate. Determine the number of people who have left the job during the past 12 months. Write that number on Line 4.

The average cost of turnover is 25 percent of an employee's annual salary (Line 1) plus the cost of benefits (Line 2). (Average company benefits cost about 30 percent of an employee's salary.)

Turnover Cost Formula

Annual wage _____ × .25 = _____

Annual wage _____ × .30 _____ × .25 = _____

Total cost per employee (add Lines 1 and 2) =_____

Total employees who left _____

Total cost of turnover (Line 3 × Line 4) = _____

Source: Saratoga Institute and Kepner-Tregoe, Inc.

Details about employee turnover can be obtained by visiting Kepner-Tregoe's Web site at http.www.kepner-tregoe.com.

Keeping Managers Alert to Turnover

Unless team leaders and department managers are attentive to the turnover problem, it cannot be controlled. Managers should not take for granted that a certain number of new hires will quit during the early stages of their employment.

For example, when Wal-Mart realized that nearly half of new hires were leaving the company during the first 90 days, the company took action.

All managers were provided with a monthly staffing report. In it, store managers can compare turnover rates for the whole company with their store. In addition, they get details on when employees left and the reasons they gave for leaving.

As a result, managers can take action to correct problems that have lead to turnover. This has resulted in managers' awareness of the importance of retention to the company's bottom line and a significant reduction in the number of quits.

Starting on the Right Foot

One reason employees quit during the first few months of starting a job is that they are not given adequate orientation. They are just thrust into the job without really feeling welcomed. They may have only a vague concept of the company's culture, mission, and goals. They just don't feel that they "belong."

The Importance of the First Days

In most companies, before new employees actually start their jobs, the human resources department gives them a briefing about the company. They may be shown videos, be given a tour of the facilities, receive literature, or attend a lecture. They learn the history of the organization, the benefits are explained, and rules and regulations are outlined. This is a good start, but it's not enough.

The team leader or supervisor must augment this with an orientation to the team or department. The quality of the *orientation program* has an impact on the future performance of new members, the manner in which they interact with associates, their job satisfaction, and even their career progress.

Words to Work By

New employees get a better start on the job if they are made to feel like they are part of the group from the beginning. Programs designed to give them information, to answer their questions about the company and the team, and to acquaint them with their teammates are called **programs.**

What Makes a Good Orientation Program?

Here are some of the actions you can do to make the new member feel welcome:

➤ Acquaint the new member with the background and history of the team. Tell him or her about past projects and challenging assignments.

➤ Discuss the department's mission and what is being done to accomplish it.

➤ Describe the functions of other members so that, when you introduce them, the new member will have a head start in remembering who does what.

➤ Introduce the new associate to the others. When making the introduction, comment about the both parties. For example, "Alice, this is Carla, our expert in state taxes. Carla's been with the company for 10 years and in our group for the past three years. Carla, Alice will be working on developing systems for our new project."

➤ Give the new person a chance to chat with each member. Make a practice of having each member spend break time or lunch time with the new associate during the first few weeks.

➤ Choose one of the members of the group to mentor the new associate. He or she should take a special interest in the newcomer; show him or her "the ropes"; answer questions about the work, the company culture, and the other staffers; and in general be there to help the new member get started properly.

➤ You, the manager, should make a point to check with the mentor every day to learn about the new associate's progress and to determine how you can be of help.

➤ Most important, speak to the new member and take a personal interest in how he or she is doing. Visit his or her workstation, not as a boss checking the work but as a colleague who is sincerely interested in making that person feel comfortable in the new job.

Hiring Hints

Try to tailor the job to the true interests of the employee. If you find that he is a "loner," assign work that can be done alone. If she is very creative, whenever possible give her projects in which her creativity can be used. When work and interests coincide, people are less likely to quit.

Why Good People Leave

Nothing is as frustrating to a supervisor as having one of the best associates quit. It has often taken months or years to bring that person up to optimum productivity—and now suddenly he or she leaves.

Not only does this disrupt the momentum of the team's work, it also has negative effects on the other members—unless, of course, the person who quit is universally disliked.

Why Employees Say "I Quit"

You ask the person why he or she quit. Often the answer will be that it's for personal reasons. Carl decided to go back to college; Vicki's chosen to be a full-time mother; Sam's father's illness requires him to take over his business; Jane's spouse is transferred to another city.

The answer also might indicate a career move. Ben has gone as far as he can in your company; Geri is offered more money by another firm; an opportunity arises in a different field—one in which Tom is particularly interested. Hilary's going to start her own business.

Often the reason given is not totally true. Yes, Tom did go to an industry in which he has particular interest, but would he have made that decision if he were obtaining job satisfaction in his current job? Geri is leaving for more money. Sure, she would like more money, but perhaps she wouldn't have even looked for a job if she were not unhappy with the supervisor's management style.

Probing for the Real Reasons

Every time someone quits, it's important to determine the true reason. This isn't easy because it may not even be clear to the person who leaves. It may be deeply imbedded in the culture of the company, subtly making the person discontented.

People may feel that they are not making the progress they had hoped for, that their salary is too low, that working conditions are unsatisfactory, or that the job has become boring. Some are reluctant to divulge the real reason for deciding to quit. This is particularly true if the real cause of discontent lies with the supervisor or other employees. Not only is it embarrassing to tell their boss they don't like him, they also may be concerned about getting a poor reference.

Recruiting Residuals

If you decide to quit, it's only fair to give your boss adequate notice. In addition, here are some suggestions that will make your leaving less painful for the group: Inform the supervisor of the status of all projects on which you are working. Offer to assist the person taking over your work. If your work involves dealing with customers, subcontractors, or other outsiders, notify them whom to contact after you're gone. Keep in contact with the supervisor after you leave to answer questions. It pays to maintain a good relationship.

Retaining good people is essential to the success and stability of your company. Supervisors and team leaders should do their best to establish a climate that will lead to satisfied employees who will remain with the organization. Of course, you may not have complete control over these conditions. Much rests in the hands of higher-ranking managers and the long-term corporate culture.

Examine your personnel practices to determine some of the reasons why your turnover rate is higher than you would like it to be. In the following worksheet, you will find a series of questions suggested by Dr. Franklin C. Ashby in his book *Revitalizing Your Corporate Culture*.

Test Your Retention Quota

Yes	No	Is the company's compensation program (salary and benefits) at least on par with competitors for the same types of personnel?
Yes	No	Do you make employees feel that their work is vital to the company's success?
Yes	No	Do you provide training to keep your staff on the cutting edge of the technology needed in their work?
Yes	No	Do you send employees to professional development programs on a regular basis?
Yes	No	Do you keep in mind employees' personal goals and provide opportunities for them to achieve these goals?
Yes	No	Do you encourage employees to contribute their ideas and suggestions?
Yes	No	Do you provide opportunities for employees to assume more responsibility—and pay them accordingly?
Yes	No	Do employees see the career paths open to them and the steps you are taking to help them move along those paths?
Yes	No	Do you give both private and public recognition to each person's accomplishments?
Yes	No	Do you sense a feeling of pride in the work and the company among the employees?

Review your responses. Any "No" answer indicates a problem that may lead to the loss of some of your good employees.

Source: Revitalizing Your Corporate Culture, by Dr. Franklin C. Ashby, Cashman-Dudley Publishers

The Separation Interview

Too often, companies do not know why they lose good employees. Exit or separation interviews are designed to probe for the real reasons people leave a job and to obtain from the employee information about the job or the company that may cause discontent.

I have witnessed a number of exit interviews in which the questions were of such a superficial nature that no significant information was developed. To get meaningful information that will enable the company to identify and correct problems that cause turnover, a well-structured interview must be conducted.

It is best for this interview not to be conducted by the immediate supervisor of the person who is leaving. A member of the human resources staff or another manager should conduct it.

As in an employment or appraisal interview, it is best to start a *separation interview* by building rapport. Questioning should begin with a general questions that will not put the employee on the defensive. The question of why he or she is leaving the company should never be the first one asked. A better start might be to say, "Tell me about the kind of work you've been doing in your most recent assignment." This will get the conversation going, but it will also enable the interviewer to evaluate whether this is the kind of work one might expect to do in that job. One reason people leave a job is because it was not what they thought they'd be doing. A market researcher might be spending all her time on statistical compilations when she expected to be doing in-depth analyses.

Words to Work By

Separation interviews or **exit interviews** give organizations insight into the real reasons people quit their jobs.

Here are some important questions that should be asked in a separation interview and some clues as to how to interpret the responses.

About the Job

For questions about the job ...

What did you like most and least about the job?

Are these job factors or personal factors? The answer provides insight into the job by the pattern of answers obtained from people who leave it.

How do you feel about your compensation?

Many people leave their jobs for another with higher pay. Others feel they should have made more money even though they were being paid the going rate for the work. This will enable the interviewer to compare the methods used to give increases with other companies in your area or your industry.

How do you feel about the progress you've made in this company?

A number of people claim they left their jobs because of lack of opportunity for advancement. Often this masks the real reasons for leaving. However, it's important to examine what a person might have expected in terms of growth in the company and relate it to the real opportunity for advancement in the job she or he held.

How do you feel about working conditions?

Companies have picked up information from this question about matters that were unimportant in their eyes but that annoyed employees to the point of causing them to leave. Often these are easily correctable.

Supervision

For questions about supervision ...

What did you like most (least) about your supervisor's style of managing?

Because many of the problems in organizational life are due to problems with supervisors, it's important to probe this factor, particularly if there is a large turnover in that department. It will bring out whether the supervisor is dogmatic, stubborn, or authoritarian and whether he or she encourages participation.

Hiring Hints

The team leader or supervisor of the employee who is leaving cannot conduct an unbiased, objective separation interview. A member of the human resources department, another management-level person, or an outside consultant should conduct the interview.

Probe further to learn about how the supervisor deals with complaints. Some leaders tend to be defensive and take any complaint as a personal affront; others take time out to discuss even the most far-fetched grievances.

It also helps to learn the good points of each supervisor or team leader so they can be reinforced when reporting the information back to the leader.

Does your team leader or supervisor tend to favor some employees or act unfairly toward others?

Favoritism on one hand and bias on the other are major causes of discontent. The question can also point to blatant areas of cronyism or, at the other extreme, prejudice and discrimination. If this bias is based on racial, religious, national origin, gender, or age factors, it might alert you to serious potential legal problems and give the organization a chance to correct them.

Special Problems

For questions about uncovering special problems …

What might have been done differently here?

A frank answer to this question will bring out some of the real reasons the employee was not happy in the job and may give you insight into aspects of the company environment of which you were not aware.

What would have made you stay longer?

When one of my clients asked this of a highly competent technician, he was shocked to learn that the employee had discussed his discontent several times with his supervisor, had been promised that the problems would be resolved, and then nothing was ever done.

Sum Up the Interview

Often the specific questions asked may not have elicited information that might be valuable in improving the corporate culture or environment. Here are some questions that may add to the total picture:

If you could discuss with top management exactly how you feel about this company, what would you tell them?

This open-ended question often results in some interesting insights. Let the person talk freely. Avoid leading questions that might influence the response. Encourage him or her to express real feelings, attitudes, suggestions, problems, fear, and hopes about the organization.

If the applicant has accepted a job with another company, ask the following question:

What does the job to which you are going offer that you were not getting here?

The answer may repeat some of the facts already brought out, but it also may uncover some of the ways the firm failed to meet the person's hopes, goals, or expectations.

If the answers to the preceding questions have not brought out the true reasons for the employee deciding to leaving, ask more specifically:

Why are you leaving at this particular time?

Some of the problems that come out at the interview may have been in existence for a long time. Some of them may have seemed unimportant until now. Find out what precipitated the resignation at this time. Have things become worse? Is there anything that can be recommended to management to prevent the problems from becoming even more serious and causing more turnover?

A good separation interview takes an hour or more, but it can provide insight into how employees who have quit really feel about the organization, how these negatives can be overcome, and what positive aspects of the work environment need to be reinforced.

What Some Companies Are Doing to Retain Good People

In many companies, employees have been given *perks*—little extras that may not seem like much but often are significant additions to the traditional compensation package—that have been a great help in keeping people from leaving.

Words to Work By

Perks (short for perquisites) are goods or services given to an employee in addition to regular salary and benefits as an incentive to attract and retain personnel.

The Perk Buffet

Company perks vary. Here are some of the more commonly provided perks:

➤ **Company cars.** Cars are leased for executives, salespeople, and sometimes other staff members.

➤ **Memberships in professional associations.** To encourage technical and specialized personnel to keep up with the state of the art in their fields, the company may pay their dues in appropriate associations.

➤ **Subscriptions to professional and technical journals.** These are offered for the same reasons as memberships in associations.

➤ **Membership in social clubs.** Because much business is conducted on the golf course or over a meal, for years many companies have paid the enrollment fees and annual dues for country clubs and dining clubs for executives and sales representatives. In recent years, such memberships have been extended to other employees as an added incentive.

➤ **Credit unions.** Many large companies provide these low-cost banking facilities. Credit unions generally arrange mortgages, car loans and other financial deals at lower rates than commercial banks or S&L associations.

➤ **Subsidized lunchrooms.** I recently had lunch in the cafeteria of a large insurance company. My bill for a salad, an entree, coffee, and dessert was less than half of what I normally pay at a restaurant. This is a great savings for employees.

➤ **Coffee.** Many companies provide a never-empty coffee pot for employees. The company might also offer free doughnuts, bagels, or sweet rolls at break time.

➤ **Childcare.** With the great number of families in which both parents work, childcare is a major problem. Some companies have child-care facilities right on the premises or arrange for childcare at nearby facilities and subsidize the cost.

Hiring Hints

Reward longevity. Give loyalty bonuses to employees who have completed long-term projects or years of service. Let employees know you appreciate their tenure.

➤ **Transportation.** Vans or buses are made available to employees to bring them to and from work. It's cheaper for employees to use the company's transportation than to take public transportation or drive their own cars. Some companies will take employees to and from the nearest railroad station or bus depot at no cost to them.

➤ **Tuition.** Companies often pick up the entire bill for courses taken by employees—even if the courses are not specific to their job training. If the company doesn't pay in full, it may pay a portion of the cost of education.

➤ **Scholarships.** Some companies provide funds for college scholarships for children of employees.

➤ **Flextime.** A very effective perk is giving team members control over their own time. Some companies have company-wide flexible hours; others allow supervisors or team leaders to set the hours for their staffs. For example, if there is a lot of pressure to complete a project, don't insist that everybody be on the job from 9 to 5. Some people may be more productive if they can work at home for a few hours before reporting to the office. Others may want to complete work away from the office during the day. Still others may do their best work in the evening. Letting each person set his or her own schedule during the project gives that person control over his or her hours and usually pays off in higher productivity.

Now let's look at some of the less common perks that companies provide:

➤ **Birthday celebrations.** There are a few companies that give employees the day off on their birthday. That's a nice gesture, but it can disrupt team production. Many more companies celebrate the birthday on the job—during a break, at lunch, or after work—with a mini-party: cake (no candles, age is confidential), soft drinks, and a little fun. When the group is relatively small, people may go out together after work for a little party.

➤ **Pets at work.** Bringing pets to the office can be very distracting, especially if they get restless. However, some companies permit employees to bring their dog or cat to work if they are kept under control. One company sets aside one day each week as "pet day" for employees who wish to take advantage of it.

➤ **Casual-dress days.** Offices have always been formal places. Men wore suits and ties; women wore conservative outfits. Today, many companies—particularly in the high-tech fields—have no dress code. Employees can wear whatever they feel comfortable in—except perhaps beachwear or "indelicate" attire. Most offices still have traditional dress codes, however, although they're modified somewhat. Sports jackets and slacks are okay for men as are blouse-skirt outfits or slacks for women. To appease and attract the younger generation, companies have instituted casual-dress days, usually Fridays, in which men can replace business suits with open-necked sports shirts and slacks and women can wear sporty outfits.

Recruiting Residuals

According to the U.S. Chamber of Commerce, the fastest growing areas of benefits over the past five years have been daycare for working parents and flexible hours.

➤ **Exercise rooms.** With so many people engaging in regular exercise routines, many large firms have built complete gymnasiums for employee use. Smaller organizations, of course, have neither the space nor funds for a gym, but an exercise room with a stationary bike, a treadmill, or other equipment for employee use is feasible.

➤ **Recreation rooms.** To give employees a chance to relax after work, during breaks, or at lunch, some organizations have recreation rooms. In an article in *The Wall Street Journal,* one firm reported that it provided a billiard table and a Ping-Pong table; another firm provided beanbag chairs; still another, a Velcro wall at which employees can throw sticky toys.

➤ **Financial counseling.** Companies sometimes provide seminars on managing money, investment basics, credit management, and means to achieve financial security. Some companies arrange for private counseling of employees by experts in the field.

Perks vs. Cash

Why do perks motivate people to stay on a job? Why not give employees cash bonuses and let them purchase or lease their own car, pay their own dues to the country club, or buy what they wish?

Companies have found that most employees like receiving perks. If they did get a cash equivalent, they'd probably use it to pay bills or fritter it away. Perks are a constant reminder that the company is giving them something. Every time they step into the company car, it reinforces their loyalty to the company. Every time they pass the daycare bill to the accounting department, they thank the company for taking that burden off them.

Perks should not be confused with benefits. Benefits such as pensions, health care, and life insurance are part of the compensation package. Today, almost all large companies provide these standard benefits. Perks usually are add-ons to make life more pleasant for employees.

Teams That Play Together Stay Together

One way to develop company loyalty is to engage in recreational activities as a team. Companies frequently sponsor bowling leagues, softball teams, and other sports activities. If team members or associates in the same department enter these programs as a team, it could add a little fun to the job and cement the relationship among the associates.

Carrie was not much of an athlete, so when her department entered the relay race at the company picnic, she was afraid she would do badly, embarrass herself, and lose the respect of her teammates. She confided her worries to her colleague, who promised that her teammates would help her. Before the picnic, the team practiced running and gave Carrie some tips on improving her techniques. When her turn came to run, the team cheered her on, and she did fine.

Sandy, a department manager, invited his staff each year to a Christmas party and a summer barbecue. The staff looked forward to these events, and Sandy attributed the very low turnover in his department to the personal rapport that was built and reinforced by these parties and other recreational activities in which the group participated.

Hiring Hints

Recreational programs need not be formal. It's not necessary for team members to spend much of their free time together. Occasional parties or attending sports events or concerts, however, can help the members know each other as total humans, not just co-workers.

Overcoming the "Peter Principle"

It's not unusual for very good people to leave a company after they've been promoted. Why does this happen? Caroline was one of the best financial analysts in her company. However, when she was promoted to divisional controller, things began to change. Her new position required skills and expertise that she didn't need in her former job and for which she was not prepared. Laurence J. Peter, in his book *The Peter Principle*, noted that, "In a hierarchy, every employee tends to rise to the level of his own incompetence." This may sound ironic, but many people like Caroline are promoted because of competence in their current jobs, not because they have the skills or strengths required in the new job. Some of these people are fired, others are demoted, and many just quit in frustration.

Words to Work By

The **Peter Principle** states that, as people are promoted, sooner or later they will be moved into a job above their level of competence.

Prepare People for Promotion

Before promoting a person, make sure he or she is fully aware of the responsibilities and activities that the new job entails. Point out the aspects of the new position that are keys to success, and discuss the candidate's background as it relates to those facets. Determine whether the new job fits in with the candidate's career goals. If there's an interest, work out what additional training would be needed to help the individual succeed.

Work with the Incumbent

If possible, arrange for the person tapped for the promotion to work with the incumbent for several months before taking over the job. This will enable you to evaluate fitness before the final promotion decision is made, and it gives the candidate an opportunity to decide whether this is a job he or she can and really wants to do.

The Trial Period

If circumstances require that the new job be started immediately, make the individual "acting" manager for several months. During this time, you or the manager to whom the job reports can work very closely with the promoted person to train, guide, and observe him or her in action.

Provide Necessary Training

Special training in areas in which the individual needs added know-how should be arranged. Caroline's problem was a lack of experience in supervision and interpersonal relations. She was a whiz in financial matters, but her analyst job required little people contact. With proper training in the soft skills, she at least would have had learned the fundamentals to start her on the road to success.

Career Planning Programs

To avoid Peter Principle turnover in the long run, companies should have an ongoing career evaluation and training program for their employees. This way, you will have a corps of qualified and prepared people ready to move into jobs in which they will be productive and happy.

The Least You Need to Know

➤ Unless team leaders and department managers are attentive to the turnover problem, it cannot be controlled. Managers should not take for granted that a certain number of new hires will quit during the early stages of their employment.

➤ Every time someone quits, it's important to determine the true reason. This isn't easy because it may not even be clear to the person who leaves. It may be deeply imbedded in the culture of the company, subtly making the person discontented.

➤ Prepare good questions that will uncover problems within the organization. A good separation interview can take an hour or more, but it can provide insight into how employees who have quit really feel about the organization, how these negatives can be overcome, and what positive aspects of the work environment need to be reinforced.

➤ In many companies, employees have been given perks—little extras that may not seem like much but often are significant additions to the traditional compensation package—that have been a great help in keeping people from leaving.

➤ Overcome the Peter Principle. Many people are promoted because of competence in their current jobs, not because they have the skills or strengths needed in the new job. Some of these people are fired, others are demoted, and many just quit in frustration. Proper preparation and training for the higher-level job can ameliorate this problem.

Glossary of Terms

active listener   One who not only pays close attention to what the other party says but asks questions, makes comments, and reacts verbally and nonverbally to what is said.

blind ads   Employment ads in which the name of the company is not listed. Applicants reply to a box number.

bona fide occupational qualification (BFOQ)   Exists when the gender of the employee is essential to performing the job. Some jokesters have commented that the only undisputed bona fide occupational qualifications are a wet nurse (for a woman) and a sperm donor (for a man).

campus recruiters   See *college recruiters.*

career pathing   Employees are assessed to determine their potential and what steps they must take to move up into positions that will be of greatest value to both the company and themselves.

chronological resumé   Presents an applicant's background by listing jobs by dates of employment.

classified ads   Ads placed in a special section of the paper that contains the help-wanted ads. The format is usually limited to a specific typeface and allows no artwork.

closed shop   A company is required to hire *only* members of the union with which it has a contract. See also *union shop.*

college recruiters   Sometimes called *campus recruiters*, these are specialized members of the human-resources department whose major function is to contact and visit colleges all over the country to seek graduates to fill their companies' ever-growing demands for college-trained people.

credit bureaus   These provide information about a person's financial stability, lawsuits, bankruptcies, and related matters.

culturally biased test   A test that includes questions related to matters more likely to be familiar to people coming from a white, majority culture than to people from minority cultures.

diagnostic interviews   See *structured interviews*.

display ads   Can be placed anywhere in the paper. Display ads can be designed with borders, artwork, photos, and a variety of typefaces.

diversity in the workplace   A culture in which people from a variety of different racial, ethnic, religious, and gender groups work together to achieve common goals.

empathetic listener   One who listens with one's heart as well as one's head. Empathetic listeners not only listen to what other people say, they also try to feel what other people are feeling when they speak. In other words, they put themselves in the applicant's shoes.

employment agency counselor   Staff members who take job orders, interview applicants, and make referrals. They are also called *consultants* or *account executives*.

employment at will   A legal concept under which an employee is hired and can be fired at the will of the employer. Unless restricted by law or contract, the employer has the right to refuse to hire an applicant or to terminate an employee for any reason or no reason or all.

executive order   This is not a law; it is an edict publicized by the president without being passed by Congress. Executive orders do not apply to the entire population—only to government agencies or organizations who do business with the government. Violation of an executive order can lead to loss of the contract.

executive recruiters, executive search organizations   Consultants who specialize in recruiting and screening executives and other top-level personnel. Often called *headhunters*.

exit interviews   See *separation interviews*.

expats (expatriates)   Americans who work abroad.

flextime or **flexible hours**   Instead of all employees working the same hours (8 A.M. to 4 P.M. or 9 A.M. to 5 P.M.), the hours are staggered so some employees come in and leave early; others come in and leave later in the day.

functional resumé   Presents an applicant's background by listing duties, responsibilities, or accomplishments without regard to the job or company in which they were performed.

guided interviews   See *structured interviews*.

gut feelings   Feelings that are not purely emotional. They develop during your years of experience in interacting with other people on and off the job. You have built up a treasury of reactions to people, and your gut feelings have been formed by these experiences.

halo effect   The assumption that, because of one outstanding characteristic, all of an applicant's characteristics are outstanding (that person "wears a halo"). See also *pitchfork effect*.

headhunters   See *executive recruiters*.

impats (impatriates)   Foreign nationals who are imported to work in the United States. Americans who work abroad who are called *expats* (expatriates).

Internet referral services   The equivalent of classified ads in the newspapers. Companies post job listings, applicants list their backgrounds, and matches can be made.

interview   Derived from *inter* meaning "between" and *view* meaning "a look." An *interview* is not a one-way interrogation but a look at a situation (in this case, a look at a job) between the interviewer and the candidate.

investigative agencies   These agencies check on an applicant's reputation in the community, criminal records, and verification of employment history.

jargon   Those special initials, acronyms, words, or phrases used in your field or company and nowhere else. A statement like "We booked a perp on a 602A" won't mean anything to someone who is not in law enforcement in your city.

job analysis   Includes a description of the responsibilities that fall within a job (*job description*) and a list of the skills and background required to perform a job effectively (*job specification*).

job bank or **skill bank**   A database listing all the skills, education, experience factors, and other background of all employees. This can be searched to match job openings against the current work force.

job description   A list of the duties, responsibilities, and expected results a job entails. Other terms used are *position results description* or *job results description*.

job sharing   Two employees share one job. Work time is scheduled so the position is always covered. Each is paid at the same rate but only for the time worked.

job specifications   The qualifications a person should have to perform a job.

knockout factors   Unless the applicant has these qualifications for the job, there's no point spending another second reading that resumé.

nepotism   Preference shown in promotion or treatment on the job by higher-level managers to relatives or close friends.

networking   A means of identifying and cultivating people who may be valuable resources for you in obtaining information, developing ideas, suggesting customers, and referring prospects for your open jobs.

nondirective interviewing   Instead of making a substantive remark after an applicant's response, the interviewer makes a noncommittal comment such as "uh-huh" or just nods or remains silent. This encourages the applicant to continue talking and brings out information not directly asked about.

open-ended questions   Instead of asking "Have you worked with Excel?" ask "Tell me about your experience with Excel."

orientation program   Helps new employees get a better start on the job by making them feel they are part of the group from the beginning.

panel interviews   A group of interviewers sit down with the applicant and collectively conduct the interview.

patterned interviews   See *structured interviews*.

perks   Short for *perquisites*, these are goods or services given to an employee in addition to regular salary and benefits as an incentive to attract and retain personnel.

Peter Principle   States that, as people are promoted, sooner or later they will be moved into a job above their level of competence.

pitchfork effect (the symbol of the devil)   The opposite of the *halo effect*. Because one characteristic is poor, you assume the person is not satisfactory in every aspect of his background.

polygraph test   Records changes in heartbeat, blood pressure, and respiration and is used to detect whether a person is telling the truth.

position results description   See *job description*.

prescreening   The aspect of the screening process that precedes inviting an applicant for an interview.

religious practices   As defined by the EEOC, these include traditional religious beliefs, moral and ethical beliefs, and beliefs individuals hold "with the strength of traditional religious view."

separation interviews or **exit interviews**   Interviews given to employees who are leaving the company to provide insight into the real reasons people quit their jobs.

serialized interview   All applicants who are not eliminated at the first screening are seen and rated by several interviewers. The decision is made after reviewing all the ratings.

shepherd   An employee who guides the candidate through the screening procedures to resolve any questions or doubts about the company and the job and to follow through to encourage the candidate to accept an offer. Some companies refer to them as *hand holders* or *catchers*.

structured interviews   A list of questions that must be asked in exactly the same way in exactly the same order. They are also called *patterned interviews, diagnostic interviews*, and *guided interviews*.

teams   A group of workers who collaborate and interact to reach a common goal. The team is made up of a team leader who coordinates the work of team members, often referred to as associates.

temps (temporary personnel)   People who do work for the company but are not employed by the company. They are on the payroll of a temporary-staffing or employee-leasing service. Usually they are used for short-term assignments such as filling in for absent employees or augmenting permanent staff when needed.

union shop   A company can hire nonunion members, but they must join the union within a specified time after being hired. (See also *closed shop*.)

Resources

In this appendix you will find a list of publications that contain articles on recruiting, a list of professional associations that can provide you with helpful information on this subject, and a list of useful Web sites.

Publications

Managers, team leaders, and others who deal with people problems must keep up with what's going on. The best way to be on the cutting edge of change is to regularly read several of the magazines and newsletters that cover these matters.

Almost every industry and profession have periodicals devoted to their fields, and most have occasional articles on employment and recruiting. This is an excellent source of information.

Here is a list of some of the better general publications that either specialize in or have significant coverage of human resources matters.

Across the Board
The Conference Board
845 Third Ave.
New York, NY 10022
Phone: 212-339-0345
Fax: 212-980-7014
Web site: www.conference-board.org

Business Week
1221 Avenue of the Americas
New York, NY 10020
Phone: 1-800-635-1200
Fax: 609-426-5434
Web site: www.businessweek.com

Forbes
60 Fifth Ave.
New York, NY 10011
Phone: 1-800-888-9896
Fax: 212-206-5118
Web site: www.forbes.com

Fortune
Time-Life Building
Rockefeller Center
New York, NY 10020
Phone: 1-800-621-8000
Fax: 212-522-7682
Web site: www.fortune.com

Harvard Business Review
60 Harvard Way
Boston, MA 02163
Phone: 1-800-274-3214
Fax: 617-475-9933
Web site: www.hbsp.harvard.edu

HR Magazine
Society for Human Resources Management
1800 Duke St.
Alexandria, VA 22314
Phone: 703-548-3440
Fax: 703-836-0367
Web site: www.shrm.org

INC
477 Madison Ave.
New York, NY 10022
Phone: 212-326-2600
Fax: 212-321-2615
Web site: www.inc.com

Management Review
American Management Association
P.O. Box 319
Saranac Lake, NY 12983-0319
Phone: 1-800-262-9699
Fax: 518-891-3653
Web site: www.amanet.org

Manager's Edge
Briefings Publishing Co.
1101 King St.
Alexandria, VA 22314
Phone: 703-548-3800
Fax: 703-684-2136
Web site: www.briefings.com

Success in Recruiting and Retaining
National Institute of Business Management
P.O. Box 9206
McLean, VA 22102-0206
Phone: 1-800-543-2049
Fax: 703-905-8040
E-mail: customer@nibm.net

Training
50 South 9th St.
Minneapolis, MN 55402
Phone: 612-333-0471
Fax: 612-333-6526
Web site: www. trainingsupersite.com

Training and Development
American Society for Training and Development
1640 King St.
Alexandria, VA 22314
Phone: 703-683-8100
Fax: 703-683-9203
Web site: www.astd.org

Workforce
245 Fischer Ave.
Costa Mesa, CA 92626
Phone: 714-751-1883
Fax: 714-751-4106
Web site: www.workforce.com

Working Woman
135 West 50 St.
New York, NY 10020
Phone: 1-800-234- 9675
Fax: 212-445-6186
E-mail: wwmagazine@aol.com
Web site: www.workingwomanmag.com

Helpful Web Sites

More and more information has become available about organizations through their Web pages. Most major companies now have Web pages that tell a good deal about them and often list job openings. In addition there are Web sites for organizations and government agencies that provide helpful information. You will also find here a list of Internet sites to list your job openings and access resumés of persons seeking employment.

Job Listings

To advertise your open jobs or to search for applicants who may qualify for your jobs, use the following Web sites:

www.monster.com	www.hotJobs.com
www.careerpath.com	www.dice.com
www.careerMosaic.com	www.careerBuilder.com
www.headHunter.net	www.nationJob.com
www.jobSearch.org	www.jobs.com

Sources for Interns

www.summerjobs.com   Listings for unpaid internships are free. Paid internship listings cost $100 per job per year.

www.coolworks.com   Seasonal openings for retailers and resorts. Cost: $50 per month per job.

www.internship programs.com   Free postings nationwide.

www.jobweb.org   Sponsored by the National Association of Colleges and Employers. Cost: $80 per month per listing.

Information

For information about equal employment laws, see the following Web site: **www.eeoc.gov.**

For statistics on jobs, try the U.S. Department of Labor: **www.bls.gov.**

For information about the Americans with Disabilities Act (ADA), see the following Web site: **www.janweb.icdi.wvu.edu.**

Associations

American Management Association
www.amanet.org

American Psychological Association
www.apa.org

American Society for Training and Development
www.astd.org

American Staffing Association
www.staffingtoday.net

International Foundation of Employee Benefits Plans
E-mail: pr@ifebp.org

National Organization for Women
www.now.org

Catalyst
www.catalystwomen.org

National Association of Personnel Services
www.napsweb.org

Society for Human Resources Management
www.shrm.org

Interviewer Quiz

How good an employment interviewer are you? Here's a challenge for you to find out. Take this quiz *before* you read this book. Don't check your answers. After you have read the book, take it again. To get the most out of the quiz, don't look at your first answers until you have completed the second go-around. Then compare your answers with the solutions.

Pre-Book Quiz

Take the quiz on this page *before* reading the book.

True	False	1.	You should study the application form before inviting the applicant in.
True	False	2.	It makes little difference whether the applicant has a favorable impression of you.
True	False	3.	In the information-gathering part of the interview, you should do about 50 percent of the talking.
True	False	4.	A company application form should be completed even if the applicant has a resumé.
True	False	5.	The best way to start the interview is to challenge the applicant.
True	False	6.	Specific questions should be framed to elicit a "yes" or "no" answer or similar simple responses.
True	False	7.	You can obtain additional information from the applicant after he or she has responded to your question if you remain silent or make noncommittal remarks.
True	False	8.	You should set traps to catch the applicant in lies or inconsistencies.
True	False	9.	One way to obtain more detailed information is to ask the applicant for specific examples of his or her experience in the area under discussion.
True	False	10.	The applicant's motivation and attitudes are secondary to his or her technical qualifications for the job.
True	False	11.	If the applicant fails to meet every job specification, he or she should be rejected.
True	False	12.	Nonverbal clues can help you evaluate the applicant.
True	False	13.	To be sure you remember the interview, take detailed notes on what the applicant tells you.
True	False	14.	If an applicant has questions to ask you, you should respond, "I ask the questions; you answer them."
True	False	15.	You have a responsibility to describe the company and the job to the applicant in whom you have interest.

Post-Book Quiz

Take the quiz on this page *after* reading the book.

True	False	1.	You should study the application form before inviting the applicant in.
True	False	2.	It makes little difference whether the applicant has a favorable impression of you.
True	False	3.	In the information-gathering part of the interview, you should do about 50 percent of the talking.
True	False	4.	A company application form should be completed even if the applicant has a resumé.
True	False	5.	The best way to start the interview is to challenge the applicant.
True	False	6.	Specific questions should be framed to elicit a "yes" or "no" answer or similar simple responses.
True	False	7.	You can obtain additional information from the applicant after he or she has responded to your question if you remain silent or make noncommittal remarks.
True	False	8.	You should set traps to catch the applicant in lies or inconsistencies.
True	False	9.	One way to obtain more detailed information is to ask the applicant for specific examples of his or her experience in the area under discussion.
True	False	10.	The applicant's motivation and attitudes are secondary to his or her technical qualifications for the job.
True	False	11.	If the applicant fails to meet every job specification, he or she should be rejected.
True	False	12.	Nonverbal clues can help you evaluate the applicant.
True	False	13.	To be sure you remember the interview, take detailed notes on what the applicant tells you.
True	False	14.	If an applicant has questions to ask you, you should respond, "I ask the questions; you answer them."
True	False	15.	You have a responsibility to describe the company and the job to the applicant in whom you have interest.

Quiz Answers

The following are the answers to the quiz:

1. **True.** By reviewing the application, you can plan what will be covered in the interview.

2. **False.** The interview is a two-way process. To get the most out of the interview, the applicant must respect you. If you've made a favorable impression, you will increase the likelihood of the applicant accepting an offer if one is made.

3. **False.** This is a major problem with some interviewers. Always remember that you can't learn anything if your mouth is open. Let the applicant do most of the talking. Keep your part down to about 20 percent.

4. **True.** Resumés are written by the applicant to emphasize his or her strengths and to minimize limitations. The company application form is more objective.

5. **False.** This will only make the applicant more tense. A tense applicant is a noncommunicative applicant.

6. **False.** Open-ended questions elicit more and better information.

7. **True.** These nondirective techniques can be effective in getting applicants to tell more than originally volunteered in response to the question.

8. **False.** If you are Perry Mason, this is okay. But not in an employment interview.

9. **True.** Specific examples of the work the applicant has done give you deeper insight into the depth of experience acquired.

10. **False.** Intangible factors are at least as important to job success as technical know-how.

11. **False.** There are few "dream" applicants. Trade-offs often must be made.

12. **True.** Watch an applicant's body language, facial expressions, and so on. Good interviewers learn to understand and interpret them.

13. **False.** It's best to write down only key factors during the interview. After the interview has concluded, write down comments and an evaluation. Too much writing during the interview prevents you from fully listening and inhibits the applicant.

14. **False.** Encourage questions. You can make significant judgments based on the type of questions the applicant asks. Also, your answers can help the applicant decide whether this job is right for him or her.

15. **True.** A good description of the organization and the available job can do much to sell the applicant on accepting an offer. If you hire the applicant, it serves as the first step in orientation. Caution: Don't tell too much too soon.

Index

A